Arlan K. Gilbert

HISTORIC HILLSDALE COLLEGE

PIONEER IN HIGHER EDUCATION, 1844-1900

Published by Hillsdale College Press
33 East College Street, Hillsdale, Michigan 49242
517.437.7341 phone   517.437.3923 fax
www.hillsdale.edu

HISTORIC HILLSDALE COLLEGE:
PIONEER IN HIGHER EDUCATION, 1844–1900

Third Printing 2011
Second Printing 2002
First Printing 1991

©1991 Arlan K. Gilbert

Library of Congress Catalog Card Number 91-072649
ISBN 0-916308-79-0

Printed in the United States of America

Cover design by Ben Santora

Printed and bound by Edwards Brothers, Ann Arbor, Michigan

May earth be better and Heaven be richer
because of the life and labor
of Hillsdale College.

Enclosed in the 1853 and 1874 cornerstones

Contents

Illustrations

Foreword

In this book we find the story of the founding of a college, and in that story the relation of a college to a free country.

In the winter of 1853, a slender man rode his horse about the countryside of southern Michigan. He visited several towns in his search for a new home for a struggling college located in Spring Arbor since 1844.

Among the towns that this man entered was Hillsdale, located along the central southern border of the state. When he arrived, he checked into the larger of two country hotels, and asked to meet the town's leading citizens, people who might be interested in education. The hotel staff fetched a physician, and the physician took the man first to his surgery, and then to the town courthouse. Along the way they gathered others to join a discussion. At the courthouse, the visitor made a speech to explain the purpose of the college that would become Hillsdale. The College, we know from the original Articles of Association, would propagate freedom and the Christian faith. It would stand for "civil and religious liberty" alike and together, essentially connected. Because of this it would abhor slavery, and it would admit men and women, black and white impartially. This was something more than unusual. It was the first time that a college was founded on these commitments in its charter.

Though these elders of Hillsdale and their visitor met in the courthouse, and though they spoke of principles public and political, these people acted without government sanction. They used a public building for purposes of high civic benefit, conducted entirely by private citizens. Such things were common in those days of American history. No one filed for a permit to use the courthouse. No one applied to the governor for funds. No one in Washington, D.C. had an inkling of what they were doing.

You will read in these pages about the man who made this journey. His name was Ransom Dunn. He would work at Hillsdale College, as it would be called, for a total of fifty years. He would travel for months at a time to raise funds from farmers, five or fewer dollars at a time. All his life he would teach and preach and speak with force and fire along a consistent theme, preserving always the power to move and instruct and uplift.

Before this man was done his influence would be written through the political and military history of the country. It would be written deeply, but seldom in his name. Rather the names of his students, and the famous men and causes they supported, would be recorded on battlefields and in the records of the great political conventions. He would educate his sons at the College, and they would go, with nearly all their classmates, to fight for the Union Army in the Civil War. One of them, and many of their classmates, would not come back. Those who did would join their classmates in building the businesses, the farms, the schools, and the churches that would spread America across the continent and its influence around the world.

On the night that Dunn rode into Hillsdale, the College was little more than a lone man on a horse and a few friends struggling elsewhere through the snowy dark. That was but a few years before their college would have consequences that would move the nation and finally change the world.

It is no easy thing today to understand how a thing so patriotic and so significant to the nation can be accomplished in the absence of official action. This absence of official action did not however diminish—indeed it enhanced—the civic purpose and effect of the meeting. This was a thing done by citizens, intending to carry their project to success by their own efforts, seeking for themselves only the chance to serve. They believed that limited government requires a society distinct from the government. They believed that representative government requires an independent people to be represented. They believed that an independent people possess their own property, answer themselves to God for their own salvation, raise their own children, and—yes—build and run their own schools and colleges if it pleased them. These private actions amounted to public actions in a higher way because they were the actions of free people, practiced in the art of providing for themselves and their neighbors. Training in the liberal arts is not the same thing as a course in modern public administration.

Although the most famous of the consequences of this meeting in Hillsdale in 1853 would be political and military in their nature, the aim of the meeting was political and military in an indirect sense only. "Civil and religious liberty" was the goal. "Sound learning" was the means. Ransom Dunn and his colleagues were teachers. Those they influenced were students first, before and as a condition of their becoming soldiers and statesmen. These teachers would drill their charges well, but in Latin and not in tactics, in history and not in artillery, in astronomy and not in political canvassing. They had an instinct and an argument that the study of fixed and enduring things would lead most effectively to the accomplishment of urgent and changing things. Thinking came before fighting. The student so trained proves to be a formidable soul upon a battlefield. But the soldier, they thought, is for the student, and not the student for the soldier.

Of course the world of 1853 was a very different world than the one we know today. Today the principle of central organization has been taken to new heights, and nowhere higher than in government. Today the fingers of one hand are more numerous than the colleges that refuse the largess of the federal taxpayer. Excepting these tiny few, each and every of these colleges must sign an agreement to abide by detailed regulation, regulation that consumes several hundred pages of documentation, that is altered annually and at will, that expands every year in volume and complexity. The farmers who gave their five dollars to Ransom Dunn demanded nothing like this despotism over details. The private people who support the real private college that survives with their assistance today also grant freely the latitude to run the College in accordance with its first and only mission.

We can measure in this winter's story of 1853 something that has been lost. What has been lost, or rather nearly lost, is the action of the free men and women who support liberty through education by their own efforts. Not so common today is the free citizen entering a town for the purpose of starting a college. Today that person must also correspond with powerful people in Washington for his permits and his subsidies.

Hillsdale College survives today. In recent decades it has become once again famous, just as the original College soon became famous. The modern College attracts many of the leading statesmen of freedom to its campus, just as the original College did. Frederick Douglass came in his day; Clarence Thomas has come in his. Edward Everett came in his day; Ronald Reagan came in his.

The modern Hillsdale College is famous for its refusal of federal government aid. To avoid the regulation of its operations in detail, it must also require that its students refuse the aid available to them, and it must replace that public money with privately funded grants. The cost of freedom in the first days of the College would be measured in the Peach Orchard and the Wheat Field outside Gettysburg. The modern cost is so far not so dear, but still it is dear to keep the principles of Frederick Douglass alive today.

If we survey the politics of America today, we will see that the experience of this old College and its beginning is not irrelevant. Its independence is relevant. It is relevant to any institution that wishes to preserve its own liberty against the ceaseless pressure of regulatory impairment. In this very year, the Congress has passed and the president has signed a bill to forbid private citizens to criticize public officials in proximity to an election. This very Foreword could be an illegal act, if it is published in the autumn and if we name the author of that ugly legislation. We have come very far since 1853. It is not plain that we Americans today with our encompassing government are any wiser, any more charitable, any more loyal to the principles of our republic than those who met in Hillsdale in 1853.

The love of learning of these men who met in Hillsdale is also relevant to our time. Listen to contemporary political discourse. In the first paragraph that he spoke, our 42nd President proclaimed that our Founders knew that "each generation of Americans must define what it means to be an American." This he said of the generation who submitted themselves to the "laws of nature and of nature's God" in forming our nation. This he said of the man who had the "forecast and capacity to introduce into a merely revolutionary document an abstract truth, applicable to all men and at all times." There was not a soul in prominent places to remind our people that Jefferson and Adams and Washington did not think the principles of right to be malleable.

Those men knew this as well: "If a nation expects to be ignorant and free, in a state of civilization, it expects what never was and never will be."

The men who met in Hillsdale in 1853 believed that the salvation of our freedom is a task to be begun in the classroom. Their own times demonstrated that they were right. Our time stands as a negative demonstration of the same point.

A teacher of mine, the great Harry Jaffa, is—like those who met in Hillsdale in 1853—a follower of Lincoln. He has written that there can be no progress without return. Arlan Gilbert, whose retirement I had the honor to interrupt, has laid the ground sublimely for progress by accomplishing the return. We are proud to offer his history of our College as something more even than the history of this fine old place. It is a window, too, into the soul of our nation.

LARRY P. ARNN
President
Hillsdale College
May 2002

Foreword to the First Printing

Peculiar to the United States, the liberal arts college probably is America's chief contribution to higher learning. Beginning with Harvard and William and Mary, such colleges have given to the people of what is now the United States intellectual and moral leadership.

I had never visited Hillsdale College, which had its origins in villages on the Michigan frontier, until invited to the inauguration of my friend, Dr. George Roche, as president. Nevertheless that very independent institution of learning had been cherished in my imagination during the 1950s. I had admired the College's refusal to accept funds from government, and its strong stand against such dubious benefactions. I knew that the College stood rather picturesquely in the southernmost tier of Michigan's counties—where, H. L. Mencken instructs us, the most typically American speech is to be encountered. I had been told that until Henry Ford invented the Model T and so took the bottom out of the horse market, the abandoned Indian reservation called the Lost Nation, a few miles from Hillsdale, had been the rendezvous of the most successful horse thieves east of the Mississippi. (They were not under the patronage of the Freewill Baptists of Hillsdale College, I hasten to add.) I fancied that Hillsdale town must be a county seat, virtually unspoilt, of interesting buildings and pleasantly old-fangled ways. In my mind's eye, indeed, Hillsdale began to look like a bit of the Terrestrial Paradise.

I was not disappointed when at last I made my way to college and town. The tall Italianate buildings of the college, the tree-lined streets of the county seat with its classical courthouse, pleased me much. And the courage with which Hillsdale College set its face against the follies of the time pleased me equally.

Arlan Gilbert's thorough and interesting history of the College during six decades of the nineteenth century makes clear the College's repeated readiness to champion causes temporarily unpopular—its opposition to slavery, its interest in higher education for women, its prolonged attachment to the classical literary curriculum. If later Professor Gilbert gives us another volume on twentieth-century Hillsdale, no doubt he will tell in some detail of the College's resistance to the Behemoth state.

For half a century, Hillsdale was the biggest and best-reputed Michigan college—second in size only to the University of Michigan, that is. It was unflinchingly Christian in character, but not denominational merely, for the College welcomed any able student or able professor who professed the Apostles' Creed. In recent years the program of Christian studies has been revived at Hillsdale—and a program of classical studies, too. It must be confessed that the College has not restored the tuition fees and the board-and-lodging rates of the middle of the nineteenth century, when, as Professor Gilbert records, "no other college in the country offered such superior facilities for a liberal education at so low an expense." (Male students paid no more than $6.50 per term for tuition; female students, $4.25.)

Beyond formal learning, the Hillsdale College of that time imparted to its young men and women a moral discipline and a sense of duty. Some 420 Hillsdale students and graduates served in the Grand Army of the Republic; Professor Gilbert's description of their performance in the field is one of the more moving chapters of this book.

More than ninety years after Arlan Gilbert's chronicle comes to its conclusion, Hillsdale still maintains a strong defense of traditional education. The College does not embrace malign fads such as "multicultural education"; it stands by our inherited culture. The College does not pay lip-service, or any other sort of service, to what have been called "the evil benefits of the welfare state." The College does not subscribe to the notion that all books published before the year 1900 are obsolete. Against odds, the College speaks up, as it did during the nineteenth century, for the Permanent Things.

RUSSELL KIRK
Mecosta, Michigan

Preface and Acknowledgments

This volume describes Hillsdale College in the nineteenth century. The small western college played a unique role in higher education in some ways unlike that of any other institution during the middle period of American history. The following qualities illustrate a distinctive record: nonsectarian Christian goals, early devotion to abolitionism, national prominence in educating blacks and women, political leadership in the new Republican party, strength to endure both a change of physical location in 1853 and a catastrophic fire in 1874, deep patriotism exemplified by an extraordinary Civil War record, emphasis upon a traditional classical curriculum, dedication to leadership in public service, and financial frugality. Based largely on primary sources, the pioneering role of Hillsdale College unfolds in the following pages.

Describing the emotions and aspirations of the early professors, administrators, supporting public, and students is perhaps more difficult than presenting a factual record of Hillsdale from 1844 to the turn of the century. The western college was absolutely unwilling to accept failure. Despite limited financial resources, Hillsdale College confidently remained self-sufficient. The independent institution from its inception also nourished self-reliance by the students. My major purpose in this volume is to describe distinctive characteristics of the hilltop college.

The students themselves were largely without funds, but with education and discipline in the preparatory department and the college, they became judges, businessmen, physicians, generals, ministers, attorneys, professors, politicians, and other leaders by the hundreds. The college and its graduates never intended their accomplishments to be pretentious, because prevailing middle-class values seldom emphasized worldly fame. A century and a half later, I modestly suggest that the early leaders of Hillsdale College built better than they knew. The institution established a reputation for a rigorous classical curriculum and for outstanding literary societies. With good reason, Dr. L. A. Crandall in 1900 commented to alumni: "I hope that some historian will arise who shall write the [nineteenth-century] record of Hillsdale College out of full knowledge and sympathetic interest."

During more than three decades of teaching history at the college, I have been particularly fortunate to work with divisional chairmen Windsor Hall Roberts, Louis C. Pitchford, Jr., and John Willson. Each of these historians, in an exemplary way, is described as an extraordinary teacher. Together they shared with generations of twentieth-century students their understanding of the traditions and principles of Hillsdale College.

The college awarded me two summer leave grants and a sabbatical to provide time and funding for research and writing. I extend appreciation to colleagues of the Hillsdale College faculty and administration for their encouragement. Joe McNamara deserves major credit for his contributions: editorial skills, valuable advice, and supportive attitude. Kendall Brown gave helpful suggestions. Lissa Roche handled publication details and expedited the release of this book. I also appreciate staff support from the fifteen archives, historical societies, and libraries where I did my research. Most importantly, I dedicate the book to my wife, Carolyn, for her constant encouragement in seeing the work to completion.

ARLAN GILBERT
Hillsdale, Michigan
April 1991

Introduction

Good histories do not come from the pens of naysayers, and not very often out of the minds of the merely curious. To tell a good story requires passion, almost always a loving passion toward its object. Institutions are like people in this respect: if they are lovely (to paraphrase Dr. Johnson), then they are loved. Arlan Gilbert loves the little college which is the object of this inspiring story, and that relationship is worth mentioning here.

Professor Gilbert is Hillsdale's senior faculty member. For over three decades he has served the College, and no other, during his professional career. He has taught more than 10,000 students in his classes, advised many hundreds, chaired his department for ten years, sat in over six hundred committee meetings, and done the thousand other things a dedicated teacher is required to do. He is intimate with the object of his scholarly affection. In a very real sense this book is what Arlan Gilbert was placed at Hillsdale thirty years ago to do.

They have been invigorating and exhausting years. Arlan arrived at a college slowly rising out of financial ashes, much as the earlier Hillsdale had to rise out of the cinders of its 1874 fire. Sound business practices, a fierce sense of independence and order during the turmoil of the sixties, and a dedicated core of faculty, coaches, administrators, and alumni pulled Hillsdale up, but just barely. Beginning in 1971 with the presidency of George Roche, Arlan and the College have seen the longest period of sustained growth in its history.

As Professor Gilbert has witnessed that growth and been part of the struggle to achieve it against many of the strongest negative forces of the contemporary culture, he has become increasingly respectful of the *sources* of the College's determination and grit. He finds them in Hillsdale's nineteenth-century origins, in the founding decades, when the College was constantly tested in triumph and loss against the forces of nature and rapid change. Its challenges were legion, but four are especially notable.

Hillsdale was a frontier college. People were few, and they were poor. Travel was hard, as life was hard. Every institution of frontier society was conditional; more towns failed than survived, and many more colleges failed than survived. They hung on by threads—often the threads of accidental politics, as whether a railroad decided to build through the town—but mostly they hung on by the will of the founders. This force of will is present in contemporary Hillsdale. Professor Gilbert tells the inspiring story of how the College came by it honestly.

Hillsdale College survived a fire that destroyed most of its material assets. Fire had destroyed Chicago just three years before it destroyed the Hillsdale campus. Chicago rebuilt, and so did the College. In earlier days Bowdoin, Williams, and Wabash colleges had disastrous fires, and survived to become great institutions. Hillsdale "deposited the Bible from the original 1853 structure in the new cornerstone," and asked God's blessing on its missions and those who served it.

Hillsdale College survived two depressions and in general adjusted to the rapid changes of the industrial revolution. Hillsdale began its life in an agricultural village society. Henry Adams once remarked that an American boy born in 1850 was closer to the year zero than to the year 1900. It may have been the College's biggest achievement to learn the conditions of the newer world (especially the financial conditions) while keeping its institutional feet planted firmly in the old.

Hillsdale College survived the most destructive war in American history. The Civil War took so many of its students that the College should have, according to the dictates of cool rationality, closed. Instead, it vigorously supported the Union cause and actually prospered because of its war effort. Wars always decimate colleges: so the Civil War, and later World War II. The former was followed by a proliferation of state universities; the latter, by a great infusion of federal monies through programs such as the National Defense Education Act. Hillsdale remained strong by resisting both trends and staying independent.

The length of time since World War II is roughly the span covered in this book, and it is part of Professor Gilbert's passion to show that the prosperity of the earlier period was based upon the same principles that have given Hillsdale the prosperity of today. "Much of the recent progress," he insists, "reflects principles basic to Hillsdale College during the nineteenth century." The college met the tests of the nineteenth century and is meeting the tests of the twentieth century because it has *a clear sense of its identity and mission and because it has an abiding concern for its students.*

One of our current political scientists wrote recently to me: "My courses are designed to help fulfill the Hillsdale mission to pass on our intellectual and spiritual inheritance from Jerusalem and Athens, and show how those traditions find expression in the American experiment in self-government." Professor Gilbert would agree that this is a sufficient (if not necessarily complete) statement of the College's mission, applicable in 1891 and in 1991. He says that "Hillsdale, by retaining traditional values, was not susceptible to the new progressive 'reforms' in education," referring to the year 1900. Yet this was not educational sclerosis, but an organic unity between past and present, based on truths timeless and transcendent.

What were those truths? Belief that real truth and wisdom and knowledge come from God. That much about civic virtue and beauty and philosophic good sense comes from Classical Greece and Rome. That the Anglo-American history of liberty under law has taught us to be "no respecter of persons," so that education and citizenship should be open to all regardless of race, sex, and nation. That education was to pass along the culture, and especially to prepare men and women for citizenship and duty, freedom, and service. That the College would hold fast to these truths and this mission *only* by holding fast to its independence from all governments and corporations.

Much of this book is devoted to the story of these principles, told in fascinating and loving anecdotal detail. Readers who are familiar with Hillsdale's current struggles and successes will recognize most of the sources of principles still intact, and the characters who hold to them. We may not find a George Roche in the nineteenth century (although President Fairfield approaches him in power and lucidity), but there is a Ransom Dunn. Professor Dunn served the College for two decades longer even than Professor Gilbert. His life and career represent what I consider to be the heart and soul of this book, an emphasis so natural to Arlan Gilbert that he modestly neglects to mention it as a major theme.

It is also the students. Not just that they were black as well as white, female as well as male: of those distinctions Hillsdale is justifiably proud. *The students were the reason Hillsdale College existed.* Professor Gilbert says that Hillsdale withstood the tests of its formative years "because Christian leaders shaped the institution through sacrifice, plain habits, and lack of self-interest." Their interest was the students. *Historic Hillsdale* fairly brims over with evidence to that fact.

They were just plain folks, men and women, white and black and Native American. They were "rural, religious, and conscientious." Most were poor, so that it was a good thing, as a student publication put it, that Hillsdale was "a piece of practical philanthropy." College officials struggled to supply endowment so that tuition could remain low. (Contrast present costs with those of Williams or Swarthmore.) Rules were strict, because the faculty "took particular pride in strengthening the moral values of self-supporting Christian students." Studies dominated their time, but literary societies gave them polish, and social fraternities provided friendships and fun (despite the faculty's reluctance to welcome them).

It is not incidental to the story that as traditional and religious as the atmosphere tended to be, students were taught and encouraged to make decisions and to serve; God, the Union, equal rights, Republican ideals, enterprise were the main themes. The faculty interpreted service *in the world* to mean that the curriculum should reflect the world to a practical degree. By the 1870s, accordingly, there were five "courses" open to students: classical, ladies', scientific, theological, and commercial. All of them but the last emphasized teaching. Hillsdale from its beginning has tried to so define the liberal arts as to give place and honor to the arts of business and the classroom.

It is also not incidental that Professor Gilbert's story shows that early Hillsdale was enthusiastic about athletics for men and women: "Duncan M. Martin, professor of mathematics, used statistics to indicate that 75 percent of those who participated in Hillsdale sports were superior students; he denied that athletics and scholarship were incompatible." Then and now, the college understands that plain men and women who would serve and be leaders must understand honorable combat. And they became leaders: clergy, lawyers and judges, physicians and scientists, teachers, journalists, and businessmen. Some order of this same list describes Hillsdale's graduates to this day.

I must commend you to this loving book. It contains no sentimentality (although it has much advocacy of Hillsdale ways); it aspires to the highest standards of scholarship; and it tells a story the depth of which will, perhaps, surprise even the most committed veterans of Hillsdale's recent struggles in the war of ideas. Professor Gilbert quotes a typical reaction of visitors to the college, printed in the *Hillsdale Herald* in 1882: "I never dreamed there was *so much of a college here*." Here you can find the first chapter of why that is still so.

JOHN WILLSON
Department of History
Hillsdale College

Abbreviations
in Endnotes, Bibliography, and Illustrations

ABAC   The American Baptist Historical Society, Archives Center, Valley Forge, Pennsylvania

ABHS   The American Baptist Historical Society, Rochester, New York

AKG   Author's collection

AWM   Archives and Special Collections on Women in Medicine, The Medical College of Pennsylvania, Philadelphia, Pennsylvania

BHC   Burton Historical Collection, Detroit Public Library, Detroit, Michigan

CHS   Chicago Historical Society, Chicago, Illinois

HC   Hillsdale College Archives, Hillsdale, Michigan

HCVPA   Hillsdale College Vice President for Administration, Hillsdale, Michigan

IHS   Indiana Historical Society Library, Indianapolis, Indiana

JG   President James Garfield Library, Mentor, Ohio

JPL   Jackson Public Library, Jackson, Michigan

LM   Library of Michigan, Lansing, Michigan

MHC   Michigan Historical Collections, Bentley Historical Library, University of Michigan, Ann Arbor, Michigan

MHI   United States Army Military History Institute, Carlisle Barracks, Pennsylvania

MPL   Mitchell Public Library, Hillsdale, Michigan

NA   The National Archives and Records Administration, Washington, D.C.

NL   The Newberry Library, Chicago, Illinois

RHC   Regional History Collections, Western Michigan University, Kalamazoo, Michigan

SAM   State Archives of Michigan, Lansing, Michigan

Chronology of
Nineteenth-Century Hillsdale College

1844: Michigan Central College was organized independently at Spring Arbor by Freewill Baptist individuals and small congregations, and it immediately took a leading role in the abolition of slavery. Official denominational endorsement of the college took place in 1847, although no church ever has held legal title to either Michigan Central College or Hillsdale College.

1850: Michigan Central College became the first successful private college in Michigan to be chartered by the legislature with authority to grant degrees, with the provision that standards equal to those of the University of Michigan. *The college charter was the first in the United States to prohibit discrimination because of race, sex, or religion.*

1853: The college moved to Hillsdale because of (1) financial support from the community and (2) services of the Michigan Southern Railroad, which had reached Hillsdale in October 1843, and became the first railroad into Chicago in February 1852.

1854: President Edmund Fairfield and other Hillsdale College leaders took an active role in founding the Republican Party at Jackson, Michigan.

1856: Hillsdale became the largest college in Michigan and remained so for most of the nineteenth century.

1861–1865: *Hillsdale College contributed a higher percentage of her young men to military service in the Civil War than any other college in the West.*

Half became officers, three received the Congressional Medal of Honor, and three became generals.

1866: General Clinton B. Fisk, an early alumnus, opened his Fisk School for Freedmen at Nashville, Tennessee, on January 9. The following year the school was chartered as Fisk University, a leading liberal arts college for blacks.

1860s and 1870s: Speakers at the college included Wendell Phillips, William Lloyd Garrison, Frederick Douglass, Charles Sumner, Edward Everett, Zachariah Chandler, Henry Ward Beecher, Lew Wallace, Susan B. Anthony, and Booker T. Washington.

1870: The college baseball club on May 17 defeated the state champions on the University Grounds at Ann Arbor, 29–28.

1870s: As the largest private college in Michigan, Hillsdale College had an average enrollment of 750 students in the 1870s.

1874: The college survived a catastrophic fire on March 6 during the economic panic of 1873. Only 182, or 20 percent, of colleges founded before the Civil War have survived until the present.

1879: On July 11, four former Hillsdale Colllege students won the first of three successive national amateur rowing championships at Saratoga.

1885: Hillsale dedicated the first college gymnasium in Michigan.

1891: Description of Hillsdale College by a *Chicago Herald* reporter: "Hillsdale has a college, second in standing to no denominational college in the country."

1893: Hillsdale College won its first M.I.A.A. football championship. Joseph Manus, a full-blooded Cherokee Indian, played left guard.

1895: Hillsdale College rejected a proposal to affiliate with the University of Chicago.

❧ONE❧

Freewill Baptists on
the Michigan Frontier

The college was fortunate in its location, the period in which it
began and its denominational setting. On account of these it
drew to itself a marked type of young men and women, scions of
a hardy and vigorous stock. It was a Christian college, sustained
and patronized by the middle classes—farmers, ministers and
mechanics, for the most part. Thus these boys and girls came
from country homes, from log houses. . . .[1]

—Alumnus H. M. Ford, 1910

The pioneers on the Michigan frontier of the 1840s arrived primarily
from western New York, which had been inhabited by New England-
ers from Vermont, New Hampshire, Massachusetts, and Connecticut
since the 1780s.[2] Comparatively few settlers came to Michigan from
Pennsylvania, New Jersey, and Ohio. Most of the Freewill Baptists
who founded Michigan Central College at Spring Arbor in 1844 had
moved from New Hampshire, and they were part of the New
England–New York–Michigan nexus. The earliest presidents of the
college, relocated at Hillsdale in 1853, arrived directly from New
England. Pushing into the wilderness, they "fashioned it into the
semblance of their former homes. The houses they built were New
England houses; they brought with them their deep religious faith,
their customs, their zeal for education."[3]

Ransom Dunn, the "Grand Old Man" of Hillsdale College, expressed the appeal of the frontier as he left Vermont: "At the East I have fared well. . . . But I could not rest. A cry was in my ears from the West, and I am now on my way again to that field of labor. . . . To that land, and even beyond to the cabins of the wilderness, I hasten with delight. . . . "[4] Daniel M. Graham, first president of Michigan Central College, temporarily lived in a log hut when the college opened at Spring Arbor on December 4, 1844. Hardship accompanied the college founders' moves to Michigan, but they renewed their commitment to abolitionism and maintained active interest in current political issues such as the division of the national Baptist denomination into northern and southern branches in 1845.

The earliest students, called "ancients" by later alumni, were also pioneers; some walked more than a hundred miles to reach Spring Arbor. It was not uncommon to furnish a dormitory room with an empty nail keg for a chair, a bundle of straw for a bed, and a window sill for a table.[5] Most college students, at Michigan Central until 1853 and at Hillsdale afterward, supported themselves by manual labor. Enrollment always was lowest in the spring, when many returned home to help with farming. Some worked at trades, and others did odd jobs for the townspeople (for example, chopping wood).

Although the opening of the Erie Canal in 1825 had made Michigan much more accessible to pioneers, the territorial population by 1830 was only 31,640. The Old Sauk Trail, or the Chicago Military Road, connecting forts in Detroit and Chicago, opened in 1835 and was 254 miles long. Admitted as a state on January 26, 1837, Michigan presented frontier conditions (defined by the Census Bureau as two to six persons per square mile) to the new college in the south-central location. The United States census of 1840 counted a farm population of 56,521 persons in Michigan, more than six times the number of all other occupations. The rural population of the new state was located primarily in the four southern tiers of counties. As late as 1850, over 98 percent of the Michigan population lived in the southern quarter of the state's total area.[6]

The University of Michigan began offering higher education at Ann Arbor in 1841, although it earlier had operated a secondary school in Detroit. The first class graduated from the university in 1845, a year after the establishment of Michigan Central College.

Horace Wellington, of the college faculty, observed in 1847 that his train time from Jackson (eight and a half miles northeast of Spring Arbor) to Boston was four days. Professor Wellington also described being detained by flooding streams, or freshets, on a journey from Massachusetts to Michigan. Most of the bridges had been swept away at Cleveland, where he was delayed three days. Wellington, professor of Greek and Latin, exhibited the perseverance of Freewill Baptist faculty: "No accident attended me but I felt that the goodness of God was manifested to me. It is in many respects quite a self-denial to live here, so far from my relatives and early associations there but the conviction that I can be most useful here balanced all the rest. We have many privations and hardships here to endure at present, but better days are coming."[7] Travellers moving west from Detroit or Toledo had to pass through the "black swamp," described in 1838 as a "much dreaded place with a large extent of low wet land with much standing water."[8]

When Michigan Central College was founded, the only states that had been admitted to the Union west of the Mississippi River were Missouri, Arkansas, and Louisiana. The confident nation was on the brink of Manifest Destiny, a popular enthusiasm for vigorous nationalism and altruistic physical expansion. The annexation of Texas came in 1845, Iowa achieved statehood in 1846, and the California gold rush followed in 1849. Financial failure of the Michigan Central and the Michigan Southern railroads, organized by the state under an 1837 internal improvements law, temporarily retarded transportation to south-central Michigan. Officials used excuses such as the tamarack swamp near Hillsdale, west of the "black swamp" in southeastern Michigan, to rationalize repeated delays.[9] Because the railroads failed as state enterprises, Michigan sold them in 1846 to private investors from Boston and New York. Progress followed, and by 1852 both lines reached Chicago after years of keen competition.[10]

Facing the hardships of the southern Michigan frontier, the founders of Michigan Central College at Spring Arbor gained motivation and strength from their Freewill Baptist religious beliefs. Benjamin

Randall, who rejected the doctrine of predestination because it denied freedom of the human moral will, had formed the denomination in 1780. Freewill Baptists, like some Methodists, Lutherans, Presbyterians, and Moravians, adopted the "Arminian doctrines of free will, free grace, and unlimited hope for the conversion of all men."[11] Part of the Second Great Awakening, the sect endorsed open communion and immersion as the only form of baptism.

By 1830 Freewill Baptist membership in New Hampshire equaled that of regular Baptists, and approximately 400 Freewill churches nationally had 16,000 communicants. Of the total, almost 60 percent lived in rural New England. Unlike many older denominations, the Baptists (including Freewill) in America did not inherit the tradition of an educated clergy from Europe. Nevertheless, the Baptists soon supported higher education, at a time when one-fourth of the nation's adult population was illiterate. The six denominations establishing the largest number of permanent colleges before the Civil War were: Presbyterians, 49; Methodists, 34; Baptists, 25; Congregationalists, 21; Catholics, 14; and Episcopalians, 11. Brown University was founded in 1765, and the next Baptist college, Colby, was established 55 years later.

Of the 25 permanent Baptist colleges organized before the Civil War, all but Michigan Central College and Alfred (Seventh Day Baptists) belonged to the main body of the denomination. Until the founding of Michigan Central in the 1840s, the Freewill Baptists had lost many dedicated ministers for failure to provide them a formal education. By the opening of Hillsdale College in 1855, denominational membership had increased to 51,775. The Freewill Baptist movement peaked in 1900 with almost 90,000 followers. By 1911 the belief in predestination had weakened among regular Baptists, and the Freewill Baptists willingly joined the major sect, the American (Northern) Baptist Convention.[12]

In spite of small membership, the evangelical Freewill Baptists exercised a strong influence upon contemporary issues such as the abolition of slavery.[13] They were "second only to the Friends in terms of early religious antislavery prominence."[14] Almost from its beginning, the denomination barred slaveholders from membership, a strong position taken by few antislavery churches even by the mid-1840s. The Freewill Baptists in 1827 courageously authorized the ordination of black ministers. Their periodical, the *Morning Star*, advocated immediate emancipation in 1834. The *Emancipator*, a publication endorsing the liberation of slaves, hailed the Freewill Baptists' prosperity as "an example to other denominations that abolitionism would not conflict with a church's well-being."[15]

At an antislavery convention on May 19, 1838, the Freewill Baptist churches in Michigan adopted a resolution "to do all that its members could consistently do to advance the cause of the abolition of slavery."[16] By 1842, two years before the founding of Michigan Central College, the national denomination organized the Antislavery Society of the Free Baptists, which endorsed immediate emancipation. Most communicants rejected their traditional Democratic loyalties to support the Free Soilers, a powerful third political party launched in 1848 to contain the spread of slavery. William Goodell in 1852 credited the Freewill Baptists with taking an antislavery position since the beginning of agitation on the issue,[17] and some extreme abolitionists endorsed them. The Baptists were one of the evangelical denominations giving the strongest support to the new Republican party in 1854.[18] After the outbreak of the Civil War, the Freewill Baptists began sending teachers and agents to work with southern blacks.

What was the specific record of Freewill Baptists on the Michigan frontier? They formed their first church near Ypsilanti on March 14, 1831. Elders Samuel Whitcomb and Elijah Cook, Jr. came from western New York and settled in 1835 at Cook's Prairie (between Homer and Marshall), where they organized a Freewill Baptist church on March 12, 1836. Whitcomb and Cook then joined Henry S. Limbocker to establish more churches in Calhoun, Jackson, Oakland, and adjacent counties. These pioneer evangelists, who farmed their land during the week and preached several times each Sunday, founded the Freewill Baptist denomination in Michigan.[19] In one year Limbocker traveled 2,900 miles (often on foot) and preached three hundred sermons, and the three leaders organized the denomination's state meeting at Leoni in 1839. Most importantly, by 1835 Whitcomb, Cook, and Limbocker began the movement to develop a formally educated ministry for their evangelical religion. Although Hillsdale College was not established specifically as a training ground for clergy, it turned out 64 missionaries and more than 400 ministers during the nineteenth century.

The leading Freewill Baptist evangelists in south-central Michigan believed that their denomination "would be compelled to raise the standard of education to enable it to keep up with the times, and to build up and maintain its interest in intellectual centers. They recognized education as the handmaid of religion."[20] In 1855 Henry S. Limbocker became chairman of the Hillsdale College Board of Trustees. The educational aims at first seemed overly ambitious, because Freewill Baptist churches were few and the members impoverished. Many frontiersmen did not even appreciate the necessity and advantages of a denominational college. Fortunately, laymen such as Daniel Dunakin, a native of western New York and one of the wealthier men in Michigan, joined the crusade for improved education. A founder of Michigan Central College, Dunakin became chairman of the Hillsdale College trustees in 1858 and remained on the board until his death in 1875. Another strong sponsor of the Freewill Baptist college was Eli T. Chase, a New York native who settled at Cook's Prairie. Additional college advocates living in Calhoun and Jackson counties were Thomas Dunton, Herman Cowles, Joseph Blaisdell, Roosevelt Davis, Jonathan Videto, Joseph Bailey, and William Smith. These and other deacons led Freewill Baptist churches in neighboring counties to become the driving force behind establishing a college in Michigan.[21]

Cook's Prairie Freewill Baptist Church exemplifies the small congregations that independently founded Michigan Central College. Families came to services at the frontier church in ox-drawn lumber wagons. Morning sermons were two hours long, followed by lunch, Sunday school, and another sermon. Humble leaders from churches such as these gave us Michigan Central College. They reflect well Hillsdale College President George Roche's description of much of the nineteenth century as "pioneer and frontier, self-reliant and courageous. . . . "[22] Many founders of the college, including pastor Elijah Cook, the first trustee named in the original charter of 1845, Samuel

Whitcomb, and Daniel Dunakin are buried in the beautiful little cemetery at Cook's Prairie in Calhoun County.[23] Other supporters lived farther than 25 miles from Spring Arbor. Becket Chapman, for example, moved from Vermont to Boston, where he served as deacon of the Free Baptist Church for 21 years. In 1844 he settled in Ionia County and promoted the early college.[24] A decade later, several of the Michigan Central founders, including Eli Chase, E. H. Cook, and Daniel Dunakin, attended the Jackson convention that organized the Republican party in 1854.

Small churches and individuals thus independently created the small college on the Michigan frontier in 1844, seven years after Michigan joined the Union as the twenty-sixth state. Action by synod, presbytery, or state convention established most other church colleges in the West. In 1916, President Joseph W. Mauck of Hillsdale College disproved the belief that the 1844 Michigan Yearly Meeting of Freewill Baptists had organized Michigan Central College.[25] The record book of the June 7, 1844, state session at Franklin Center clearly contains no reference to plans for establishing a college.[26] The Michigan Freewill Baptist Yearly Conference first mentioned the college on June 11, 1847: "Resolved that the Board of Trustees of the Michigan Central College earnestly solicit the Freewill Baptist Ministers everywhere, and especially those in this State, to exert their influence by preaching and otherwise, on behalf of this Institution."[27] The same yearly meeting donated $500 to the college for the purchase of materials. The independence of the small congregations and elders who established Michigan Central without endorsement by a church hierarchy would permanently influence the ideals of the new frontier college.

Endnotes

1. H. M. Ford, "Alumni History of Hillsdale College," 1910. Ransom Dunn Collection, MHC.

2. *Bulletin of the University of Wisconsin Historical Series*, I, No. 4, as quoted by Kathleen Gillard, *Our Michigan Heritage* (New York, 1955), p. 157. By

1850, the Michigan population of 397,654 included 133,756 born in New York.

3. Willfred Mauck, typewritten memoirs entitled "Hometown," n.d. HC.

4. Helen Dunn Gates, *A Consecrated Life: A Sketch of the Life and Labors of Rev. Ransom Dunn, D.D.* (Boston, 1901), pp. 71–72.

5. John Hopkins, "A Full and Reliable History of the Alumni and Alumnae of Our Alma Mater," in *First Quinquennial Record of the Alumni Association of Hillsdale College* (Hillsdale, 1876), p. 21.

6. Willis Dunbar, "Frontiersmanship in Michigan," in *Michigan Perspectives*, edited by Alan Brown, John Houdek, and John Yzenbaard (Dubuque, IA, 1974), p. 40.

7. Jackson in the 1840s was variously known as Jacksonopolis, Jacksonburg, and Jacksonville. Horace Wellington to friends at Lynn, Massachusetts, April 19, 1847. Michigan Central College Collection, MHC.

8. E. W. Bovee, "Chronicles of a Pioneer Family," *The Sauk Trail Historian* (January 1991), p. 5.

9. Robert J. Parks, *Democracy's Railroads: Public Enterprise in Jacksonian Michigan* (Port Washington, NY 1972), p. 125. The Michigan Southern Railroad was an early railroad on the western frontier; Philadelphia merchants did not begin construction of the Pennsylvania Railroad, an eastern trunk line, until 1846.

10. George Rogers Taylor, *The Transportation Revolution* (New York, 1951), p. 100; Thomas Weber, *The Northern Railroads in the Civil War, 1861–1865* (Westport, CT, 1970), p. 3.

11. Timothy L. Smith, *Revivalism and Social Reform: American Protestantism on the Eve of the Civil War* (Gloucester, MA, 1976), pp. 88–89. Dr. Michael Bauman, associate professor of theology and culture at Hillsdale College, assisted me greatly in defining the beliefs and roles of the Freewill Baptists.

12. Edwin Gaustad, *Historical Atlas of Religion in America* (New York, 1976), p. 58; Donald Tewksbury, *The Founding of American Colleges and Universities before the Civil War* (New York, 1932), pp. 90, 117–19.

13. David Moberg, *The Great Reversal: Evangelism and Social Concern* (Philadelphia, 1977), p. 28.

14. John R. McKivigan, *The War against Proslavery Religion: Abolitionism and the Northern Churches, 1830–1865* (Ithaca, NY, 1984), p. 28.

15. Ibid., p. 44.

16. John C. Patterson, "History of the Freewill Baptist Church of Cook's Prairie," (n.d.), p. 38. John C. Patterson Collection, MHC.

17. William Goodell, *Slavery and Anti-Slavery* (New York, 1852), p. 197. AKG.

18. William E. Gienapp, *The Origins of the Republican Party, 1852–1856* (New York, 1987), p. 434.

19. Coe Hayne, *Baptist Trail-Makers of Michigan* (Philadelphia, 1936), p. 90.

20. John C. Patterson, "History of Hillsdale College," 1883 article reprinted in *Collection of the Pioneer Society of the State of Michigan*, VI (1907), p. 139.

21. Ibid., p. 141.

22. George Roche, *Going Home* (Ottawa, IL, 1986), p. 179.

23. The Rev. Elijah Cook, Revolutionary War veteran and first trustee of Michigan Central College, was an ancestor of the Jane and David Elliott family of North Adams, Michigan. Jane Elliott is also a direct descendant of Mrs. Sophia E. Baker Randolph, from Sturgis, Michigan, who entered Hillsdale College in the 1850s. In the first Hillsdale commencement exercises on June 18, 1856, Miss Baker delivered an essay, "Every Beginning Is Shrouded in a Mist."

24. Becket Chapman's obituary was provided by his great-granddaughter, Mrs. Clarence Chambers, Lakeland, Florida.

25. Joseph W. Mauck, untitled paper on Michigan Central College, November 7, 1916. Freewill Baptist papers. Michigan Association Collection, MHC.

26. The most important record book of the Michigan Yearly Meeting of Freewill Baptists at Franklin Center on June 7, 1844, is located in the Freewill Baptist papers, Michigan Association Collection, MHC.

27. The Constitution and Records of the Michigan Yearly Conference of Freewill Baptists, 1847. Freewill Baptist papers, Michigan Association Collection, MHC.

TWO

The Formative Era:
Michigan Central College

We have rarely witnessed an examination that has given so good
evidence of ability and fidelity on the part of the professors and
teachers, and of untiring industry on the part of the students, as
this . . . . The [collegiate] class is composed of both ladies and
gentlemen, all of whom evinced a maturity of scholarship that is
unusual with persons of their age and progress, even in older
institutions. . . . In the compositions of the young ladies, and the
orations of the young gentlemen (as well as in the papers of the
literary societies), some of which we have never seen surpassed,
we were gratified to see so many good moral and religious sentiments inculcated.
                    —State Board of Visitors' report, June 1848

Freewill Baptist churches throughout Michigan continued to contribute small donations to their new college during the summer and fall
of 1844. Elder Chauncey Reynolds presented the largest individual
gift, eighty acres of land.[1] Cook's Prairie, Leoni, Jackson, and Spring
Arbor competed for the college site. Spring Arbor, formerly a Pot-
tawatomie Indian village, earned the location by offering 210 acres of
land and the most funding. Pottawatomies had remained in the area
until removed by the federal government to Green Bay, Wisconsin,
in 1839 and 1840. The trustees, meeting in October 1844, chose the
name Michigan Central College over Spring Arbor Seminary and es-

tablished the first Freewill Baptist collegiate institution in the United States. The beginning was humble and unpretentious.

The college of five students opened on December 4 with Daniel McBride Graham, Oberlin College graduate, as president and sole faculty member. An old, small wooden building formerly used as a store was the campus, and snow sifted through the roof.[2] Graham, who lived in a log hut, used his first speech at the college to attack slavery, advocate temperance, and praise education. In earlier preaching at Spring Arbor, he had denounced slavery as a national sin and curse. Walking out of one of Graham's sermons, a pro-slavery advocate in the congregation shouted loudly, "I will not listen to such talk!" Graham quickly called to him, "The wicked flee when no man pursueth!"

A statewide canvass among Freewill Baptists brought in additional small subscriptions for building and development. Farmers with heavily mortgaged land and ministers living on annual salaries of $200 to $300 contributed far beyond their means. The trustees exchanged Chauncey Reynolds' donation of eighty acres of land for lumber to construct two college buildings. The two new structures, at a total cost of $2,000, were ready for occupancy by the fall of 1845. Each was 35 feet by 60 feet, with the first floor used for classrooms and the second for dormitories. The construction of a central building with the two original structures as wings was never completed.

The founders realized the significance of securing a charter from the state legislature. Unfortunately, supporters of the University of Michigan waged a strong battle against aspiring denominational colleges during the first eighteen years of statehood.[3] The Michigan Constitution of 1850 prohibited granting charters to church colleges. In effect, the University of Michigan established a monopoly over higher education more rigid than any other state in the Union. Ohio, Indiana, and Illinois encouraged the formation of private colleges, but many of these early institutions were weak and only feigned full accreditation. Because the state university maintained the exclusive right to confer collegiate degrees in Michigan, an act of March 19, 1845, authorized the Michigan Central College trustees only to hold property to the amount of $30,000, to sue and be sued, to have a seal, to appoint and remove teachers, and to admit and dismiss students. The religious toleration clause illustrated the college goal to be Christian and nonsectarian: "No person shall be excluded from any privilege, immunity or situation in said college on account of his religious opinions."[4]

Michigan Central College secured authority to confer collegiate degrees when the state legislature amended the original charter on March 20, 1850.[5] The institution thus became the first permanent private college in Michigan with authority to grant liberal arts degrees, with the stipulation that academic standards equal those of the University of Michigan.[6]

Accordingly, Michigan Central College was one of 119 colleges included in the U.S. Census of 1850. The faculty already had anticipated receiving a full college charter from the state legislature, and students pursued a rigorous schedule. The first catalogue of 1845–46 adopted a strong classical curriculum. With no allowance for electives, it emphasized the ancient classics, ethics, and rhetoric. The freshman year offered such courses as trigonometry, Livy, Vergil, and physiology. The sophomore curriculum included Cicero, Homer, botany, and writing of Latin and Greek. The junior year presented natural philosophy, astronomy, chemistry, zoology, Tacitus, Hebrew, French, and psychology. Senior year studies were geology, calculus, moral philosophy, weekly declamations and compositions, and monthly original speeches. A board of visitors administered public examinations after each of three terms per year.

By 1852 the growing preparatory department offered the following courses, among others: Latin grammar, Cicero, Vergil, Greek, United States history, and geography. The standard for student conduct was brief and direct: "In government, great reliance is placed upon the sense of propriety and obligation; and when means of this nature do not suffice, there must of course be a removal of offenders."[7] The catalogue included a requirement that each student complete a probation of six months before full admission as a regular student.

Because a college gains full legal status only by obtaining the right to confer degrees, it is significant to contrast Michigan Central's charter of March 20, 1850, with later dates when other private colleges in Michigan were formally established.[8] Kalamazoo College, begun by Baptists as the Michigan and Huron Institute in 1833, obtained a collegiate charter in 1855. Congregationalists in 1844 started Olivet, which received degree-granting power under the general college law of 1855. Adrian College, founded by the Methodists, was fully incorporated by 1859. Methodists also established Albion College, which gained power to confer degrees on February 25, 1861. Hope College (Dutch Reformed) was incorporated in 1866, and Alma College (Presbyterian) obtained formal recognition in 1887. Calvin College, supported by the Christian Reformed Church, was not authorized to grant collegiate degrees until 1894. Most educational institutions incorporated by Michigan before the Civil War, however, never became chartered colleges. The "failures" included schools with such little-known names as St. Philip's College (Catholic), Marshall College (Presbyterian), Tecumseh Academy, Grand River Seminary, Grass Lake Academy, Allegan Academy, Grand Rapids Academy, Clinton Institute, White Pigeon Academy, Howell Academy, Tecumseh Literary Institute, Clarkston Academic Institute, and St. Mark's College.[9]

Evangelist Edmund B. Fairfield, at age twenty-seven, became president of Michigan Central College in 1848.[10] His New England family background is significant. His father, Micaiah Fairfield, was born in New Hampshire, graduated from Middlebury College and Andover Theological Seminary, and became a home missionary on the Ohio frontier. In spite of poverty and hardship, traveling preacher Micaiah Fairfield gave his nine children a most important legacy— education. Edmund learned English grammar at age five, and two years later began the study of Latin under his father's direction. Because his family lacked funds, Edmund supported himself through college (Denison, Marietta, and Oberlin) by sawing wood, making brooms, setting type, and coopering. His college courses prepared him for the Christian ministry. In his junior year, he was licensed to preach by the Baptist church. A brilliant student, Fairfield graduated from Oberlin in 1842. Within two years, he returned to New England to teach at the Freewill Baptist academy at Strafford, New Hampshire. Here he met Ransom Dunn, who joined the Michigan

Central College faculty in 1852 and later became the "Grand Old Man" of Hillsdale College. Edmund Fairfield accepted pastorates at Roxbury, Massachusetts, and Canterbury, New Hampshire. In the summer of 1848, he received a call to the presidency of Michigan Central College. A biographer later explained: "Rev. Mr. Fairfield was made to understand that this academic infant of days was, after all, a college, bona fide, free from debt, with $10,000 endowment, and would pay its new president the munificent salary of $400!"[11] A career as head of a new educational institution in the West must have appealed to the young scholar, in spite of probable poverty and hardships.

Unfortunately, the college turned out to be less than he had expected. Michigan Central lacked authority to grant degrees, carried a debt of $1600, had no endowment, and received limited income from tuition and rent. The fall term of 1848 opened with only twenty students, but the University of Michigan had begun in 1841 at Ann Arbor with only two professors and six students. Fairfield rose to the challenge by traveling long distances to lecture, to preach, and to recruit students; and he paid off the debt of $1600 immediately. Fairfield's most important accomplishment during his early presidency was persuading the legislature to grant Michigan Central College the power to confer degrees by 1850, as described above. *Now* there was a bona fide Freewill Baptist college in the West! Although the financial credit of the college corporation was weak, President Fairfield raised money in western New York to build a new dormitory for forty students. Edmund Fairfield's reputation later increased when he provided political leadership for the new Republican party. By 1858 the *Detroit Advertiser* described him as a worthy scholar and one of the most eloquent men of the Old Northwest.

Michigan Central College rapidly attracted a stronger faculty (a total of fourteen by 1852) and larger enrollments. Classes graduated in 1851, 1852, and 1853. Amasa Walker, who gained a reputation as an outstanding economist, was an early instructor in 1849. Michigan Central recognized the value of teaching political economy.[12] Walker served as examiner in political economy at Harvard University from 1853 to 1860 and lecturer at Amherst College from 1860 to

1869. An early supporter of the antislavery movement and president of the Boston Temperance Society, he was elected as a Republican to the Thirty-Seventh Congress. An admirer of Adam Smith, Walker was best known as author of several books on political economy. In *The Science of Wealth,* published in 1866, he concluded that "government cannot furnish a new power in man, or a new agency in nature."[13] Walker favored paper currency based on 100% specie reserve, contraction of the currency, and a minimal economic role for government.[14] In 1874 he denounced excessive intervention by the national government in the Civil War economy.

Another outstanding faculty member was Austin Blair, born in a log cabin at Caroline, New York, in 1818. As a young lawyer, he moved from New York state to Jackson in 1842. A member of the state legislature in the 1840s, Blair was one of the earliest western politicians to advocate black suffrage. His House Judiciary Committee strongly protested a Senate report denying civil rights for Michigan blacks.[15] Blair was delegate to the Free Soil national convention at Buffalo, New York, in 1848, and in the same year he campaigned as an abolitionist for Judge of Probate. Because the 1850 Michigan constitution prohibited the granting of special charters, Blair presented a successful bill for the general incorporation of colleges in Michigan in the state senate on January 12, 1855.[16] He specifically introduced the measure to recognize the new college at Hillsdale, which recently had been transferred from Spring Arbor.

Known as the "War Governor" of Michigan, Blair for two terms was one of the most effective northern politicians in organizing domestic support for President Abraham Lincoln. In his annual 1863 message to the legislature, Governor Blair described slavery as the "vilest crime of the world." In June 1864, Hillsdale College awarded him an honorary LL.D. The statue of Blair outside the Capitol in Lansing bears the following citation: "He gave the best years of his life to Michigan and his fame is inseparably linked with the glorious achievements of her citizen-soldiers." An early leader of the abolitionist wing of the Republican party, Blair in 1867 successfully filed a writ of mandamus in the state Supreme Court that led to a decision to strike down public school segregation in Michigan. Serving three terms in Congress as representative from the Third District of Michigan after the Civil War, Blair endorsed the Thirteenth, Fourteenth, and Fifteenth Amendments for black rights.[17]

From opening on December 4, 1844, to closing on July 6, 1853, Michigan Central College had 13 graduates and a total of about 700 students. Many young students came to Spring Arbor from distant Freewill Baptist, Quaker, and antislavery families in New Hampshire, Vermont, Massachusetts, Rhode Island, New York, Ohio, Indiana, and Wisconsin. A sectional schism of the Baptist Church had occurred in 1845, and the abolitionist stance of Michigan Central strongly attracted northern Baptists and other antislavery denominations.

Students' financial costs were extremely low, as indicated by a notice in the *Jackson Patriot* on April 10, 1849: "Tuition for all branches $3 per qr. [quarter]. Tuition is reduced to this extremely low standard, because we would endeavor to encourage, rather than discourage by extra charges, those who may wish to pursue an extensive course of study. Board $1 per week. Room rent $1 per qr. Incidental expenses, 25 cents per qr., lodging, lights, and fuel, extra."

Two literary societies, the Eunomians and the Philogrammatians, contributed greatly to student life. Their meetings, featuring debates and original papers, were open to the public. After attending a literary society presentation, a reporter from the Jackson *American Citizen* invited his friends to attend the next "intellectual feast, to partake not only of the solid food of philosophical and scientific research, but the ever welcome desert of good advice, moral sentiment, and ... pure, original, rib-straining *wit*."[18] Rivaling the appeal of literary society meetings were commencement exercises. Tents protected the public from sun or rain as well-known politicians addressed the graduates. The Spring Arbor Temperance House supplied food and the Jackson Brass Band entertained.[19]

Donors, including Boston industrialist Amos Lawrence, contributed volumes to the college library collection. Leader of the early New England textile industry and member of one of America's wealthiest families, Lawrence was an early nineteenth-century philanthropist.[20] His motive in aiding Michigan Central was to promote abolitionism, and his son Amos A. Lawrence helped to raise black troops for the famous 54th Massachusetts Infantry in the Civil War.[21] Edward Everett, then president of Harvard College, donated books of high quality to the Michigan Central library. Supporting the college because of his antislavery convictions, Everett wrote to Charles Sumner in 1850, "I think I do not yield to any man in my abhorrence of slavery."[22] The college library contained 1700 volumes, and the reading room held from twenty-five to thirty periodicals.[23] Horace Wellington, professor of Latin, Greek, and Hebrew, accurately described the growing college on April 19, 1847: "This Inst. is quite popular in these parts and in general is very prosperous."[24]

The college trustees proudly declared in 1851 that their educational facilities were "unsurpassed in the West."[25] Referring to the "flourishing condition of the institution," the *American Citizen* in 1852 claimed that "no place in the State affords equal advantages to those desirous of pursuing a Collegiate course."[26] A committee of local citizens requested additional funding in March 1852, because with an "accessible, pleasant and healthful locality—the sympathy of the community in which it is located—the ability and exemplary energy of its faculty—its prudence and honesty in pecuniary liabilities—the correctness of its moral influence—and its freedom from a narrow sectarianism, it [Michigan Central] promises well to accomplish such ends as should be sought by a literary institution of a thorough and practical character."[27]

The only college to file a report with the Superintendent of Public Instruction in 1852, Michigan Central was "in a flourishing condition, owning real estate, with two college buildings substantially built of two stories, containing rooms for recitations, apparatus, libraries &c." Scientific equipment was "superior to any other at present in the State: consisting in part of an electrical machine, with a three feet plate and its accompaniments, a powerful magneto-electrical machine, galvanic batteries, air pump, orrery [planetarium], tellurium, magic lantern, with astronomical slides, microscope, globes, &c."[28] President Fairfield confidently wrote to Ransom Dunn in 1852, "2 yrs. from now we shall have 300 students all provided for and 300 more knocking and not being able to come in. Three cheers for M. C. College!!!"[29]

In less than a decade, Michigan Central had compiled an enviable record as a frontier college. The courage of various congregations, donors, and founders battling hardships on the Michigan frontier made success possible. Michigan Central opened only six months after initial proposals by local churches, and hardy pioneers built their college in the wilderness with the same enterprise and religious zeal that had characterized Puritan towns in colonial New England.

Michigan Central clearly was one of the small colleges in the West that represented the "very essence of American civilization, for in their founding was combined the westward movement, the religious diversity and passionate faith of American individualism and Protestantism, and a devotion to the ideal that every aspiring youth should find the means of acquiring whatever measure of education he desired."[30] Patriotism and moral ideals were major motives of its creation and existence.[31] Emphasizing religious goals, Michigan Central College prided itself upon being nonsectarian. Students of all denominations were invited to attend. By 1856 seventy-two Freewill Baptist churches in Michigan provided a stronger base for their college. The other successful Freewill Baptist institution of higher learning, Bates College in Maine, received its charter after the Civil War.[32]

Three Civil War generals (Clinton B. Fisk, Jasper Packard, and William Humphrey) illustrate the high educational quality of Michigan Central College.[33] Besides providing sound classical education, the frontier institution took an active interest in crucial political issues. Many Freewill Baptists who had founded the college in 1844 actively supported James Birney, presidential candidate of the Liberty party that year.[34] From the start Michigan Central College was antislavery and coeducational.[35]

Richard Bartlett, historian of the American frontier, argues that the American four-year college was primarily a western phenomenon.[36] The Freewill Baptist institution on the Michigan frontier provides an excellent example of his thesis. Michigan Central combined religious faith with the individualism of the American West. The peak years for founding colleges beyond the Appalachians were the 1850s and 104 of these institutions became permanent. To maintain their rapid rate of progress, the Michigan Central College trustees recognized the need to obtain both a construction fund and an endowment. An additional third building was essential.

Energetic and highly capable professors who recently had joined the faculty (Charles H. Churchill, 1851; Ransom Dunn, 1852; and Henry E. Whipple, 1853) raised the expectations of the college, but the community did not support the building program. "By the early 1850s Michigan Central had outgrown the meager resources of this country village. . . . "[37] Spring Arbor was not directly on the Michigan Central Railroad, and the eight and a half miles to the rail station in Jackson posed a major handicap. The value of farms in Jackson County was less than the state average, and Jackson had not even organized a Freewill Baptist church until 1849.[38] The Fairfield administration knew that inadequate funding at the present location would prevent the college from fulfilling its mission, and agitation to move from Spring Arbor began in the early 1850s.

On January 5, 1853, shortly after the publication of Harriet Beecher Stowe's *Uncle Tom's Cabin, or Life among the Lowly,* the trustees voted 9 to 2 to consider removal to a more suitable location and appointed a committee to examine possible sites.[39] Plans soon were underway to close the doors on July 6, 1853, and to transfer the college with its strong potential to Hillsdale. Other early Baptist colleges had rejected all removal offers. Colgate had considered Rochester as a possible new site; Bucknell, Philadelphia; Franklin, Indianapolis; Denison, Cincinnati; and Mercer, Atlanta.[40] In spite of relocation, the small institution begun at Spring Arbor would leave a permanent legacy, according to *The Michigan Baptist:* "Anti-slavery and co-educational from the start, sympathetic with students who earned their way by cutting firewood and otherwise, liberally responsible to the nation's call in 1860, loyal to their institution in trying times of 1874 when college halls were destroyed by fire, the fervent spirit of service which characterized its beginning has permeated its development since."[41]

Endnotes

1. Rev. Chauncey Reynolds' home was a station on the Underground Railroad. Nine of Rev. and Mrs. Reynolds' eleven children survived to maturity; all nine attended college at Michigan Central or at Hillsdale.

2. S. W. Norton, "Hillsdale College, Hillsdale, Michigan," *Michigan Pioneer and Historical Society Historical Collections*, XXXII (1903): 452–53. Not until the 1850s did framed houses generally replace log cabins in the Jackson and Hillsdale area.

3. Lawrence A. Cremin, *American Education: The National Experience, 1783–1876* (New York: 1988), p. 165; Howard H. Peckham, *The Making of the University of Michigan, 1817–1967* (Ann Arbor, 1967), p. 58.

4. An Act to Incorporate the Michigan Central College at Spring Arbor, *Acts of the Legislature of the State of Michigan, Passed at the Annual Session of 1845* (Detroit, 1845), pp. 36–37. The charter also provided that the state Superintendent of Public Instruction (soon replaced in this function by boards of visitors) attend examinations each year and report to the legislature on the condition of the college. Annual reports by boards of visitors for the next half century are extremely valuable in evaluating Michigan colleges.

5. An act to amend the act to incorporate the Michigan Central College at Spring Arbor, *Acts of the Legislature of the State of Michigan, Passed at the Annual Session of 1850* (Detroit, 1850), pp. 105–6.

6. The Michigan legislature was the first west of the Appalachians to establish minimum standards for a college before it could incorporate. On April 16, 1839, Marshall College (a Presbyterian school in Marshall) and St. Philip's College (a Catholic institution in Detroit) each received a charter granting the power to confer degrees. Both colleges, however, experienced brief and unsuccessful histories.

7. *Catalogue of the Officers and Students of Michigan Central College, at Spring Arbor, 1845–6* (Jackson, 1846), p. 12. MHC. The concise code regarding student conduct at Michigan Central resembles the advice given to freshmen by Robert E. Lee as president of Washington College following the Civil War: "Young gentlemen, we have no printed rules. We have but one rule and it is that every student must be a gentleman."

8. "The date of 'founding' of a college has been defined as the date on which the legal right to confer degrees was granted to the institution either by implication or by explicit reference." Donald G. Tewskbury, *The Founding of American Colleges and Universities before the Civil War* (New York, 1969), p. 30.

9. *System of Public Instruction and Primary School Law of Michigan* (Lansing, 1852), p. 637.

10. Micaiah and Hannah Fairfield, Edmund's parents, are buried at Oak Grove cemetery, north of the Hillsdale College campus. Hannah was born to slave-owners in Virginia in 1787. The Reverend Micaiah Fairfield, her second husband, was a veteran of the War of 1812. When he saw slaves firsthand in Virginia, Rev. Fairfield immediately opposed slavery and adopted views which influenced his son, Edmund. *Addenda to Memorabilia of the Class of 1881* (Number Five, 1944), p. 41.

11. "Lives of the Founders and Builders of Hillsdale College," *The Advance* (June 23, 1886): 306.

12. Yale University, on the other hand, did not have a chair of political economy until 1872.

13. President D. M. Graham of Hillsdale College formally endorsed the seventh edition of this well-known volume in 1872 and adopted it as a textbook. *The Science of Wealth*, 7th edition (Philadelphia, 1872), p. 2.

14. Francis A. Walker, "The Hon. Amasa Walker, LL.D.," *The Historical and Genealogical Register*, XLII (April 1888), pp. 133–41; Joseph Dorfman, *The Economic Mind in American Civilization, 1606–1865* (New York, 1946), II, p. 751. Amasa Walker taught at Michigan Central College largely because he endorsed the antislavery views of the institution. Walker had helped to organize the New England Anti-Slavery Society in 1831. His son, Francis Amasa Walker, also became a well-known economist.

15. Eric Foner, *Free Soil, Free Labor, Free Men: The Ideology of the Republican Party before the Civil War* (New York, 1971), p. 283. As late as April 1868, Michigan voters defeated a new state constitution that included black suffrage by a 3 to 2 ratio.

16. *Report of the Superintendent of Public Instruction of the State of Michigan for the Year 1863* (Lansing, 1863), p. 15. "The new Constitution of the State having forbidden the granting of special charters for any private corporation

whatever, and a project being on foot to establish a College at Hillsdale, a general law for the incorporation of Colleges was asked of the Legislature. On 12th day of January 1855, Hon. Austin Blair presented, in the Senate, a 'Bill for the incorporation of Colleges and other institutions of learning.'" Blair's bill passed the Senate unanimously, and the House of Representatives voted in favor, 54 to 14. AKG.

17. *History of Jackson County, Michigan* (Chicago, 1881), p. 594; George S. May, *Michigan: An Illustrated History of the Great Lakes State* (Northridge, CA, 1987), pp. 84–85. When the new state capitol was occupied in 1879, two portraits—Governor Austin Blair and the Marquis de Lafayette—were placed at the front of the Senate chamber. Blair is buried in Jackson, Michigan, which was his home. He rode by horseback to teach at Michigan Central College.

18. *The American Citizen* (Jackson), February 4, 1852.

19. Ibid., June 30, 1852.

20. William R. Lawrence, ed., *Extracts from the Diary and Correspondence of the Late Amos Lawrence* (Boston, 1855), observes on p. 198: "Nearly every day, at this period [1845], bears some record of his charities; and among others was a considerable donation to a Baptist college, in another State." There are no available records to indicate whether or not this gift by Amos Lawrence was the one to Michigan Central College.

21. Dudley Taylor Cornish, *The Sable Arm: Black Troops in the Union Army, 1861–1865* (Lawrence, KS, 1987), p. 108.

22. As quoted by Paul R. Frothingham in *Edward Everett: Orator and Statesman* (Boston, 1925), p. 355. In the antebellum era, Edward Everett was elected to each house of Congress, and in 1860 he campaigned for Vice-President on the Constitutional Union ticket. One of the most outstanding orators in the nation, Everett delivered the principal speech of an hour and fifty-seven minutes at the dedication of the Gettysburg national cemetery. Everett sensed immediately that he had been overshadowed by the brilliance of President Lincoln's shorter and more majestic prose. He later wrote to the President, "I should be glad if I could flatter myself that I came as near to the central idea of the occasion in two hours as you did in two minutes."

23. *The American Citizen* (Jackson), August 20, 1851.

24. H. Wellington, letter from Spring Arbor to friends at Lynn, Massachusetts, April 19, 1847. Michigan Central College Collection, MHC.

25. *The American Citizen* (Jackson), November 12, 1851.

26. Ibid., February 25, 1852.

27. Ibid., March 31, 1852.

28. *System of Public Instruction and Primary School Law of Michigan* (Lansing, 1852), pp. 192, 284.

29. President E. B. Fairfield to Rev. Ransom Dunn, December 4, 1852. Ransom Dunn Collection, MHC.

30. Alice Felt Tyler, *Freedom's Ferment* (New York, 1962), p. 257.

31. *Free Baptist Cyclopaedia* (Boston, 1886), p. 264.

32. Bates College awarded Ransom Dunn the honorary degree of D.D. in 1873. *General Catalogue of Bates College*, 1931.

33. College pranks were common even on the Michigan frontier in the 1840s. A student at Michigan Central College occasionally stole food sent by Clinton B. Fisk's mother. Fisk finally caught the student helping himself to homemade pie. He told the offender that the pie contained poison to kill rats in the dormitory. Fisk and a friend then administered a strong medical "remedy" that made the transgressor physically ill!

34. Floyd Streeter, *Political Parties in Michigan, 1837–1860* (Lansing, 1918), p. 216.

35. Helen Dunn Gates, *A Consecrated Life: A Sketch of the Life and Labors of Rev. Ransom Dunn, D.D.* (Boston, 1901), pp. 104–5; *Michigan Baptist* (May 1923). Mrs. Helen Gates, Professor Dunn's daughter, served as second president of the Hillsdale College Women's Commission from 1897 to 1902.

36. Richard A. Bartlett, *The New Country: A Social History of the American Frontier, 1776–1890* (New York, 1974), pp. 393–94.

37. David B. Potts, *Baptist Colleges in the Development of American Society, 1812–1861* (New York, 1988), pp. 61–62.

38. *Fourteenth Annual Report of the Freewill Baptist Home Mission Society* (Dover, NH, 1848).

39. Minutes of January 5, 1853, Records of the Proceedings of the Board of Trustees of Michigan Central College at Spring Arbor, from the year 1853 to July 9, 1855. HCVPA.

40. Potts, *Baptist Colleges,* p. 300.

THREE

The "Oak Openings" of Hillsdale in the 1850s

To you who so efficiently helped to plant in the oak openings of Michigan an abolition college which has blessed and helped thousands—that is glory enough for one man.[1]
—Anonymous student to Professor Ransom Dunn

Ransom Dunn was primarily responsible for influencing the faculty and administration to support removal of the college from Spring Arbor.[2] Bitter debate marked the so-called "stormy session," when the trustees, on January 5, 1853, considered a resolution for relocation. Amid great excitement, students left their classes and citizens called off business affairs to attend the crucial meeting. By 9 to 2, the trustees voted to consider the expediency of moving the college to a more suitable location.[3] The board on January 19 selected Jackson, Adrian, Coldwater, Hillsdale, and Marshall as potential sites.[4]

President Fairfield and Ransom Dunn, leading committee members, first visited Coldwater, where they were warmly received and given promises of liberal contributions to secure the college. On his own initiative, Professor Dunn decided to return home through a severe snowstorm by way of Hillsdale, although no Freewill Baptists lived there. On January 14, Dunn, a total stranger, inquired at the Hillsdale House, the larger of two hotels in town, for names of citizens interested in education. Dr. Alonzo Cressy assured Dunn, "The

people will wish to see you, sir." Cressy invited the leading citizens
to his physician's office. The leaders then attended a public meeting
at the courthouse that same evening. To twenty persons, not one of
whom belonged to his denomination, Professor Dunn explained his
plan for building a first-class college. In forty brief minutes, Ransom
Dunn secured the educational future of those determined to play a
leadership role in nineteenth-century American education.

Dunn specified these goals: "One thing must be distinctly understood that the school from the first is to be a denominational one
but not [narrowly] sectarian, furnishing no special advantages to any
denomination, nor refusing favor to any; neither does it propose to
make distinctions on the ground of sex or color."[5] An observer later
described Dunn's impact at the meeting: "You so satisfactorily presented the subject as to satisfy us all with the feasibility of the project. . . . I have always regarded you as the principal founder of
Hillsdale College and its most steadfast friend, and as having raised
more money than any one else for its endowment."[6] The citizens
enthusiastically voted to acquire Michigan Central College. As an
historian summarized in 1883, "Hillsdale had captured the professor,
and the professor had captured Hillsdale."[7] President Fairfield later
credited Dunn with having "discovered" Hillsdale.

The next day Dunn, with three local citizens, examined four
potential building sites. To reach the last one, the men waded in their
boots through mud on the one north-south road, now Hillsdale Street,
over the St. Joseph River, and through a small alder swamp at the
base of the future "College Hill."[8] No east-west crossroad existed
north of the swamp and the open pasture, and one small frame building and an orchard dotted the barren landscape. The present campus,
on the crest of the hill north of the alder swamp, then was a half-
cleared pasture, surrounded by a split rail fence. "Stumps, wild grass,
and browsing cattle held rule."[9] Deer and other wildlife ran across the
openings that became part of "College Hill." (Partridges, turkeys,
and quail would be hunted by students a few hundred yards from the
new college building.[10]) A deep sinkhole, a frog pond, and woodland
were located west of the future campus, and strawberries grew on the
surrounding hills. Dunn recognized the potential of this magnificent

elevation north of town, soon to become the permanent home of the college. Because President Fairfield, meanwhile, had been favorably impressed by his visit to Coldwater, Professor Dunn's confidence in Hillsdale soon would have to be backed by strong evidence of local commitment.

The Board of Trustees decided to hold classes at Spring Arbor until the close of the academic year, but a faction at Michigan Central College chose not to give up without a fight. An unfortunate series of charges and countercharges followed. There is irony in the situation, because the citizens of Spring Arbor at an earlier meeting to retain the college had been able to raise only $350, plus pledges from the professors themselves. On January 29, 1853, citizens opposing the removal of the institution drew up an accusation: "*Resolved,* that the attempt on the part of the Faculty, connected with the Michigan Central College, at Spring Arbor, to change its location, is an act of gross injustice and ingratitude. . . . "[11] On February 9, the same pro-Spring Arbor group argued:

> The entire faculty, and every Freewill Baptist on the board of trustees except one, have determined not to patronize or sustain longer than to the end of the next term, the Michigan Central College at Spring Arbor. . . . We pledge a sacred regard to the original intentions of the donors, to built up a literary institution at Spring Arbor. No religious denomination is named in the charter, but the Freewill Baptists have had a majority of the board of trustees. . . . We say the funds were contributed for educational purposes, exclusively by the friends of education of all religious creeds, and of all political parties and should not be used to advance the interest of one at the expense of another.[12]

Having received positive reactions from Coldwater and Hillsdale, the site committee next appointed five trustees to select among Hillsdale, Coldwater, Jackson, Adrian, and Marshall, with the stipulation that the new college community contribute $15,000 toward construction. Many friends of Michigan Central favored Jackson, one of the four largest towns in the state, because of its proximity to Spring Arbor; but proslavery sentiment there rejected the abolitionist college. Hillsdale secretly took the initiative by sending four leading citizens incognito (Daniel Pratt, Dr. George Underwood, C. J. Dickerson, and Dr. Daniel Beebe) to Spring Arbor. They concluded that, although the physical plant was worth little, Hillsdale should acquire the college because of an excellent faculty backed by an energetic denomination.[13] The Hillsdale delegation returned home determined to obtain the college, although Coldwater still remained the probable choice.

After receiving a firm offer of $10,000 from Coldwater, the Michigan Central College relocation committee came to Hillsdale. Informed about Coldwater's bid of $10,000, citizens led by Dr. George Underwood directly asked the relocation committee to name a price for obtaining the college. After conferring, the committee settled upon $15,000 for construction. The Hillsdale citizenry replied in the affirmative, with the stipulation that the college itself raise another $15,000 for building purposes.[14] Although the sum of $30,000 seems meager, other permanent colleges at the same time were begun with less than $10,000 in subscriptions. By gentlemen's agreement based on honor, the deal was sealed. (One wonders how many documents and how much legalistic bickering would be required today!) The Michigan Central College Board of Trustees ratified the arrangement on February 16, 1853, the deadline previously chosen for a decision.[15] To carry out the ambitious plans, the board appointed trustees Daniel Dunakin, Edmund Fairfield, Henry Limbocker, Henry Whipple, and Charles Churchill as the Prudential Committee, which immediately became a permanent and vital part of the institution.[16]

The Michigan Central College Board of Trustees officially met as a body for the first time at Hillsdale on May 25, 1853. The trustees promptly appointed a committee to examine the possibility of consolidating with Geauga Seminary, which Freewill Baptists had established in 1842 near the village of Chester, Ohio. The goal of the seminary (more accurately, an academy) was to offer both a basic classical education and an introduction to the cultured life. The founders included Ransom Dunn. Opposed to slavery, the Geauga trustees had rejected their first charter from the Ohio legislature in 1843 because it excluded blacks as students. The academy was relatively weak, and the Freewill Baptist Conference thought it advisable to combine their western educational work in one institution. After a year of discussion, Geauga Seminary was sold and the funds (over $2000) were transferred to Hillsdale College; institutions dating from 1842 and 1844 had merged. Hillsdale gained some faculty, books, and scientific apparatus.

The most noteworthy student at the Geauga Seminary was James A. Garfield, a soldier-politician who would later serve as Union general, congressman, and president of the United States. S. D. Bates, future Hillsdale College trustee, had influenced the young man in 1849 to begin his formal education at the Freewill Baptist academy; and at age seventeen Garfield left his work as driver and helmsman on the Ohio Canal.[17] Garfield rented a room with two other young men in an old frame house near the Geauga campus. During his attendance for four terms during 1849 and 1850, he studied under several future Hillsdale College faculty, including Geauga principal Spencer Fowler. The Geauga catalogue listed 252 students (140 males and 112 females) and a staff of five men and three women.[18]

Fundraising for the college to be constructed at Hillsdale proceeded well in 1853. The Prudential Committee reported in May that Hillsdale County residents already had exceeded their goal of $15,000 for construction. No church ever owned independent Hillsdale College, which consistently supported strong religious goals. Congressman Esbon Blackmar of Newark, New York, a prosperous Episcopalian merchant who owned a thousand acres of land adjoining Hillsdale village on the north, contributed a twenty-five acre campus to the Baptist college, plus $500 in cash.[19] The land previously had been used as a wheat field and a sheep pasture. Blackmar stipulated that his property, worth from $10 to $20 an acre, always be used for education and that a majority of the trustees be Hillsdale County residents.[20] The college trustees formally accepted his gift on May 26, 1853.

At its May meeting, the Board of Trustees resolved to raise $100,000 for endowment, with only the interest to be spent. This decision by the college trustees was the first of many to reveal frugality and careful management of assets.[21] On principle, the trustees refused to go into debt. Only available funds were used to pay faculty salaries. The cause of financial distress among many early Baptist colleges was the "pressure of debts incurred while acquiring facilities and a corresponding lack of endowment."[22] Despite the financial panic of 1857, the $100,000 goal for endowment was met by 1861, although the Civil War caused a loss of at least $25,000 in the form of personal securities. Later in the century Hillsdale frequently described itself as the "college which does more with the money at hand than any other school in the U.S." At the May meeting, the trustees also appointed a committee of fifteen to receive the deed for the new site and created a building committee of six members.

Laurens B. Potter, one of the earliest students at Michigan Central College and later a trustee, defended the transfer of the college to Hillsdale: "It is proposed to secure facilities and advantages [for the college] . . . that its prosperity may still continue, that its sphere of usefulness may be enlarged. . . . *Resolved,* That we, as friends of the Michigan Central College, possessing a true knowledge of the real worth of our Professors, do most earnestly remonstrate against *any*thing and *every*thing tending to cast a stain upon their moral character as *men.* . . . "[23] [Emphasis is Potter's.]

The last commencement at Michigan Central in Spring Arbor took place on July 6, 1853, two days after the cornerstone was laid in Hillsdale. A Michigan Central College faction, however, continued some instruction at Spring Arbor until the close of the academic year in July 1854.[24] At this point, Hillsdale College was eager to obtain the secretary's record book of Michigan Central College dating from 1844. The Spring Arbor faction persuaded the constable to deliver a search warrant to L. J. Thompson, Michigan Central secretary who favored the Hillsdale location. Laurens B. Potter, however, already had obtained the record book and concealed it under straw in a friend's barn at Spring Arbor. When the constable failed to locate the book, Potter carried it to an old store in Jackson and finally to Hillsdale.[25] Possession of the record book lacked legal significance, but Hillsdale College had gained something of a psychological victory.

Hillsdale, new site of the ambitious college, was first settled in

1835 by New England and New York pioneers who faced wolves and panthers while farming the virgin soil. In 1847 Hillsdale became an incorporated village. A Hillsdale native, who became a college student in 1862, described the community as he remembered it twenty years earlier: "Roads were things unknown. . . . There were no schools or churches. Hillsdale village consisted of a gristmill, an old log tavern, and three or four dwellings situated south of the place it now occupies. . . . Jonesville could boast about the same importance. . . . The farmers, as soon as able to raise wheat, drew it with ox teams to Adrian, and those with horses often [went] to Toledo or Monroe, and received from thirty to sixty cents per bushel. They were generally poor. . . ."[26]

Politically, the village in the early 1850s was strongly Democratic and opposed abolitionism. The arrival of the college brought an immediate and drastic political change. People like Ransom Dunn, former president of the Free Baptist Antislavery Society, influenced Hillsdale by 1855 to support the Free Soilers, a political party opposed to the extension of slavery into western territories. Hillsdale County became a leader in the Republican ranks of Michigan. In the five elections for governor from 1856 to 1864, the county generally voted Republican by a ratio of 2 to 1 or larger.

Physical development of the village by the early 1850s extended only slightly north of the railroad, but construction of homes beyond the St. Joseph River accompanied the transfer of the college from Spring Arbor.[27] Years later, President Willfred Mauck still could describe the Hillsdale of his youth in the early twentieth century as "more like a community of tiny farms, set close together. Behind every house there was a barn, with a horse or two, and perhaps some cows. . . . Every house had its fairly large kitchen garden. . . . So, you see, we had the best of town living, and the country, too."[28]

Townspeople sometimes referred to "College Hill" as "Piety Knob," but they soon recognized that the institution stimulated growth and prosperity. When the site was chosen, land as far as seven miles from Hillsdale immediately rose in value by two dollars an acre. In ten years, 1850 to 1860, the population of the village doubled from one to two thousand. Ransom Dunn believed that the town was small enough for the residents to appreciate the college and large enough to provide adequate support. A majority of Baptist colleges at mid-nineteenth century, incidentally, were located in towns of one to two thousand residents.[29] (Spring Arbor also had been a village of about a thousand people in 1850, but the growth rate already had leveled off.)

Dunn reminded the community at the end of the century that the greatest worth was not economic prosperity but educational gain: "The real value of colleges and universities is not to be estimated by the magnitude of buildings or endowments, but by the increase of mental power and moral force."[30] Oratorical contests, musical recitals, commencement exercises, students' lecture courses, and public meetings of the literary societies offered Hillsdale residents opportunities generally unavailable to westerners. Particularly unique on the Michigan frontier were speeches by women undergraduates. The first annual exercises on June 18, 1856, included essays by Caroline Ford on "Our Country's Prospects"; Etta Vance on "Personal Responsibility"; and Clariet Capron on "The Sphere of Woman."[31]

Approximately the population center of antebellum Michigan, Hillsdale was an advantageous location for the college and the village. The absence of any other colleges on the Michigan Southern Railroad was beneficial.[32] Completion of the section of the Michigan Southern from Monroe to Hillsdale in October 1843 stimulated economic prosperity. Strap iron rails, three-quarters of an inch thick, were used to construct the original track. Hillsdale for the next decade was the railhead, a thriving storage center for domestic business. A significant railroad terminus with large warehouses, the village became the shipping point for three counties. Farmers brought grain by wagon from surrounding towns such as LaGrange, Angola, Bryan, and Homer. The Michigan Southern expanded eastward by leasing the privately financed Erie and Kalamazoo, which was the first railroad built west of the Appalachian Mountains.[33] The state of Michigan, recognizing the failure of public enterprises, sold the Michigan Southern in 1846 to private investors from New York, who successfully extended the line westward from Hillsdale. With excitement at a high pitch, the Michigan Southern raced the Michigan Central to reach Chicago first. The *Chicago Daily Journal* reported on February 20, 1852, that the

Michigan Southern, the first eastern train into Chicago, arrived that morning. In the following year, the railroad earned profits exceeding a million dollars.[34] Cornelius Vanderbilt acquired the Lake Shore & Michigan Southern in 1873 as the western extension of his New York Central system, and Hillsdale gained a position on the trunk line from New York City to Chicago.

With the completion of the Michigan Southern into Chicago, Hillsdale village leaders recognized that they might lose some of their former storage business, and this made them more enthusiastic about the transfer of the college from Spring Arbor. The railroad helped to attract students by providing reduced rates. Of the sixteen antebellum Baptist college towns studied by David Potts, only Hillsdale had rail transportation.[35] As an alternative route, Hillsdale County also had the Chicago Military Road, now U.S. 12, which grew out of the need to connect forts in Detroit and Chicago. The road, extending 254 miles west from Detroit, in effect served as an extension of the Erie Canal and became the main route into southern Michigan.[36] The other early Baptist college towns depended upon coach roads, canals and/or rivers for transportation.

Area residents soon oversubscribed the $15,000 goal to relocate the college from Spring Arbor. Citizens of the township and the county contributed $22,500, and inhabitants of the village an additional $7,000. Progress was so rapid that Fairfield could write on June 7, 1853, "We have contracted for 1,000,000 of brick. The buildings are to be enclosed this fall. Plenty of money even for my largest plan without basement. [Sufficient funds permitted the construction of a large building with four floors and a basement.] All moves right."[37] The construction contract was signed on June 13, 1853, and laborers received fifty cents a day. The cornerstone-laying ceremony on July 4, 1853, attracted more than 6,000 people, four times the size of the village and the largest crowd that Hillsdale ever had hosted. Dust-covered people arrived from miles around by oxen and wagons to witness the event. Placing a cornerstone in the middle of a frontier pasture symbolized the college founders' pioneering fortitude.

In his oration on the seventy-seventh anniversary of American independence, President Fairfield praised the community's cooperation: "The cordiality, the unanimity, and the liberality with which they have contributed to the erection of the building whose corner-stone is now to be laid, have not often been paralleled in the history of such institutions." Fairfield's major theme was a ringing endorsement of freedom: "The College is the friend of the Republic, and the Republic should be the friend of the College. Our educational establishments ever have been the faithful allies and firm supporters of all that is ennobling in our free institutions, and every lover of the Republic should see to it that they are nurtured and guarded with a sleepless vigilance."[38] By August 1853, foundations had been laid for a new building, 262 by 60 feet.

Leading faculty members, meanwhile, worked to raise endowment. To avoid legal complications, they used a simple subscription form for all pledges. The key sentence was: "We, the undersigned, agree to pay . . . for the erecting of College building, at Hillsdale, for the use of the Michigan Central College." The courts, both circuit and appellate, upheld the document in every case that arose. Agent for the New York State Temperance Society, President Fairfield travelled to New England and New York but suffered from bad health during his fund-raising efforts. He wrote from Buffalo to Ransom Dunn on November 26, 1854, "Already I begin to feel the pressure of more care than I am prepared to sustain. But I can manage to throw it off. I have been obliged as far as possible to forget that there is a college in Mich. in order to live. My tendency is to a fatal disease of the heart, and I am obliged to throw off all care as far as possible . . . . I need not tell you that this inability to labor for the college endowment has been to me the trial of my life."[39] Professor Henry Whipple, meanwhile, raised funds in Michigan, Ohio, and Indiana.

Professor Dunn accepted the most demanding assignment of all—to secure $10,000 in the territory west of the Great Lakes, including Illinois, Wisconsin, Iowa, and Minnesota. Departing in July 1853, for two years he travelled 6,000 miles by carriage and horseback over broken prairies and raised more than $22,000 in small individual pledges.[40] Dunn's original subscription list contains thousands of donors, many of whom contributed one to five dollars. He signed his impressive list of contributors with a modest summary:

"Was sent after $10,000. *Secured.*" Dunn often spoke at school-houses, where evangelists held religious services on the frontier. People of modest means, some of whom lived in log houses or shanties and lacked even the necessities of life, contributed to the early endowment. Out of this adversity rose the pioneer college and its passion for independence.

Physically frail and suffering from poor eyesight, Ransom Dunn not only raised funds but also attracted enrollment for Hillsdale College, because each contribution of $100 provided permanently free tuition for one student. O. A. Janes, later U. S. pension agent for Michigan, wrote: "I well remember you, when I was a boy, at Johnston, Wisconsin, pleading for Hillsdale College and preaching in the old stone schoolhouse. I then made up my mind that I should attend college at Hillsdale."[41] During his expedition, Dunn was elected president of the Freewill Baptist Ministry in the West, which held a convention at Marengo, Illinois, on October 12, 1854. This organization later became the Western Evangelical Missionary Association (also called the Western Ministerial Convention).[42]

A serious legal issue suddenly arose when Spring Arbor citizens on August 27, 1853, obtained a preliminary injunction in the Jackson County Circuit Court to restrain the trustees from selling or removing property from Michigan Central College. Spring Arbor citizens claimed that they were stockholders of the college corporation, because of their earlier financial contributions. A court mandate prevented the trustees from continuing work on the building at Hillsdale. Pledges were not paid, and work was suspended.[43] The court also restrained individual trustees from obtaining additional funds, and enthusiasm in Hillsdale for the new college temporarily waned. The contractor for the brickwork, a Mr. Perkins, worked alone for months. He stopped after completing the first floor and covered the walls with boards for protection. For months Hillsdale appeared to have gained little more than a skeleton college. Fortunately, the circuit court judge dissolved the original injunction with a decision in late 1854 that "there were no stockholders of the corporation [at Spring Arbor] to be protected by a court of equity."

Reports of Professor Dunn's successful fundraising in the West also boosted morale. Equally important, Professor Whipple influenced the Free Baptist Educational Society in New Hampton, New Hampshire, to raise $25,000 for Hillsdale. The successful Freewill Baptist seminary established two years before in New Hampton had hoped to receive all the denominational funds for higher education. By February 1854, the *Hillsdale Standard* informed subscribers to the college building fund that construction would resume on April first.

The impossibility of removing the Michigan Central College charter to Hillsdale was perplexing. The state legislators never would have granted that charter had they believed that the small college could fulfill the requirement of equaling University of Michigan standards. The fixed policy of the state was to reserve the power of granting collegiate degrees for the University of Michigan. John D. Pierce, who became the first Michigan Superintendent of Public Instruction in 1836, strongly opposed chartering private colleges. Hillsdale trustees decided to request the legislature to enact a general college incorporation law, rather than to amend the previous private charter of March 20, 1850, to allow a change of location. Freewill Baptists accomplished the seemingly impossible task because they had identified politically with the antislavery cause. Leaders like President Fairfield helped to organize the Republicans at Jackson; and Freewill Baptists almost unanimously supported the new political party in the 1854 campaign, when the Republicans came into power in Michigan.

The election of a Republican legislature and governor gave the college at Hillsdale an undeniable advantage, because "the friends of the institution and the denomination had claims upon the new party in power."[44] Daniel Dunakin, early trustee of Michigan Central who had built the stone foundations of the first campus with his own hands, won election to the state House of Representatives from Calhoun County in 1854 with the express goal of supporting a new general incorporation bill for colleges. Dr. Alonzo Cressy, elected to the Michigan Senate from Hillsdale, shared this aim. Austin Blair, who previously had taught at Michigan Central College, presented his general incorporation bill for private colleges to the state Senate on January 12, 1855. Blair's private college bill, passing the Senate unanimously and the House by 54 to 14, became law on February 19, 1855.[45] Although Austin Blair's purpose was to recognize the new college in Hillsdale, all future denominational colleges in Michigan would be incorporated under this act. "The history of that law is simply a chapter in the history of Hillsdale College."[46]

A meeting to incorporate the college under the new law was held on March 22, 1855, in the basement of the Presbyterian church in Hillsdale. As a "body corporate and politic," Hillsdale College became the first institution organized under the general statute.[47] Articles of Association were approved, a new board of thirty-five trustees was elected, and land and money held in trust were now turned over to the college.[48] The new articles declared that the "object of this institution is to furnish to all persons who wish, irrespective of nationality, color, or sex, a literary and scientific education as comprehensive and thorough as is usually pursued in other colleges in this country, and to combine with this, such moral and social instruction as will best develop the minds and improve the hearts of the pupils."[49]

One obstacle still remained. The trustees of Michigan Central College had packed their board with people opposing the removal to Hillsdale. The two boards of trustees now waged a final contest, in which the Spring Arbor faction retained the property of the older corporation, worth between $20,000 and $25,000. In the process, records were lost and books and scientific equipment scattered. Hillsdale College, however, had secured "the faculty, the brains, and the living soul of the old college at Spring Arbor."[50]

At their first annual meeting on July 18, 1855, the trustees voted to open the college on the first Wednesday in November. They set tuition at $20 a year, gentleman's room rent at $8 to $10 a year, lady's rent at $5 to $8, and incidentals at $2 or $3. The weekly charge for board without tea or coffee was $1.50. Some of the costs were soon reduced. Most students received income from scholarships that covered tuition, and renting a scholarship was possible for others. The low costs at Hillsdale contrasted markedly with those of Brown University, the oldest Baptist college. Tuition at Brown was $60 a year, with additional charges for items such as servants and fuel.[51] With their frontier background, Hillsdale students lacked servants and cut their own firewood. Careful accounting techniques and professorial salaries averaging from $750 to $800 enabled Hillsdale College to compensate for low income from student revenue. During the entire nineteenth century, average student costs were 25 to 50 percent lower at Hillsdale than at comparable liberal arts institutions.

The trustees learned on November 6 that the cost of construction was $33,947.12, leaving a debt of $7,565.04. To prevent endowment funds from being used for this construction debt, the board passed Ransom Dunn's resolution: "All funds raised toward the endowment of the College by donations or the sale of scholarships outside of Hillsdale County shall be held forever sacred, the interest only to be expended."[52] From 1855 to 1865, the endowment accordingly rose from nothing to $48,111.96. These figures seem small by today's standards—but in the 1850s, annual insurance costs for the college were $252, and yearly repairs averaged $300!

Although the college structure was not completed by the fall of 1855, the opening gala was held in November. Trees still had to be felled and stumps cleared. The summer had been warm and wet; ague, a malarial fever, weakened many carpenters. The dining room in the basement of the east wing was painted only two days before the grand celebration. Arriving by train or teams of horses, many trustees, donors, and clergy attended the opening festivities. By necessity, the unfinished college became a "dormitory, hotel, assembly hall, and host to both transient and permanent guests."[53]

Students began arriving for the opening of the fall term on November 17, as news about violence over the slavery issue in "Bleeding Kansas" attracted national attention. They were met by a faculty consisting of a president, six professors, one tutor, a lady principal, and student assistants. Some students found their rooms totally unfurnished, without a stove, bed, or chair. These were days of homesickness and discouragement! The men were housed temporarily on the fourth floor of East Hall because the west wing was not completed. The front campus was little more than ungraded ground, mud, and piles of lumber and brick. Wild strawberries grew on the surrounding hills, and the only evidence of technology was an old mill. A reservoir was not dug behind West Hall until 1856. Describing the hardships of these opening days, President Fairfield quoted Vergil: "Perhaps you may hereafter enjoy the recollection of these trials."

Completion of the campus proceeded rapidly in the late fall of 1855. Those who had shivered in cold rooms now received carpeting and other amenities. Standard furnishings included a bed, a table, a stove, a cabinet and two chairs. Students supplied their lights and firewood.[54] Built of brick, the majestic building had four floors and a basement. The central part contained the chapel surrounded by galleries, five recitation rooms, two society halls, and the treasurer's office. The East Hall lower level was the dining room, and on the first floor were the parlor and the halls of the women's literary societies. Ladies' dormitories filled the rest of the east wing. A reporter for the *Hillsdale Standard* claimed that "the accommodations for young ladies are unsurpassed by any institution in the country." A museum, laboratory, recitation rooms and men's dormitories were located in the west wing.

The magnificent structure contained a total of 25 public rooms and 110 dormitory rooms. Students drew lots on the first day of each term for choice of rooms. The college community was sheltered, fed, taught, and preached to in the same building, although some students obtained rooms in the village and boarded themselves. Several young men who provided their own food lived on potatoes, mush, bread, rice, eggs, tea, applesauce, and butter.[55] In spite of inconvenient kitchen facilities, women from town served a public dinner at the college for 400 persons on November 20. This was the first of many community-college projects, and the proceeds helped to furnish rooms in the new building. Visiting Hillsdale in December 1855, a *Detroit Tribune* reporter admired "the new college building, which overlooks the whole town and surrounding country from a commanding eminence at the north of the village. This is a stately and imposing structure, and catches the eye of the traveler at a distance of miles on the railroad, east and west. It was erected through the intelligent and bountiful liberality of the citizens of the village and vicinity, and is, at once, a monument of their own interest in the cause of education, and an ornament and honor to the place."[56] The college dome was the first thing seen by visitors entering Hillsdale, and the last as they left.

Attendance for the first term was 162 students. Most enrolled in the preparatory course, which was required preceding classical or scientific collegiate studies because Michigan had only seventeen high schools in the 1850s. One year of preparatory study was sufficient at first. However, classical preparatory studies at Hillsdale were increased to two years in 1860 and to three years in 1871. The scientific preparatory course remained at one year. Hillsdale village was fortunate in having a schoolhouse, built in 1847 on the courthouse yard, to provide education through the intermediate grades. The new Central School in 1868 accommodated 500 pupils and offered studies through the high school level. Hillsdale first conferred high school diplomas in 1875, but the college usually had to rely on its own preparatory school. The length of time that a student remained on the Hillsdale campus varied from one term to the seven years required for a full preparatory program plus college. During the antebellum era, Hillsdale, like most small colleges, educated more students on the preparatory than on the collegiate level.

Hillsdale operated three departments beyond the preparatory level: (1) college course, (2) English and scientific, and (3) ladies' course. All announcements clearly stated that any woman who chose could pursue the full college course, leading to the classical or B.A. degree. The four-year classical curriculum resembled the earlier program at Michigan Central College. The ancient classics, ethics, and rhetoric remained the basic subjects. Optimistic college publications and faculty speeches endorsed the strong curriculum. A student commented about his work at Hillsdale: "Looked at from every point of view, classical study secures a greater variety of important advantages than can be derived from any other branch of study."[57]

Scattered in rural areas, colleges of a dozen instructors and several hundred students characterized higher education in the West. Hillsdale was more fortunate in the size of faculty than most frontier colleges of the 1850s, though salaries were low. During their first year, professors Whipple and Churchill each received $525. Hillsdale instructors usually were trained in the classics and divinity, and they were generalists rather than specialists. During his lengthy career, Ransom Dunn taught a total of thirteen subjects.

Hillsdale, a small hilltop college, was determined to provide an integrated education, to make ladies and gentlemen as well as scholars. The result was a respect for learning all too rare in modern education. Evangelist Fairfield in 1856 added to his many responsibilities by preaching (at an annual salary of $150) at North Reading, eight miles from Hillsdale. During his first three years, he converted approximately 500 people. In May 1857, the church was formally organized; and a meeting house was completed by May 1859 from donated labor and materials. The clerk's record book of the North Reading Baptist Church contains many references to President Fairfield, including his annual acceptances of the duties of pastor. On September 21, 1867, he refused the call to the pastorate after eleven years of service.[58] Fairfield also preached for eight years at the Free Will Baptist Church of Reading, constructed in 1858.[59] He prepared his sermons by reading the Bible in Greek. Years later, at age eighty-five, Fairfield still eloquently endorsed moral standards: "Understand that to be honest with yourself, to make the most of yourself, to make the most of the faculties that God has given you, is your first and highest trust. . . . The beginning of wisdom is the fear of God, the reverential regard for God's authority."[60]

Total enrollment at Hillsdale College, large from the beginning, reached 493 by the third term of the first year and increased in succeeding terms. According to early catalogues, approximately a third of the students came from outside Michigan; another third were residents of Hillsdale County. Thirty-nine percent were women, generally excluded from American higher education until the 1880s. The college intentionally attracted students of all denominations.

Non-Freewill Baptists donated a majority of the funds for the impressive building, and the college gained strength with a minimum of denominational support. The *Hillsdale Standard* applauded the growth of the young college in the fall of 1857: "The term commences with a larger number of students than at any time previous. . . . It is highly gratifying to the citizens of this County and Village, and others interested in the welfare of this college to know that it is in a prosperous condition. Great credit is due the President and professors for their prudent management and untiring energy, to which this institution owes its popularity and success."[61] The Paw Paw *Northerner* claimed that Hillsdale College "bids fair to become a shining ornament to this our western country. . . . There are students here from ten or twelve different states, besides about half a dozen from Canada West."[62] George Fuller, a scholar of Michigan history, accurately asserted that "Hillsdale College early gained importance and interesting distinction in educational pioneering. . . . "[63]

Hillsdale was already the largest private college in Michigan and would remain so for most of the nineteenth century. By the fourth year, enrollment reached 757. The first commencement ceremony was held in 1856, and the first class of fourteen seniors who pursued the full collegiate course graduated in 1860. For the sake of comparison, Columbia University graduated an average of only twenty-four bachelors of arts annually between 1835 and the Civil War. Enrollment in the Hillsdale classical curriculum by 1860 was almost half the size of the comparable program at the University of Michigan. If the Ladies' Department is included, "Hillsdale [in 1860] matched Williams College in enrollment, and was three-fourths the size of Michigan, Princeton, or Dartmouth."[64]

Religious emphasis by the college included chapel every weekday morning at 9 o'clock, with Ministerial Association meetings and Bible classes in the evenings. In contrast to the strong moral emphasis of Hillsdale College, the Brown University [Baptist] catalogue had only the following statement: "Every student is required to attend punctually upon prayers." Hillsdale students attended one or two church services every Sunday. One young man described going to chapel on Sunday morning, hearing another sermon in the afternoon, and then attending prayer meeting in the evening.[65] Another student complained about a lengthy service: "Went to chapel . . . Mr. Reynolds preached. It was a complete bore. He kept us there two hours and twenty minutes."[66]

Although there had been no Freewill Baptists in Hillsdale in

1853, twenty members organized a church in the college chapel on November 27, 1855. Townsman E. V. Merritt expressed his doubts about the new Freewill Baptist church in Hillsdale: "I think there is enough to keep them from organizing.... They need a balance wheel."[67] Merritt's doubts were ill-founded, and membership rapidly increased from 20 to a congregation of 500. Students attended regularly. Pastor Henry E. Whipple of the faculty often preached from the pulpit about the evils of slavery, and he praised John Brown on January 1, 1860.[68] A student described baptisms in the new Hillsdale Freewill Baptist Church: "This morning at 9 o'clock a large number of people repaired to the water where five of our fellow students went forward in baptism."[69]

Hillsdale students, many in their twenties, had earlier faced great hardships on the frontier; now they accepted poverty to gain a formal education at the "oldest of the denominational colleges in the State."[70] The college willingly accepted students of little or no wealth: "Nowhere can there be found less aristocracy of wealth, or caste of position, every student taking rank on personal merit and achievement."[71] From the beginning, Hillsdale encouraged self-reliance and labor, and the college was "in a peculiar sense the home of self-supporting youth."[72] Most students worked to pay their expenses. For example, one young man walked from Pennsylvania to Hillsdale and earned money by milking cows for a local farmer. Years later he became a very successful lawyer. James Hawley hiked from his home in Groveland, New York, to Hillsdale and sawed firewood while studying a Latin text by his side. Asked how the arrangement worked, he replied, "Pretty well. I think I have sawed the first conjugation into my head." Captain in the 2nd Michigan Cavalry in the Civil War, Hawley was killed at Chickamauga. Many ladies earned extra income by providing board in the dining hall, sewing, and washing clothing.

A high level of responsibility never ruled out student pranks and misbehavior, of course. While cleaning up debris from construction in the spring of 1856, student volunteers observed twelve new hitching posts for horses on the campus lawn. Resenting the transformation of an idyllic scene into a stable, one daring youth solved the problem with his axe.[73] Wayland Dunn submitted more evidence in 1857 of unacceptable behavior: "The other day they threw a dead pig down two pair of stairs and for chewing tobacco they have had three or four fellows before the faculty. I do not know what they have done with them but I should not wonder if they got their walking papers."[74] Another student complained that he was not prepared for recitations because "the boys in our room carry on so much that I cannot study."[75] In December 1860, six adventurers obtained a sleigh and drove to Jonesville to dine at an oyster house. They bought cigars for the return trip, and some indulged in two or three. "One of the boys got sick before we got home and heaved up." Each participant contributed fifty cents to finance the venture.[76]

Student literary societies, strongly supported by the faculty and the public, reflected the highest qualities of the early college. These groups had much the same purpose as their eastern predecessors in the mid-1700s, such as the Flat Hat Club at the College of William and Mary and Critonian at Yale. Students joined together to add breadth to a formal curriculum and to balance the rigors of classical education. More than most liberal arts colleges, Hillsdale championed literary organizations as a way to complement academic study, to improve rhetoric and to provide practical discipline. Parliamentary rules, oratorical excellence, skill in debate, and general literary culture prepared many students for public service. Members also benefitted from strong fraternal ties. Michigan Central College had two societies, the Philogrammatian and Eunomian, whose aim was to provide "a higher degree of mental, moral, and social improvement." Lewis Cass, U. S. senator from Michigan who had championed popular sovereignty as a solution to the territorial expansion of slavery, became an honorary member of the Hillsdale College Eunomians.[77] A faculty order on September 17, 1856, disbanded the two societies because each admitted both men and women as members.

With the elimination of societies that admitted both sexes to membership, the Hillsdale students organized new clubs limited to males or to females. Prior to the 1856 faculty edict, Hillsdale men already had formed the Ciceronian debating club, which became the Alpha Kappa Phi Society on October 10, 1857. The Philologian society reorganized as the Amphictyons (males only) on December 7, 1857; the Theological Society (males only) was formed in the spring of 1866. The college trustees provided all societies with elegant halls. Alpha Kappa Phi added improvements, including curtains, chandeliers, carpeting, bronze busts of Daniel Webster and Henry Clay, a library, comfortable chairs, and a melodeon.[78] Professor Ransom Dunn dedicated the Amphictyons' new room on August 18, 1858; satin cloth lined the walls and a Brussels carpet covered the floor.

Soon there existed a total of five societies, three for gentlemen (Alpha Kappa Phi, Amphictyon, and Theological) and two for ladies (Ladies' Literary Union, 1857, and Germanae Sodales, 1858).[79] Each club held weekly meetings, annual contests, and two public exercises each year. Programs consisted of speeches, debates, and vocal music. Hillsdale literary societies immediately attracted prestigious honorary members. The Alpha Kappa Phi honorary members included Schuyler Colfax, Speaker of the House of Representatives in the latter part of the Civil War and Vice-President on U. S. Grant's 1868 Republican ticket; Zachariah Chandler, first Republican senator from Michigan and a leading Radical who served on the Committee on the Conduct of the War; Lewis Cass, U. S. senator and President Buchanan's secretary of state; Austin Blair, governor of Michigan during the Civil War; and James A. Garfield and Benjamin Harrison, two future U.S. presidents. (Cass and Chandler, the only two Michigan senators to be honored with places in Statuary Hall of the United States Capitol, both were honorary members of Alpha Kappa Phi.)

The quality of literary societies at Hillsdale remained consistently high for more than three-quarters of a century. One of Ransom Dunn's sons revealed a benefit of the societies when he transferred from Oberlin to Hillsdale: "There is a different spirit here among the boys than there is in Oberlin. They [the Hillsdale students] seem more closely bound together."[80] Endorsing the contributions of literary societies, the Hillsdale faculty opposed the modern fraternity system that was being introduced into many western colleges by the 1850s.[81]

The physical growth of Hillsdale College was accompanied by strong antislavery convictions that had characterized Michigan Central, although there were only 6,779 blacks in a total Michigan population of 751,110, according to the 1860 census. William Reynolds wrote in his student diary on April 30, 1857, that a Mr. Clark lectured about his journey to the southern states: "To hear one that has seen the degradation of the cursed institution of slavery tell how it is carried on in violation and daily breaking the commands of Almighty God is enough to make us shudder and cause freemen to awake."[82] A month later, Reynolds again commented on the slavery issue: "This afternoon the usual lecture was delivered by Mr. Martin, a fugitive from the South, who has been in the free states only 18 months and he uses as a general thing better language than the majority of speakers. It is surprising to hear him. He speaks the truth."[83] President Fairfield suddenly added a new political dimension when he was nominated to the state senate in the summer of 1856.

Most students were politically supportive of Fairfield and the college, but one Democratic undergraduate revealed strong dissatisfaction in a letter on November 16, 1856: "The members of the faculty here have been so bigoted, vindictive, and fanatical to be completely carried away with their love for niggerdom."[84] H. J. King, college treasurer, also opposed political activities: "Pres. Fairfield is making friends and enemies by stumping for Republicans and of course the college interest will be affected thereby, but just how much you can figure up as well as we. On the whole I regret it."[85]

Eager to defend free institutions, Fairfield had been instrumental in founding the Republican party in 1854 and actively supported John C. Fremont's presidential campaign in 1856. Within four months of organizing at Jackson, the Republicans assumed political power in Michigan. J. J. Hopkins, '62, referred to antebellum days at Hillsdale as the "golden age of politics—when the daily paper was the principal textbook. College presidents and professors left their classes to make political speeches. . . . A partisan mass meeting was a sufficient excuse for a holiday. Eloquence ran riot everywhere."[86] Although Hillsdale had long since adopted a strong antislavery position, the college rejected the beliefs and tactics of the most radical abolitionists. Rather, it subscribed to middle-class values, market capitalism, and Christian self-help.[87]

At a Hillsdale rally that attracted an immense crowd, Fairfield made a name for himself by attacking slavery in a brilliant reply to Robert McClelland, President Franklin Pierce's Secretary of the Interior and ex-governor of Michigan. Requests poured in for more public appearances. During the Fremont political campaign of 1856, John A. Bingham (Republican from Ohio who served in the House of Representatives from 1855 to 1863 and from 1865 to 1873) gave a four-hour speech. Zachariah Chandler, later an extremely influential Radical Republican senator from Michigan, added more lengthy oratory. The audience of 6,000 began shouting, "Fairfield, Fairfield, Fairfield!" In brief prose, the college president used justice as his theme in attacking the evil effects of the fugitive slave law. Observers claimed that Fairfield accomplished more in his fifteen minutes than had the two orators preceding him.

Taking his seat in the state senate in January of 1857, Fairfield backed his antislavery resolutions with a two-hour speech that had a circulation of 50,000 copies. The press also praised his endorsement of a proposal requesting Congress to admit Kansas as a free state, to repeal the Fugitive Slave Law, and to abolish slavery in the District of Columbia. Senator Fairfield opened discussion of the bill in "one of the ablest speeches to which it has ever been our privilege to listen."[88] As chairman of the committee on education, Fairfield presented a petition requesting that the state university be opened to women, although the issue was tabled by an almost unanimous vote.[89] He strongly opposed a proposal to cancel the state university's debt of $100,000 by claiming that state-supported institutions of learning had been a failure. Fairfield questioned whether it was sound policy to tax Michigan residents for educating university students from other states, and he argued that colleges backed by private enterprise had stronger reputations.

In 1858 Fairfield campaigned successfully for lieutenant-governor of Michigan. In his political endorsement, the editor of the Marshall newspaper referred to Fairfield as president of "the largest and most imposing college edifice in the western states, with an able faculty and board of teachers, and more than five hundred pupils in attendance." The *Detroit Tribune* also supported the Freewill Baptist candidate: "He was at an early day identified with the anti-slavery movement in the North. . . . At present he is president of one of our foremost educational institutions there located." The *Detroit Advertiser* claimed that Fairfield "as a political speaker has no superior, if he has an equal in the state."[90] With the press reporting that he had canvassed the state more thoroughly during the campaign than any candidate on either ticket, Fairfield guaranteed his reputation as a leading Republican platform speaker. A contemporary said Fairfield's oratory "well-nigh threw me into a chill. As a political speaker he had no superior, and during the Civil War he was constantly in demand."[91] When called out of bed at midnight by a telegram announcing his election as lieutenant governor in 1858, Fairfield delivered one of the most brilliant speeches of the campaign. He might have become a successful congressional candidate, but the Detroit Germans living in his district attacked his temperance views.[92]

President Fairfield and other founders repeatedly had taken a strong stand on antebellum political issues. Daniel Graham, the first president at Spring Arbor, condemned slavery as a national sin. In 1850, a student announced at the anniversary exercises of Michigan Central, "We like the spirit—the frank, open avowal of sentiment exhibited on this occasion against *slavery*. . . . It should be explicitly understood that our war is against *slavery* first, and *slaveholders* next, but not yet against the Southern or any other portion of our Union."[93] [Italics used by the Jackson newspaper editor.] Probably nobody could have predicted, however, the contributions by the oldest college in Michigan when civil war broke out. The Hillsdale students' rally in record percentages to the support of the Union proved their courageous support for antislavery ideals, preservation of the Union, and endorsement of the new Republican party. The college had emphasized character as the supreme aim of education. That character now would be tested under fire.

Endnotes

1. Helen Dunn Gates, *A Consecrated Life: A Sketch of the Life and Labors of Rev. Ransom Dunn, D.D.* (Boston, 1901), p. 130.

2. Both Dunn and Fairfield were the sons of veterans of the War of 1812. Dunn began his long service to the college in 1852 as professor of moral philosophy. Recognized for his dedication to teaching for more than four decades, he also raised endowment and served as interim president prior to his retirement in 1898. He was a college trustee from 1855 until his death in 1900. Five of Dunn's children and nine of his grandchildren graduated from Hillsdale College.

3. Minutes of January 5, 1853, "Records of the Proceedings of the Board of Trustees of Michigan Central College at Spring Arbor" from the year 1853 to July 9, 1855. HCVPA.

4. Ibid., minutes of January 19, 1853. Also see D. M. Fisk, "The Story of the Planting, " III, *The Reunion* (May 20, 1885), p. 33.

5. D. M. Fisk, "The Story of the Planting," I, *The Reunion* (May 6, 1885), p. 3. William Glasgow, a Presbyterian elder and one of the founders of early Hillsdale College, exemplified the religious toleration of the institution.

6. Helen Dunn Gates, *Life and Labors of Ransom Dunn*, p. 111.

7. Patterson, John C., "History of Hillsdale College," 1883 article reprinted in *Collection of the Pioneer Society of the State of Michigan*, VI (1907), p. 149.

8. Within a short distance of each other, the St. Joseph, Kalamazoo, Grand, Raisin, and Maumee rivers originate from the Hillsdale summit.

9. D. M. Fisk, "The Story of the Planting," II, *The Reunion* (May 13, 1885), p. 18.

10. Francis Wayland Dunn diary, entries for January 24 and 25, 1860. Francis Wayland Dunn Collection, MHC.

11. *The American Citizen* (Jackson), February 2, 1853.

12. Ibid., February 9, 1853.

13. The Hillsdale committee made an accurate assessment. Total assets of Michigan Central College were about $4,480, counterbalanced by old debts of $2,588.95 and costs of $1,363 for a new building.

14. Many permanent colleges founded about 1850 began with less than $10,000 in subscriptions. Carl Russell Fish, *The Rise of the Common Man* (New York, 1927), p. 214.

15. Minutes of February 16, 1853, Records of the Michigan Central College Board of Trustees, 1853–1855. HCVPA.

16. The Prudential Committee, since its organization in 1853, has played a permanent role in providing leadership on the Hillsdale College Board of Trustees.

17. *Marion* (Ohio) *Independent*, as quoted in the *Hillsdale Herald*, March 3, 1881.

18. Russell Conwell, *The Life, Speeches, and Public Services of James A. Garfield* (Portland, ME, 1881), p. 83; Harry Brown and Frederick Williams, ed., *The Diary of James A. Garfield* (East Lansing, 1967), I, pp. 39, 61. In his diary on April 18, 1850, Garfield described Spencer Fowler, who later joined the Hillsdale College faculty: "Prof. Fowler has arrived and taken charge of the Academy. He appears to understand himself in all points. I think he is a good teacher." Founded by Freewill Baptists, the Geauga Seminary was as antislavery as Hillsdale College. On October 2, 1850, afternoon classes were cancelled for the students to hear a speech by Joshua R. Giddings, leading abolitionist and member of the House of Representatives from 1838 to 1859.

19. Dr. John Willson, Hillsdale College professor of history, is an authority on the migration of settlers and their traditional ideas from Europe to New England to New York to the Old Northwest. There is coincidence in Dr. Willson's taking a position at Hillsdale College, because Esbon Blackmar's town of Newark is only a short distance from Dr. Willson's home in Phelps, New York. Furthermore, Elizabeth D. Camp, who received the first degree in the scientific course at Michigan Central College in 1851, came from Palmyra, New York, also a short distance from Phelps.

20. Dr. Daniel Beebe negotiated the gift with Blackmar in Newark, New York, in 1853. Beebe was the great-grandfather of Richard Knight, who served Hillsdale College as secretary for much of the twentieth century.

21. Bucknell, Rochester, and Furman were other early Baptist colleges in the 1840s and 1850s that handled endowments carefully.

22. David B. Potts, *Baptist Colleges, 1812-1862*, Harvard University Ph.D. dissertation, 1967 (New York, 1988), p. 182. Most early Baptist colleges operated for several decades without endowment income.

23. *The American Citizen* (Jackson), February 23, 1853. Potter eventually barricaded the doors of his home and prepared to use a shotgun to defend himself against those who favored the Spring Arbor location. Elon G. Reynolds, ed., *Compendium of History and Biography of Hillsdale County, Michigan* (Chicago, 1903), p. 71.

24. *The American Citizen* (Jackson), August 17, 1853. S. W. Norton, "Hillsdale College, Hillsdale, Michigan," *Michigan Pioneer and Historical Society Historical Collections*, XXXII (1903), p. 454. Norton makes one of several errors by reporting that Michigan Central College closed on July 6, 1853. The Spring Arbor faction started the fall term on September 7, 1853. The struggling college even proposed to raise an endowment of $100,000 and to sell tuition scholarships for students as young as sixteen years (or fourteen years with faculty consent).

25. Laurens Baldwin Potter, "Lives of the Founders and Builders of Hillsdale College," *The Advance* (April 28, 1886), pp.245–46. No institutional use was made of the property formerly occupied by Michigan Central College until 1872, when the Free Methodists took over the ten acres of land and the two buildings. Spring Arbor Seminary opened in May 1873. By the 1930s most of the instruction was on the junior college level, prior to the emergence of Spring Arbor College as a liberal arts institution.

26. P. P. Randolph, "Life in Michigan, Twenty Years Ago," *The Amateur* (June 1862), pp. 26–27.

27. The swampy and muddy St. Joseph River caused malaria in Hillsdale.

28. Willfred Mauck, memoirs entitled "Hometown," n.d. HC.

29. Potts, *Baptist Colleges, 1812–61*, p. 143; *Hillsdale Area Centennial, 1869–1969* (Hillsdale, 1969), p. 20. The village of Hillsdale grew rapidly with the arrival of Hillsdale College. The population in 1850 was 1,067; in 1860, 2,177; and in 1870, 3,518. By 1869, Hillsdale had become a city. The town of Gettysburg, site of a German Lutheran Seminary, had a population of 2,400 by the Civil War battle of July 1–3, 1863.

30. Ransom Dunn, "Financial Values of Hillsdale College," *Wolverine* (1897 yearbook), p. 29.

31. *Exercises of the First Annual Commencement of Hillsdale College*, Hillsdale, June 18, 1856. HC.

32. Robert Parks, *Democracy's Railroads: Public Enterprise in Jacksonian Michigan* (Port Washington, NY, 1972), pp. 126–28; *Lake Shore & Michigan Southern Railway System and Representative Employees* (Buffalo, 1900), pp. 31, 34; George Rogers Taylor, *The Transportation Revolution, 1815–1860* (New York, 1951), p. 100. The state began construction of the Michigan Northern, the Michigan Central, and the Michigan Southern railroads as part of an internal improvement program in 1837, but financial failures resulted in sale to private companies in 1846. The Southern Michigan Railroad Society today provides open-air excursions of the Clinton branch of the old Michigan Southern Railroad.

33. Martha Bigelow, "Michigan: A State in the Vanguard," in James H. Madison, ed., *Heartland* (Bloomington, 1988), p. 44.

34. The directors of the Michigan Southern and the Northern Indiana Railroad Companies in September 1849 solicited a subscription of a quarter of a million dollars to extend the road west from Hillsdale. The line from Hillsdale to Coldwater, a distance of 22 miles, was contracted in the spring of 1850, and the five-mile route to Jonesville opened in September 1850. *Report of the Boards of Directors of the Michigan Southern and Northern Railroad Companies* (New York, July 30, 1853). CHS. The Michigan Southern and Northern Indiana Railroad, with a gross income of more than a million dollars a year, was one of the major railroads during the Civil War. Its standard gauge of 4' 8 1/2" was an advantage; also, it had excellent machine shops and engine houses. During the war, the railroad shipped 5,000 barrels of flour daily to the East. Thomas Weber, *The Northern Railroads in the Civil War, 1861–65* (Westport, CT, 1970), pp. 6, 7, 9, 74.

35. Potts, *Baptist Colleges, 1812–61*, p. 155.

36. *Jonesville: Sesquicentennial Historical Record* (Jonesville, MI, 1978), p. 5.

37. E. B. Fairfield to Ransom Dunn, June 7, 1853. Ransom Dunn Collection, MHC.

38. Speech of 1853 reprinted in the *Hillsdale Standard*, May 8, 1855. Fairfield made a brief talk, because on the same day he delivered the Fourth of July oration at Hillsdale.

39. Edmund Fairfield to Ransom Dunn, November 26, 1854. Ransom Dunn Collection, MHC.

40. Dunn's subscription list. Ransom Dunn Collection, MHC. By the end of almost half a century of service to Hillsdale College, Dunn personally had raised over $104,000 for endowment.

41. Helen Dunn Gates, *Life and Labors of Ransom Dunn*, p. 120.

42. Records of the Western Ministerial Conventions. Western Ministerial Collection, MHC. The Western Evangelical Missionary Association accepted Lewis Tappan's antislavery views, and it closely resembled the American Reform Tract and Book Society, the American Missionary Association and the American and Foreign Anti-Slavery Society. These groups gave financial support for training antislavery clergy, and they organized the leading evangelical, church-centered movement for emancipation. Lawrence J. Friedman, *Gregarious Saints: Self and Community in American Abolitionism, 1830–1870* (Cambridge, 1982), p. 69.

43. Patterson, "History of Hillsdale College," pp. 152–53.

44. Ibid., p. 154.

45. *Twenty-Seventh Annual Report of the Superintendent of Public Instruction of the State of Michigan, with Accompanying Documents* (Lansing, 1863), p. 15.

46. Patterson, "History of Hillsdale College," p. 154.

47. Officials of Kalamazoo College, which sometimes is listed erroneously as the earliest Michigan college under the general law of 1855, agreed twenty-five years ago that Hillsdale College was first.

48. *Hillsdale Standard*, March 27, 1855. The Hillsdale College trustees previously had approved the new Articles of Association on February 9, 1855, ten days before the passage of the general incorporation law for Michigan colleges. Minutes of February 9, 1855. Records of the Proceedings of the Board of Trustees of Hillsdale College, 1855 to 1969 with Proceedings of the Prudential Committee, 1855–1870. HCVPA.

49. *Hillsdale Standard*, April 3, 1855.

50. Patterson, "History of Hillsdale College," p. 156.

51. *A Catalogue of the Officers and Students of Brown University, 1854–88* (Providence, 1854), p. 47. AKG.

52. D. M. Fisk, "The Story of the Planting," VI, *The Reunion* (June 10, 1885), p. 83.

53. "Lives of the Founders and Builders of Hillsdale College," *The Advance* (April 14, 1885), p. 225.

54. Hillsdale College circular, September 1, 1856. MHC.

55. Francis Wayland Dunn diary, entry for April 5, 1860. Francis Wayland Dunn Collection, MHC.

56. Reprinted in the *Hillsdale Standard*, December 11, 1855.

57. William Bouton, "The Study of Language," *The Amateur* (June 1861), p. 32.

58. Notes from the clerk's record book of the North Reading Baptist Church. Kevin Andrews, Hillsdale College Dean of Men, provided these informative notes and also Clara Bartlett's article on "North Reading Church History."

59. *Reading Centennial, 1873–1973* (Coldwater, 1973), pp. 25–26.

60. Edmund B. Fairfield's address at the college chapel service, May 19, 1904, as quoted in *The Collegian*, May 25, 1905, p. 277.

61. In spite of the Hillsdale professors' dedication and heavy work load, students occasionally complained about faculty performance. William H. Reynolds wrote in his diary on April 23, 1857: "This afternoon the students met for lecture but were disappointed as neither of the professors were [sic] prepared to speak." Reynolds diaries, MHC.

62. *Paw Paw Northerner*, September 20, 1857, as quoted in the *Hillsdale Standard*, September 29, 1857. Hillsdale College has a large collection of excellent cartes de visite, early photographs of faculty and students, during the 1850s, 1860s, and 1870s. Their clarity is vastly superior to most daguerreotypes, ambrotypes, and tintypes of the period. Jean Darling, whose great-grandmother Betsy Kinne attended Hillsdale College during the Civil War, donated many of these cartes de visite to the College Archives. I have purchased many additional cartes de visite from bookstores and antique shops.

63. George N. Fuller, *Michigan: A Centennial History of the State and Its People* (Chicago, 1939), II, p. 445.

64. William C. Rigenberg, "The Protestant College on the Michigan Frontier," Ph.D. dissertation, Michigan State University, 1970, p. 97.

65. William H. Reynolds diary, entry for April 19, 1857. Reynolds diaries, MHC.

66. Francis Wayland Dunn diary, entry for February 18, 1860. Francis Wayland Dunn Collection, MHC.

67. E. V. Merritt to Ransom Dunn, November 21, 1855. Ransom Dunn Collection, MHC.

68. *Twenty-Second Annual Report of the Freewill Baptist Home Mission Society* (Dover, NH, 1856), p. 117. Francis Wayland Dunn diary, entry for January 1, 1860. Francis Wayland Dunn Collection, MHC.

69. William H. Reynolds diary, entry for April 5, 1856. Reynolds diaries, MHC.

70. Educators and journalists in the nineteenth century repeatedly referred to Hillsdale as the oldest denominational college in Michigan. This specific citation was made by the editorial correspondent to the *Michigan School Moderator,* as quoted in *The Advance* (March 31, 1885), p. 213.

71. Brochure entitled *Hillsdale College: A Few Facts Concerning It,* n.d., p. 2. No classes were held on Monday, so that the women could perform domestic chores, such as washing laundry and cleaning. The men also caught up on routine matters, including patching their old clothes!

72. Hillsdale College brochure (Hillsdale, ca. 1900), p. 2. Loaned by Dr. Lilian Rick, professor emeritus of Spanish, Hillsdale College.

73. Student behavior may have influenced the college trustees, who voted in 1862 "to set hitching posts *outside* the college fence on Hillsdale and College Streets, and as many as may be needed on West St." Minutes of June 16, 1862, Records of the Board of Trustees. HCVPA.

74. Wayland Dunn to his father Ransom Dunn, January 12, 1857. Ransom Dunn Collection, MHC.

75. William H. Reynolds diary, entry for March 18, 1857. Reynolds diaries, MHC.

76. Francis Wayland Dunn diary, entry for December 28, 1860. Francis Wayland Dunn Collection, MHC.

77. *First Annual Catalogue of the Eunomian Society of Hillsdale College* (Hillsdale, 1856). Lewis Cass was almost eighty years old when he made his last public appearance in August 1862 at a recruiting rally in Hillsdale. Frank Woodford, *Lewis Cass* (Rutgers, 1950), p. 335.

78. *History of the Alpha Kappa Phi Society of Hillsdale College* (Hillsdale, 1890), p. 18.

79. *History of the Amphictyon Society of Hillsdale College* (Hillsdale, 1890), p. 10.

80. Newell Ransom Dunn, Jr., journal, entry for May 17, 1860. Newell Ransom Dunn Collection, MHC.

81. Helen Horowitz, *Campus Life: Undergraduate Cultures from the End of the Eighteenth Century to the Present* (Chicago, 1987), p. 29.

82. William H. Reynolds diary, entry for April 30, 1857. Reynolds diaries, MHC.

83. Ibid., entry for May 28.

84. Letter by anonymous student at Hillsdale College, November 16, 1856. MHC.

85. H. J. King to Ransom Dunn, October 29, 1856. Ransom Dunn Collection, MHC.

86. J. J. Hopkins, as quoted in *Hillsdale Standard*, June 23, 1885.

87. Garrisonians sometimes opened their meetings by burning copies of the Constitution, because the document permitted slavery according to the terms of the three-fifths compromise. For an excellent description of various goals within the abolitionist movement, see Lawrence J. Friedman, *Gregarious Saints: Self and Community in American Abolitionism, 1830–1870* (Cambridge, 1982), p. 5.

88. Lansing *State Republican*, as quoted in the *Hillsdale Standard*, February 10, 1857.

89. *Detroit Tribune*, as quoted in the *Hillsdale Standard*, March 17, 1857.

90. The quotations from the Marshall newspaper, the *Detroit Tribune*, and the *Detroit Advertiser* were cited in the *Hillsdale Standard*, September 14, 1858.

91. H. M. Ford, as quoted by Coe Hayne, *Baptist Trail-Makers of Michigan* (Philadelphia, 1936), pp. 95–96.

92. Fairfield was employed as agent for the New York State Temperance Society in 1853. C. H. Churchill to Ransom Dunn, January 28, 1854. Ransom Dunn Collection, MHC.

93. *American Citizen* (Jackson), July 10, 1850.

❧FOUR❧

"How like hell them college boys did fight!"

Probably no College in the country is better represented in the Union Army than this [Hillsdale College]. It has sent its young men to the war by hundreds. They have watered with their blood every battlefield of the Republic. . . . Their patriotism and love of country have won for them a fame even better than college honors.

—*Detroit Advertiser and Tribune*, June 14, 1864

At the end of the nineteenth century, President George F. Mosher of Hillsdale College praised the foundation of liberty that was "built out of the very lives, out of the devotion, out of the sacrifice of the young men who went from Hillsdale, from Harvard and Yale and other institutions of learning [during the Civil War]. . . . Whenever anything is to be won that is worth winning, it calls for heroism, for self-denial, for sacrifice of the young men and the young women, too."[1] Students who had left their classrooms to march into the long and bitter conflict well deserved such admiration. The abolitionist college motivated its young men to enlist—and to experience heartbreak and heroism. And yet, there was a sense of innocence as they left their campus. Little did they know that Hillsdale would send, arguably, a higher percentage of its male student body than any other western college. In all, some 420 young men enlisted, and half became officers. From Hillsdale College classrooms came three generals, numerous regimental commanders and high-ranking officers, and three Congressional Medal of Honor winners. At least 60 students died.

Years later, veteran Asher LaFleur characterized the college men's dedication: "I saw them fight. I saw them die, and I want to say now, with all those memories rushing in upon me, that a nobler, braver, truer band of patriots never fought for their country than these very college boys of ours ... by their superiority and enthusiastic patriotism influencing and controlling the entire command. Theirs was a noble duty, nobly performed—*the sacrifice of their lives was hallowed.*"[2] [Emphasis mine.] Civil War valor constituted a high-water mark in the history of Hillsdale College.

The total of some 420 young men enlisting from Hillsdale College is a contrast to the Civil War records of other Michigan educational institutions. The Kalamazoo College catalogue reveals that a total of 68 graduates and students participated in the "War of the Rebellion."[3] An Albion College historian concludes, "It is very likely that students, faculty members, and alumni of the institution did very little as soldiers during the conflict."[4] The first men did not graduate from Olivet College until 1867, and probably the only military activity was performed by a student company drilling three times weekly.[5] William C. Ringenberg in his Ph.D. dissertation, "The Protestant College on the Michigan Frontier," claims that Hillsdale College sent nearly as many current students into Civil War duty as did the University of Michigan from all of its undergraduate classes, 1846 to 1865. The Michigan State Normal School, now Eastern Michigan University, may have contributed a four-year total of 160 soldiers from an average annual enrollment of 500 males.[6] Michigan State Agricultural College, today Michigan State University, supplied eight graduates and ninety former students to the Union forces.[7] Hope Academy, not yet a college, provided nine known soldiers.[8] Only a handful of men from Adrian College enlisted.[9] In assessing enlistments from all northern colleges, Charles Roland recently concluded that the majority of students remained on campus and that education actually flourished during the war.[10]

The outbreak of fighting in no way discouraged Hillsdale College leaders. President Fairfield insisted in 1861, "No thought has ever been entertained of suspending any Department [sic] of the College. Every class will be kept up in the best manner. And we shall have 300 students this fall in spite of the war. We only expected 200."[11] In 1862, the second year of the conflict, the faculty was optimistic about the full enrollment (522 students) and a strong academic program.[12] The local newspaper in 1863 reported the construction of substantial houses on the vacant lots of College Hill, which was crowned by "one of the best and most beautiful institutions of learning in the West."[13]

The college catalogue contained names of students from almost every northern state, particularly Ohio, Indiana, Illinois, and Wisconsin. One reason for high enrollment was the predominance of preparatory over collegiate students; many were only fifteen or sixteen years old.[14] In addition, Hillsdale College had marketed many perpetual scholarships costing $100 apiece. These grants, which provided free tuition, by 1862 totalled 189 in Michigan, 128 in northern Ohio, and 77 in central and southern Ohio.[15] Another factor was the high number of women attracted by Hillsdale's coeducational policy.

At first glance, activities seemed to suggest an almost normal era from 1861 through 1865. Telegraph lines had reached Hillsdale in 1849, and the first county fair was held two years later.[16] Two steam-powered flour mills highlighted the local economy, and only one town on the railroad between Toledo and Chicago shipped more grain than Hillsdale. On the Michigan Division of the Michigan Southern, the thriving village of about 3,000 was connected directly with Detroit, Adrian, Hudson, Pittsford, Jonesville, Coldwater, Bronson, Sturgis, White Pigeon, Bristol, Elkhart, and Chicago.[17]

The Hillsdale business district featured eight dry goods stores, six clothing shops, a bookstore, seven groceries, three drugstores, two hardware dealers, two boot and shoe stores, three hotels, four churches, and two printing offices. The *Detroit Advertiser and Tribune* claimed that few colleges in the country could boast a better faculty than Hillsdale College. Although young trees planted by the students were not fully grown, a Detroit reporter observed that the college park possessed considerable natural beauty.[18] A transfer student claimed that Hillsdale professors were more practical, exercised sounder judgment, had a better appearance, and influenced their students to become more useful adults than did the Oberlin College faculty. Hillsdale College continued to recruit excellent new faculty, such as Fenelon B. Rice, who was expected "to lay the foundations of a musical department second to none in the West."[19] Professor Rice remained at Hillsdale until 1868 and later established the prestigious music conservatory at Oberlin College. President Fairfield and Professor Dunn took time to lecture at the Law Department of the University of Michigan. Student D. K. Allen complained, however, when Fairfield spoke for an hour and fifty minutes at the dedication of the new Amphictyon hall.

Despite the war, many college activities reflected business as usual. Henry J. King, secretary-treasurer, requested Mrs. Frederick Fowler to provide the assistance in grading college grounds that her husband had promised before leaving for the war. King needed a team of oxen with a scraper and chain, and also a wagon for unloading dirt by early November 1861.[20] Fifty students had agreed to give one day's work, as requested by the faculty. Mrs. Fowler promptly provided the team of oxen to grade an avenue almost a hundred feet wide past the campus before winter. As yet there were no walks, and Wayland Dunn protested, "We and the rest of the students will have to wade through six inches or a foot of mud all winter and spring."[21]

Cultural activities increased following the organization of the Beethoven Society, a new twenty-voice choir that printed 500 tickets for the first annual concert during commencement week of June 1862. The college in the same year celebrated the anniversary of the American Anti-Slavery Society. The first professorship was endowed in 1864, and the Hillsdale College Alumni Association organized in 1865. A local newspaper editor acknowledged that through the efforts of the college, "Our citizens are favored with a series of lectures from the most eminent orators and statesmen of the day." The editor added that it would be difficult to find elsewhere literary societies of such quality. The societies' exercises included band and vocal music conducted by Professor Fenelon Rice.[22] Playing baseball and shooting pigeons provided recreation. The men also enjoyed hunting partridges, quail, turkeys, and owls within a short distance of campus. The most shocking social news was the marriage of Julia Bailey, a college coed, to an old widower in Reading![23]

Most undergraduates continued to earn money by manual labor, including gardening and driving sheep for townspeople. Some students, as usual, were unhappy with their college board for $1.60 a week. Meals consisted of meat, potatoes, bread, butter, and water in the morning; cold meat, bread and butter at noon; and bread, butter, and applesauce for supper, with pudding, cheese, and a small piece of pie once a week.[24] Undergraduates also complained about the difficulty of academic studies. As one student informed his brother, "I had some awful hard lessons, I assure you. I have to speak a piece once in two weeks, write an essay as often. . . . I'm on for a discussion one week from today. The subject is Resolved that Congress ought to colonize the slaves as well as liberate. I am on the affirmative. Consequently, I shall make all things smoke."[25] An 1862 alumnus later characterized his campus life at Hillsdale as "the real days of chivalry." On the surface, then, college life seemed to go on very much as usual during the Civil War.

Despite the college authorities' strong determination to maintain a normal appearance, most students barely restrained their partisanship during the stormy days following Fort Sumter. A student recalled the excitement at the outbreak of the war: "Each man, each boy, felt that the appeal was to him, that the call for men was the cry of Father Lincoln to his boys to gather at Washington; to rally around the home and flag. . . . No spot could quicker answer than did this abolition college. . . . The pluck and patience, the perseverance and prayers that had built this western school almost out of nothing, amid these oak openings in southern Michigan, found instant exhibition."[26] Professor Henry Whipple, as colonel, immediately organized several drill companies, including the Volunteer College Rifles. By telegraph they replied "ready" to Governor Blair on April 13, 1861, the day after Sumter. Furnished with old muskets and bayonets, the amateur companies lacked the sufficient preparation that their prompt response to the governor suggested. Drilling on campus was a poor substitute for genuine military training; hopes for active duty motivated teenagers in the preparatory department, whose minimum age was fourteen years, as well as collegiate upperclassmen. President Fairfield, startled by the quick response, feared briefly that the college would be wholly disbanded.

Student Wayland Dunn confided in his diary on April 15, "News came today for certain that war had commenced and that Fort Sumter had been captured. . . . The Devil and all his imps got hold of me today and I am half a mind and more to enlist."[27] Reluctantly, Dunn promised his father to complete college before volunteering.[28] Another student described the war fever, "The excitement continues to increase here, a large portion of the students are volunteering and waiting to march to the conquest. Prayer meeting turned into a war discussion." On April 19, college undergraduates met to plan their response to the war and adopted a resolution "in favor of suppressing rebellion, enforcing the laws, and supporting the Constitution." Talk of volunteering became infectious. The faculty decided not to oppose enlistments, in spite of the possible adverse effect on college enrollment.

Perhaps the most moving campus scene early in the war occurred when many students in companies E and H of the Fourth Michigan Infantry briefly returned to their college for a prayer service on June 12, 1861, preceding commencement exercises. For many about to become battle-hardened veterans, and some casualty statistics, this was their last visit to "the hill." The college community, sensing the high drama, loudly applauded their recruits: Magee, Salsbury, Merrifield, Janes, Kinney, Luce, Emerson, Jennison, LaFleur. . . . Professor Henry Whipple, trying to speak, was overcome as tears rolled down his cheeks.[29] The coeds pinned on each young soldier of '61 a red, white, and blue rosette. A student later claimed that no knight of medieval Europe ever was prouder of his lady's memento. Student R. H. Pratt soon felt the terrible emptiness that permeated the Hillsdale campus until the conclusion of the war: "Commencement is over and most of the students are gone and I am unacquainted with any word or words that can begin to express the utter loneliness that pervades the college halls. Luce, Magee, Williams, Alden . . . have joined the Michigan 4 Reg. now in camp at Adrian."[30]

Deep emotion over these departed college students was well deserved. Fighting in the Army of the Potomac from Manassas to Appomattox, the Fourth Michigan gained a reputation as rowdy frontier fighters carrying Bowie knives.[31] In the summer of 1861, the Fourth was issued old-fashioned Model 1842 Springfields with bayonets, but by 1862 the regiment obtained the "New Springfield Rifle." Some men in the Fourth carried Models 1855, 1861, or 1863 Enfield rifles, or captured Confederate equipment.[32] The regiment saw action and suffered heavy casualties in over fifty battles. As early as May 1862, the Fourth Michigan got within ten miles of Richmond during General George McClellan's unsuccessful peninsular campaign. Henry Magee, who participated in forty battles, reported the following words of praise from General McClellan on May 24: "The Michigan Fourth covered themselves with glory—you have done splendidly." Meeting the enemy in close combat for the first time, the regiment suffered eight killed or wounded while inflicting losses of at least 150 on the Fifth Louisiana Tigers, a crack Confederate unit. Magee clearly was optimistic: "The boys are well, and anxious for the final conflict. Michigan men are at a premium in this army."[33]

In combat at Chancellorsville in early May 1863, the Fourth Michigan, with many Hillsdale College men, again gained recognition. General George Meade wanted his best troops to protect an important point, and he twice asked a subordinate, "Can they hold it?" The officer firmly replied, "General, they [the Fourth Michigan] can hold it against hell!" In desperate fighting at Gettysburg, the regiment lost 188 men in half an hour while charging over the Valley of Death, through the wheatfield, and as far as Devil's Den. The Fourth Michigan in this one attack suffered a casualty rate of more than one in five. A monument at Gettysburg today marks the regiment's field position. When Company E returned to Hillsdale in July 1864, after three years of duty, the courthouse bell and a bonfire on

Railroad Square announced the news at midnight. The veterans proceeded to the Western Hotel, where the proprietor, Mr. Allen, prepared a magnificent dinner.[34]

Many Hillsdale students returned to their hometowns to enlist in regiments from New York, Indiana, Ohio, Wisconsin, Illinois, and other states. They usually received brief training at camp for a month or more before being shipped to a war theater. Ohioan B. P. McKoon left campus immediately after the attack on Fort Sumter to enlist on April 18 in the Springfield Zouaves at Columbus. He explained that his act appeared rash but that he felt compelled to answer his country's call. On his way to Washington, McKoon spoke at length with former President James Buchanan at Lancaster, Pennsylvania.[35] Another out-of-state student who enlisted at home was Richmond W. Melendy from Indiana. Listed in the first Hillsdale College catalogue, Melendy used intelligence, energy, and ambition to more than compensate for his withered right arm and lack of financial means. Melendy's magnetic qualities had made him a natural leader among early Hillsdale College students. Leaving Hillsdale in the summer of 1861, he raised a company of men for the Twenty-Ninth Indiana Infantry. Unanimously elected lieutenant by the recruits, Melendy faced a superior officer who refused to muster him into service because of his deformity. Inspired by Melendy's leadership, the entire company refused to sign the roll until he was accepted. Headquarters sent back the order, "Muster in the one-armed lieutenant!"

In letters to friends on the hill and to former classmates on the battlefield, Hillsdale soldiers wrote warmly of college memories. Captain Jacob H. Stark held a stronger affection for the college than any other place, because it was where he had learned to make himself useful. "I thank God that there [Hillsdale College], a little light fell upon my mind, opening a road through the dense darkness which enshrouded it."[36] Students looked back with satisfaction to their college days; one recruit claimed that it seemed only a day or two since he had entered the preparatory school, not seven years. Future Congressional Medal of Honor winner Moses Luce wrote from Virginia on January 26, 1862, "Does the martial spirit still increase in the college? I sometimes get to thinking of the old times at Hillsdale and feel as though I should like to be back to enjoy those privileges again and then I feel that I am doing that which is my duty and by the power I'll fight it out."[37] Wayland Dunn observed from his camp in Glendale, Mississippi, that college matters had more consequence than he ever thought possible when he was a student. He hoped that there would be at least 600 students after the war, and he judged it "a pity that there is not some man with a purse as long as Astor ready to give about half a million to put the institution in good shape."[38]

Hillsdale soldiers' qualities included moral standards and religious convictions strengthened by life at the Baptist college. Lewis J. Whitcomb, formerly at Michigan Central, served as chaplain for the 13th Michigan Infantry; Robert Taylor left Hillsdale early in the war to become chaplain of the Second Michigan Cavalry; S. E. Root was chaplain in the Ninth Michigan Infantry; and G. S. Bradley became chaplain of the Twenty-Second Wisconsin Volunteer Infantry. Ransom Dunn, Jr., described the troops at Corinth, Mississippi, as "a hard set of boys, hard set every way, a drinking, brandy-sipping set. . . . They all play cards and drink when they get a chance." Dunn later complained, "The moral tone of the soldiers is very low. Stealing ceases to be a sin." He became particularly unhappy when soldiers stole all the sutler's supplies.[39] (Sutlers accompanied troops in the field and sold food, equipment, tobacco, etc.) Don A. Hubbell of the Tenth Michigan Cavalry, who soon was to die at the military hospital at Camp Nelson, Kentucky, protested against thievery: "I have been very lucky as yet as I have not lost anything but my inkstand and necktie. Others had lost their coats and blankets and even socks off their feet and money from their pockets. I have seen more playing cards here than I ever thought could be played in a year. I am the only man in our company who does not drink and play cards and swear."[40]

Hillsdale soldiers described a wide range of emotions. They commonly complained about regimental officers who were "political wire pullers, policy men who have got their positions through favor."[41] On the other hand, many students were inspired by meeting outstanding generals, such as William Sherman and James McPherson. They naturally exhibited admiration and genuine compassion for the wounded and the sick. Wayland Dunn, at Marietta during Sherman's march through Georgia, expressed anguish as long trains of ambulances and wagons carried casualties back to Kingston. Some soldiers revealed a bit of humor. Lieutenant James Hawley of the Second Michigan Cavalry joked on August 24, 1862, that for anyone with taste or liking for horses, cavalry was "far superior to infantry. Long marches are made on *four* legs instead of *two*."[42] Many Hillsdale students would join the cavalry because of prior experience with handling horses.[43] Soldiers complained about boredom in camp, and one youth claimed that it was all lost time. The college men liked to read, but that was difficult to do in a tent with ten or twelve fellow soldiers laughing and talking. Some requested books, including dictionaries and German grammars, from home. Because the Hillsdale students were accustomed to college life and books, the worst privations of a soldier's life for them were not the usual complaints such as lack of feather beds and chairs, but rather mental and social factors.

Hillsdale College volunteers revealed a wide range of reactions to combat. Lieutenant Richmond Melendy's account of his first military action resembled that of many inexperienced students. On December 17, 1861, his regiment met some 400 Confederate cavalry at Green River, Kentucky. Melendy described his emotions: "I have seen a battle, have heard the cannon roar, seen the polished steel glisten as it performed its work of death, and smelt the smoke of powder burned in battle. When the order to march was given, I felt some as I did in Hillsdale College when I was going on the stand to make my first speech—a little excited; but this soon wore off. . . . I felt as though I could walk through their whole Confederacy, without stopping to eat."[44] Franklin H. Bailey, who graduated from Hillsdale College and joined the faculty after the war, was only seventeen years old when he "saw the elephant" (i.e., experienced combat) at Shiloh in April 1862. Bailey graphically described his emotions: "It was the first battle I have seen, and I hope that it will be the last one. . . . The more men I saw killed the more reckless I became; when George Gates was the first man shot in the battle, and he stood next to me on my right hand, I was so enraged I could have tore the heart out of the rebel could I have reached him."[45]

Sergeant Andrew N. Buck of the Seventh Michigan Cavalry, who had entered Hillsdale College in 1860 to prepare for the ministry, wrote to his family several days after the battle of Gettysburg, "We are now practicing war not theorizing it. We have been in seven battles and skirmishes. . . . The object our cavalry forces have had in view has been the detention of the retreating rebel army and the destruction of his trains." The Seventh Cavalry was part of colorful Brigadier General George A. Custer's highly regarded Michigan Cavalry Brigade. Total losses in Custer's brigade at Gettysburg were so severe that only ten percent later reported for duty. After his horse was shot and fell on him, Sergeant Buck concluded that "our Reg. led a charge at the battle of Gettysburg and suffered severely, but repulsed its antagonist. . . . Cavalry never did such fighting before in America."[46] Another Hillsdale student recorded his battle experience with more modesty, "We were the first upon the field, and the last to leave it."[47]

Of more than 400 students who entered military service from Hillsdale College, about 60 died. Some of these slain were buried as unidentified corpses in mass graves, hastily dug at night following battle. Many found their final resting place in national cemeteries, and other corpses were shipped home. Hillsdale men were killed in well-known battles like Antietam, Fredericksburg, Gettysburg, Chattanooga, Chickamauga, Kenesaw Mountain, Atlanta, the Wilderness, Spotsylvania, and Petersburg. Others paid the supreme sacrifice at places less recognizable—Island No. 10, Alatoona, North Anna, Corinth, Pleasant Hill, Yellow Tavern, and Cedar Mountain. The Confederate prison at Salisbury, North Carolina, was a death camp for E. S. Steadman of the 26th Michigan Infantry on December 12, 1864.

Jerry Arnold of the Second Michigan Cavalry died in an army hospital at New Madrid, Missouri, on April 14, 1862. Lieutenant James Hawley contributed $70 in an unsuccessful attempt to ship the body home to Hillsdale, but Arnold was buried instead in a rough board coffin. An Amphictyon brother fired his revolver over the grave. Wayland Dunn eulogized Arnold's sacrifice, "His name is unknown to fame. There were no epaulettes on his shoulders, no solemn procession followed his remains to the grave, no sculptured monument marks his resting place but in that great record kept above is written

'Jerry Arnold—one that always did his duty.' What more could we ask?"[48]

The Alpha Kappa Phi Society learned that brother Lieutenant W. W. Wallace of the Twenty-Fourth Michigan had been killed leading his company at the battle of Gettysburg. With 80 percent losses, the Twenty-Fourth suffered the largest number of casualties of more than 400 Union regiments fighting at Gettysburg. A member of the legendary Iron Brigade, Wallace (who earlier had lost an eye at the Battle of Fair Oaks) refused to leave the battlefield as ordered when wounded on the first day of fighting.[49] His Alpha brothers on campus adopted a resolution that "while we lament the crisis which has caused the sacrifice of our noble brother and friend, we recognize the justice and righteousness of the cause in which he fell and hold ourselves in readiness to make the same sacrifice."[50]

A remarkable example of collegiate brotherhood involved Sewell Jennison of the Fourth Michigan Infantry, a unit with many Hillsdale students. Jennison survived twelve encounters unharmed but died of exposure after the bloody battle at Antietam. Four of his Alpha Kappa Phi brothers carried him into the woods, wrapped his martial cloak around him, and folded the stars and stripes over his heart. They marked Jennison's grave with a simple board, penciled with his name. The brothers then set into the board a piece of bone on which they had carved the Greek letters of their society. After firing a final salute over his grave, the four Alphas left Jennison behind to sleep beneath the sun.[51]

Another emotional incident involved Professor Dunn's two sons, Wayland and Ransom, Jr., who waited to enlist until they had graduated from Hillsdale College. Ransom's unit, the 64th Illinois Infantry (Yates' Sharpshooters), participated in the Battle of Corinth, Mississippi, on October 3 and 4, 1862. The Dunn brothers' regiments remained near Corinth, where typhoid fever and pneumonia weakened Ransom, Jr., by the middle of March 1863. Wayland was allowed to visit the military hospital, and he repeatedly wrote home about Ransom's illness. Ransom requested Wayland on March 27 to cut him a piece of bread for communion and to repeat the phrase, "Do this in remembrance of me." The next day Wayland shared with his father the "saddest news that I can write. . . . He died Thursday morning about 6 o'clock. I was with him from one in the night until that time. . . . The doctor came in and gave him some stimulant and put a poultice on his breast. . . . After this he did not speak. About half past five his breathing grew easier . . . but just at sunrise I noticed a sudden change in his countenance. . . . I knew it was the last and gave him some stimulant in hopes that he would revive and speak. He could only drink two or three swallows and then I asked him, 'Is it all right, Ransom, is it all right?' He turned his eyes upward and kept them so until they were clouded over. . . . He went to rest without a murmur and without a struggle either of body or soul. . . . Now, father, let us be resigned and trust in that source of all comfort."[52]

Wayland Dunn immediately went to the superintendent of the railroad but could not get permission to ship the corpse home. Wayland finally obtained approval directly from General G. M. Dodge and placed the wooden coffin with his brother's corpse on the train at Jackson, Mississippi, to be transferred at Memphis. Professor Dunn replied to Wayland from Hillsdale on April 2, "The corpse arrived all safe this evening and I have telegraphed for Pres. Fairfield or Prof. Whipple to preach the sermon next Sabbath." Ransom Dunn, Jr., who had enlisted less than a year before his death, was buried at Oak Grove Cemetery north of campus. His father and brother later were placed by his side.

Some college veterans received increased pensions because of illness or wounds related to the war. Byron A. Dunn (not related to Wayland and Ransom Dunn), '70, of the Ninth Indiana Infantry, was severely wounded at Chickamauga. At the battle of Nashville, a minie ball passing through his right shoulder and chest maimed Dunn for life. According to his pension certificate, Captain Francis M. Bissell was wounded during a charge by his brigade on September 20, 1863, at the Battle of Chickamauga. A shell killed his horse, shattered the saddle, and passed through his left ankle. During later action at Missionary Ridge, Bissell again was wounded when a minie ball passed through his body.[53] The examining surgeon verified that the wounds totally disabled Bissell for military duty.[54] Major Myron Baker of the 74th Indiana Volunteers complained to his sister in 1862 about infectious Union hospitals: "If I was to get into a hospital I should at once make my will and order my coffin—I have a cold in my lungs now."[55] He also gave a low opinion of his troops' diet, which consisted of salt "sow belly" and "union shingles," a combination of baked flour and water.

Probably the most significant Civil War personality from Hillsdale College was Clinton B. Fisk, who had supported the underground railroad at Spring Arbor when he was one of the first five students at Michigan Central College.[56] Following graduation, he failed as merchant, miller, and banker during the panic of 1857–1858. He moved to St. Louis in 1859 and became a personal friend of both Abraham Lincoln and Ulysses S. Grant before the war. Devout Methodist, avowed abolitionist, and original member of the United States Christian Commission, Fisk frequently was described by contemporaries as the most religious general in the Union army. He kept his headquarters well stocked with Bibles and hymnals and posted the following sign prominently at his headquarters: "SWEAR NOT AT ALL." After Fisk recruited the 33rd Missouri Infantry in 1862, he regularly conducted religious meetings at the St. Louis fairgrounds. At one of these services, the entire regiment stood up and agreed to let Fisk alone do all the swearing for the unit![57]

Strongly opposed to slavery on moral grounds, General Fisk wrote to President Lincoln in 1863: "I believe slavery to be the cause and strength of the rebellion, and I desire that *slavery should die.*"[58] As commander of the District of Southeast Missouri and later the Department of North Missouri, he fought Confederate raiders including Sterling Price in the Missouri-Arkansas area. His major responsibility was to control bushwhackers and guerillas.[59] Fisk in 1864 instructed his commander of the Sixth Missouri Cavalry, "Strike with vigor and determination. Take no prisoners. We have enough of that sort on hand now. Pursue and kill."[60] Responding to serious factionalism in Missouri, he insisted that Union forces always be alert for serious trouble because so many towns, railroad bridges, stations, and trains were vulnerable to destruction by raiders. Late in the war, Fisk was promoted to Major General.

Clinton B. Fisk, whom President Lincoln had wanted to head

the Freedmen's Bureau, accepted President Johnson's request to become commissioner of the Freedmen's Bureau for Kentucky and Tennessee after the war. President Johnson commented, "Fisk ain't a fool; he won't hang everybody."[61] Fisk began relocating blacks on 65,000 acres of land, an attempt at providing assistance that was uncommon during Reconstruction. He also published *Plain Counsels for Freedmen*.[62] Fisk reported that many of the 25,000 black soldiers, after returning to Kentucky, were "scourged, beaten, shot at, and driven from their homes and families."[63] Sergeant John Sweeny, a former slave, wrote to Fisk in 1865 that his regiment of former slaves needed a school to make "ourselves capable of business in the future." Sweeney's home was in Kentucky where "Prejudice reigns like the Mountain Oak." His black regiment already had organized a literary association before the march to Nashville, and the men desired "to become a people capable of self-support as we are capable of being soldiers. . . . What we want is a general system of education in our regiment for our moral and literary elevation."[64]

Responding to such requests, the general on January 9, 1866, opened an abandoned army barrack and began his Fisk School for Freedmen in Nashville, chartered the next year as Fisk University, with a curriculum including Tacitus, Horace, Sophocles, and the Bible in Greek.[65] The fame of the Fisk Jubilee Singers spread rapidly, and within seven years the choir raised $150,000 for their college.[66] In a study of black higher education in 1917, Thomas Jesse Jones identified only Fisk and Howard universities as offering strong college-level work in the liberal arts.[67]

In his later years, Clinton B. Fisk made a fortune as an official of railroad and insurance companies. Head of the Board of Indian Commissioners from 1881 to 1890, Fisk campaigned for the presidency on the Prohibition ticket in 1888. He returned to Hillsdale to speak at the Underwood Opera House on April 3, 1888, when the college faculty honored him.[68] Upon his death in 1890, Fisk was buried in Coldwater, Michigan, his early home.

After combining farming with studying at Michigan Central College, ex-schoolmaster William Humphrey rose to fame in the Civil War by participating in a total of 54 battles. He became regimental commander of the Second Michigan at the battle of Malvern Hill on July 1, 1862. Commissioned a colonel on February 16, 1863, Humphrey was an outstanding brigade commander at Jackson, Vicksburg, Knoxville, Richmond, and Petersburg. A memorial on the Vicksburg battlefield commemorates his leadership. The Second Michigan of Humphrey's brigade courageously seized Confederate rifle pits near Fort Sanders at Knoxville on November 24, 1863; in fierce action, the regiment lost 83 of 160 soldiers and 5 of 11 officers.

Humphrey was the most brilliant military tactician from Hillsdale College during the war, and his Second Brigade, Third Division, Ninth Corps, compiled an outstanding record. Colonel Humphrey on May 12, 1864, led his brigade at Spotsylvania, classified by generals of both armies as one of the bloodiest battles of the war. Wounded in action but "cool as an iceberg and resolute as fate," Humphrey led his men as they stopped the Confederate advance.[69] Humphrey's brigade also repulsed three attacks at the battle of Weldon Railroad (Globe Tavern) on August 18 through 21, 1864. Upon General George Meade's recommendation, Humphrey was brevetted a brigadier general on August 1, 1864, for conspicuous and gallant service both as regimental and brigade commander.[70] ("Brevet" refers to a battlefield commission.) After the war, he became editor of the Adrian *Times* and then auditor general of Michigan in 1866. A third Civil War general, Jasper Packard, was a student at both Michigan Central and Hillsdale College. He began his Civil War career as a private in the 48th Indiana. During a visit in 1863 to Glendale, Mississippi, Packard expressed appreciation to Wayland Dunn for Professor Dunn's excellent preaching during his college days.[71] Wounded in action at Vicksburg, Colonel Packard later served as regimental commander of the 128th Indiana Infantry during General Sherman's Carolina campaign.[72] Brevetted a brigadier general, he later became a prominent newspaper editor and Indiana legislator.

Only fourteen years old when he entered Hillsdale College, Sergeant Moses A. Luce served in Company E of the Fourth Michigan Infantry. On the morning of May 10, 1864, his regiment received orders to lead an assault on the Confederate works at Laurel Hill during the battle of Spotsylvania. Forced to fall back under heavy fire,

Luce heard a wounded soldier's cry near the Confederate rifle pits. Ignoring a volley of bullets, he rescued Asher LaFleur, company commander and former Hillsdale student whose leg had been shattered.[73] Luce's reckless daring impressed even the southerners. The following day General Grant made his well-known statement, "I propose to fight it out on this line if it takes all summer." For his valor at Laurel Hill, Sergeant Luce became one of three Hillsdale students to win the Congressional Medal of Honor. A total of sixty-four men from Michigan received the Congressional Medal of Honor for action in the Civil War. When Luce returned to Hillsdale College to graduate in 1866, it was more than fitting that he should win the major oratorical prize with a speech on American valor. Luce later practiced law in San Diego, California, and became a judge in 1875.

Before the dramatic rescue by his fellow collegian Luce, Asher B. LaFleur already had become a hero in his own right. Having left Hillsdale College to enlist in the Fourth Michigan, LaFleur fought in sixteen engagements and was left to die on the Gettysburg battlefield in July 1863. The Confederates carried him to a barn, where he lay for three weeks with little assistance. Whatever food he ate passed through a wound in his abdomen. Finally discovered by Union soldiers, LaFleur received medical attention at the military hospital in Harrisburg and returned to the Fourth Michigan. While leading his company into heavy combat at Spotsylvania on May 10, 1864, he was rescued by Moses Luce. LaFleur successfully underwent three amputations, including the loss of his right foot.

The second Medal of Honor winner from Hillsdale College was Sergeant Cornelius M. Hadley of the Ninth Michigan Cavalry, hospitalized for three months in 1862 because of illness and a wound. After regaining his health, Hadley earned his medal by carrying a message from General Ulysses S. Grant at Chattanooga to General Ambrose Burnside, besieged at Knoxville in November 1863. Grant's dispatch was, "I shall attack Bragg on the 21st, and if successful, will start immediately to the relief of Knoxville if you can hold out." Written upon tissue paper and placed in Hadley's revolver, the message was to be destroyed in case of danger. Hadley wore the disguise of a captured Confederate uniform to bypass 20,000 southern troops; if captured, he might have been hanged as a spy. After riding in the saddle for nineteen hours, he reached Burnside's headquarters with the message. Following a short rest, Hadley was sent back by General Burnside with four dispatches for General John Wilcox, General Ulysses S. Grant, Secretary of War Edwin Stanton, and Mrs. Ambrose Burnside. Fired upon by rebels during his return trip, Hadley was forced to dismount and walk. Completely exhausted, Hadley traveled a total of more than a hundred miles through Confederate territory.[74]

Another distinguished Hillsdale soldier, Frank D. Baldwin, became the first regular army officer ever to receive two Congressional Medals of Honor.[75] At twenty-one years of age, Baldwin enlisted at Coldwater early in the war. As captain of Company D, Nineteenth Michigan Infantry, Baldwin earned his first medal by leading a countercharge on July 12, 1864, at Peach Tree Creek, Georgia. Ahead of his men and under heavy fire, he singly entered Confederate lines and captured two commissioned officers. Baldwin won his second medal during the Indian war of 1874, when Cheyennes crossed into western Kansas, killed part of the Germaine family, and carried off three young daughters. Against superior numbers, Baldwin led two companies into the Indian camp at McLellan's Creek, Texas, and rescued the two younger Germaine girls.[76]

Through a remarkable coincidence, three Hillsdale College regimental commanders helped to lead the spectacular attack on the crest of Missionary Ridge on November 25, 1863. Captain Francis M. Bissell led the Eleventh Michigan across an open field and took the Confederate rifle pits at the base of the ridge. Hit with a torrent of bullets from the top of the slope, his regiment kept climbing. Bissell led the unit double-quick in a successful charge to the crest. Debates followed about which unit won the race to the summit, but the Eleventh Michigan was among the first. During the charge, Captain Bissell was struck by a minie ball that entered his left hip, passed through his body, and came out near his spinal column. Surviving the wound, he was discharged on June 4, 1864.[77] Former Hillsdale student Colonel Myron Baker also helped to lead the famous assault on Missionary Ridge. With his 74th Indiana Volunteer Infantry, Baker charged up the ridge, six hundred feet high. He later reported, "Advancing as rapidly as possible, [my regiment] soon reached the brow of the ridge, and with fixed bayonets contributed their share to the work of driving the rebels from their rude fortifications."[78] On August 5, 1864, Colonel Myron Baker was killed immediately when hit by a musket ball fired from the Confederate picket line at Utoy Creek near Atlanta, Georgia. "Leaving a sentence uncompleted, Myron raised his arms quickly, fell backward, straightened his body, gave one gasp, and without a groan or struggle, his brave and noble spirit had taken its flight."[79]

Captain Edward P. Bates, commander of the 125th Ohio Infantry, was the third regimental commander from Hillsdale College to participate in the decisive attack at Missionary Ridge.[80] His men took cover behind logs and stumps until the final charge. Colonel Emerson Opdycke reported that Bates was "cool and judicious. I commend him for handling the regiment so that it performed nobly the part assigned to it, and with such small loss."[81] General Grant's plan had been to take the Confederate rifle pits at the base of the slope; no one planned for the troops to storm the forbidding slope. Grant sharply asked General George Thomas, "Who ordered those men up that ridge?" The soldiers had attacked spontaneously, and much credit for the brilliant Union victory belonged to the heroic regimental commanders from Hillsdale and elsewhere who led their troops by personal example. Was this chance or providence? In the spectacular charge up Missionary Ridge, the fate of both armies had been taken from the generals and thrust into the hands of college students, farm boys, and clerks. The Confederate line broke, General Braxton Bragg's army turned in full retreat, and Union forces won the important battle of Chattanooga, a turning point of the war.

Colonel Jasper M. Dresser, Sr., Hillsdale College student from 1855 to 1858, was another outstanding officer. Born in nearby Litchfield, he moved to Lafayette, Indiana. When President Lincoln issued his first call for troops at 9 a.m., April 15, 1861, Dresser enlisted in the National Rifles regiment before noon. As Chief of Ordnance, he organized General John A. McClernand's artillery (Dresser's battery), which played a critical role in the battles of Forts Henry and Donelson.[82] General McClernand commended Captain Jasper Dresser to

General U. S. Grant for alacrity in carrying out orders during danger-
ous action before Columbus, Kentucky, on November 7, 1861. Colonel James Fyffe on January 5, 1863, reported the action of the Second
Brigade before Murfreesboro, Tennessee. He singled out Major Jasper
Dresser of the 86th Indiana Regiment, promoted to Lieutenant-Colonel, for particular commendation. Injured earlier at Bull Run, Dresser
was "severely wounded in the engagement of the first day" when
struck by a piece of shell, but was saved from falling off his horse by
Lieutenant Richmond Melendy. Regaining consciousness, Dresser recognized Melendy as his former Alpha Kappa Phi brother, whom he
had not seen or heard from since both left campus at the beginning
of the war. Without the other's knowledge, each had entered a different command in the army. There were countless other times when
former Hillsdale students met by coincidence on the battlefield, as
fact became stranger than fiction.

Lieutenant-Colonel J. H. Newbold commanded the Fourteenth
Iowa Infantry that fought at Fort Donelson, Shiloh, Corinth, and
other major battles. On April 9, 1864, Newbold was killed at the
battle of Pleasant Hill during the Red River campaign. Confederates
had trapped his regiment on the right flank, and Captain Warren
Jones described how "in this deadly crossfire our lamented lieutenant-
colonel, J. H. Newbold, fell from his horse mortally wounded, the
ball passing through his body from the right breast, disabling his left
arm." Brigade commander Colonel William Shaw described Newbold
as "a Christian gentleman, and a brave, industrious, and conscientious
officer, whose loss to his regiment is irreparable."[83]

George L. Cornell, a Michigan Central student whose father was
one of the first members of the state legislature, graduated from
medical school at the University of Michigan. As medical officer and
assistant surgeon at Camp Douglas, Chicago, he was assigned to care
for Confederate prisoners. He later was transferred to the First Michigan Sharpshooters, and "his rare skill as a surgeon was exercised to
the greatest advantage on many a bloody battlefield."[84] Albert
Hartsuff, who entered Hillsdale College in 1856, became an M.D.
and joined the Medical Corps as assistant surgeon with the rank of first

lieutenant. Remaining in the regular army after the Civil War, Hartsuff received promotion to brigadier general.[85]

Levant C. Rhines, a second Hillsdale student at Camp Douglas, became Union commissary of Confederate prisoners in 1863.[86] Transferred from the prison camp, Rhines was hospitalized for smallpox in early 1864 but recovered. He became regimental commander of the First Michigan Sharpshooters, and his men fought in the front lines at the costly battle of Cold Harbor in June 1864. Trapped later within Confederate lines at Petersburg, his sharpshooters tried to fight their way out. With slightly fewer than a thousand troops, the regiment suffered 156 losses, including Rhines who was killed in action on June 17, 1864. According to the *Official Reports,* "After dark the First Michigan Sharpshooters, Major Levant C. Rhines commanding, was ordered to charge upon the angle of the enemy's works. . . . The enemy, however, were not disposed to yield the point and soon returned to the fight, which now became a fierce hand-to-hand conflict, in which Rhines, who displayed the greatest gallantry, lost his life." General O. B. Willcox reported that Major Rhines fell at the Confederate works just as his men began cheering after they carried the point. Most of the First Michigan Sharpshooters surrendered later when surrounded by superior numbers.[87]

As a Hillsdale student, James Hawley told President Fairfield that he planned to quit college and walk home seventy-five miles because he lacked money. Fairfield replied that he used to walk as far as 150 miles, and the struggling youth decided to remain in college. After the fall of Fort Sumter, Hawley, at age twenty-three, left classes and rose rapidly to the rank of captain in the Second Michigan Cavalry. His regiment saw action from New Madrid and Island Number Ten to Nashville and Iuka. The Hillsdale trustees on June 16, 1862, unanimously awarded Hawley his classical degree. Their rationale was that "Mr. Hawley was a leading member of the College Class graduating at this time. He has been here from the first term that the College opened until last fall when he became 2nd Lieutenant in Company G of the 2nd Regiment of Michigan Cavalry. Mr. Hawley has always been a successful student with much maturity and strength of mind."[88] This probably is the only time in the history of the college that a student intentionally was graduated without fulfilling requirements. Shot from his horse while trying to rally the Fourth Ohio at Crawfish Springs near Chickamauga, Hawley died on September 20, 1863. General Robert Mitchell, Chief of Cavalry, reported that "in battle, he was brave almost to a fault. A stranger to fear, his delight was to be amid the strife. Thoroughly patriotic, with no motive but duty to his country and his God he has fallen where he often expressed his desire to fall, if fall he should during the war, in battle, his face to the foe and nobly performing his duty in a trying hour."[89] The regimental chaplain claimed, "We can hardly realize that the best and truest friend we had in the army is indeed dead."[90]

Hillsdale students also performed superbly at the Battle of Malvern Hill, last of the Seven Days' Battles, near Richmond on July 1, 1862. General Robert E. Lee's outstanding troops had forced the Army of the Potomac back to the James River during the peninsular campaign, and the Fourth Michigan received orders to hold the left position of the Union line against General John Magruder. Stonewall Jackson's corps could not turn the Union flank; three times the rebels charged, and three times they were driven back. In resisting these attacks, the Fourth Michigan expended their cartridges and took more from dead comrades.[91] Sergeant Henry Magee graphically described how college students held their ground in the front ranks, where every man to his right except Moses Luce was shot. "Then no college boy flinched, and each held his place, full to the front, on that awful death line, fighting until the battle was won. . . . Every college boy did his whole duty. That night, when bivouacked on that bloody field, a couple of us overheard a conversation between some of the town boys discussing the battle, and one says to the other, with a soldier's language and grammar, 'How like hell them college boys did fight!'"[92] During the five days of fighting at Gaines' Mill and Malvern Hill, the Fourth Michigan lost 252 men.

Lafayette Young, sergeant in the 27th Michigan Infantry, compiled an outstanding war record. Wounded at Malvern Hill on July 1, 1862, he was taken to Richmond as prisoner and exchanged. Young returned to his studies at Hillsdale College but re-enlisted when partially recovered from his injury. Rejoining his army in the field as Grant opened the spring offensive of 1864, Young was hit while leading a charge at the Battle of the Wilderness and died eleven days later. Another fatality was Lieutenant Hartman S. Felt of the 7th Michigan. After crossing the James River, he died on August 24, 1864, from wounds received in action at Strawberry Plains, near Petersburg.[93] The last college casualty of the war was Lieutenant William E. Smith of the Tenth Michigan Cavalry, who was severely wounded on April 8, 1865, at Henry Court House, Virginia. General W. J. Palmer praised him for gallantry in action.[94] On the following day, General Lee surrendered his Army of Northern Virginia at Appomattox Court House.

Throughout the war, President Fairfield continued his tireless efforts to support the military effort, the Republican party, and the antislavery movement. On February 22, 1863, he spoke to a large audience at Representative Hall in Lansing. The press termed it "a thrilling and masterly effort. Everybody was captivated. That sermon should be preached in every city, village, and hamlet in the land, where there is any opposition or indifference among the people to carrying on the war until the rebellion is crushed."[95] State legislators were so impressed that they published the speech in a pamphlet entitled "Christian Patriotism." When President Fairfield delivered a series of three addresses at Oberlin College in 1865, a student responded, "I think I can say with truth that it was the most interesting lecture to which I ever listened."[96]

Fairfield played an active role in Lincoln's re-election campaign of 1864. On October 22, Governor Austin Blair, a strong supporter of the college, spoke at a mass meeting that attracted 20,000 people to Hillsdale. Delegations came from surrounding communities including Jonesville, Litchfield, Pulaski, Reading, and Camden. From his location between the courthouse and the post office, President Fairfield "addressed the meeting, holding them spellbound by one of his masterly impromptu efforts." The huge crowd again cheered as the Hon. Schuyler Colfax, Speaker of the House of Representatives, delivered the next oration.[97]

The faculty contributed in various ways to the war effort. Ransom Dunn, Sr., who wanted to command troops, was rejected because of impaired eyesight. A friend reassured him, "I think you are not needed to engage in this conflict by your personal appearance on the battlefield. I think you can do more good to stay at home and give your influence to aid on the work of emancipation by 'speechifying.'"[98] Governor Blair on July 7, 1864, notified Dunn of his appointment as military agent for Michigan under the "act for the relief of sick, disabled, and needy soldiers" passed on February 18, 1863. With the Army of the Cumberland as his field of operations, Dunn was responsible to the U. S. Sanitary Commission,[99] which provided medical care. His specific duty was to evaluate the sanitary conditions of Michigan troops at the front, and in July 1864, he visited soldiers at Kenesaw Mountain. Dunn also was active in the Northwestern Freedmen's Aid Commission. Professor Henry Whipple served with the U. S. Christian Commission, which provided chaplains in army camps and cared for the wounded. He accompanied Governor Blair on an inspection of Michigan regiments in the Army of the Cumberland in July 1863.[100]

A series of speeches delivered by some of the most influential Republicans and abolitionists of the Civil War era partially overshadowed the participation by the Hillsdale faculty and by the local Freewill Baptist Church in political and humanitarian activities. Several factors explain the role of the college as a leading center for wartime oratory, where more than a dozen nationally known public figures spoke. Through its president and some trustees, Hillsdale College had been active in the formation of the Republican party at Jackson in 1854. Supported by Freewill Baptists, the institution had been a primary force for abolitionism since the 1840s. Even after the war, Hillsdale College continued to select leaders who had opposed slavery. James Calder, called to the presidency in 1869, "was an abolitionist when it meant something, helping fugitives from the Tory hotbeds of south-central Pennsylvania."[101]

Both major political leaders in Michigan, Governor Blair and Senator Chandler, were Radicals putting pressure on the Lincoln administration to end slavery; and these two men had strong connections with Hillsdale College.[102] Senator Zachariah Chandler, a college pa-

tron, campaigned three times in Hillsdale. He spoke at the railroad
depot on the afternoon of September 19, 1860. In the evening, Chandler led a torchlight parade to college hill, where a huge bonfire and
Roman candles set off by students illuminated the campus. In his
re-election campaign of 1862, the Senator became the personification
of Radical Republicanism. The current phrase was that "Chandler
carried the Republican organization in his breeches' pockets."[103] In
1879 Hillsdale College awarded Chandler an honorary Doctor of Laws
degree, for reasons described by President DeWitt Clinton Durgin:
"In consideration of the long and valuable services rendered by you
during the critical and bloody period of our nation's history . . . in
defense of those principles which have ever been dear to the friends
and founders of this institution."[104]

Senator Charles Sumner, prominent Republican, appeared at the
college on January 28, 1861. In the spring of 1856, Sumner had
delivered in the Senate his "Crime against Kansas" speech, during
which he launched an intemperate attack upon Senator Andrew P.
Butler of South Carolina. Congressman Preston Brooks, Butler's
nephew, responded by knocking Sumner unconscious with repeated
blows to the head. The emotional incident had done much to drive
North and South apart. Student James Hawley, killed later at Chickamauga, wrote in 1860 that the assault on Sumner more than anything
had aroused the ire of the North.[105]

Carl Schurz, an antislavery Republican, lectured before a full
chapel on February 4, 1861. President Lincoln appointed him general
during the Civil War in a political attempt to gain German support
in the West. Wendell Phillips, brilliant spokesman for abolitionism,
lectured at the college in April 1862. Students and citizens of
Hillsdale County crowded the college chapel early, because Copper-
heads ("Peace Democrats" opposing abolitionism) in the vicinity had
attacked Phillips and his college hosts the day before. Phillips proclaimed that slavery caused the war, and many students regarded him
as the most polished speaker they ever had heard.[106] Edward Everett,
usually rated as the greatest orator of his age, was an early benefactor
of Michigan Central College. Editor of the *North American Review,*
Everett resigned as Secretary of State in protest over the Kansas-

Nebraska Act and was a strong Unionist during the war. In May of 1862, he spoke to a large Hillsdale audience on "The Origin and Character of the War."[107]

President Fairfield introduced Senator Lyman Trumbull of Illinois in October 1862. Trumbull served in the U.S. Senate from 1855 to 1873. With the other two powerful Radical senators (Benjamin Wade and Zachariah Chandler), Trumbull formed the "Jacobin Club." Artemus Ward (pen-name for Charles Browne, famous humorist for the *Cleveland Plain Dealer*) appeared at the college in November 1862. President Lincoln enjoyed Ward's writings so much that he recited them at cabinet meetings. "Parson" William Brownlow, another featured college speaker, launched anti-Confederate tirades in his *Knoxville Whig* early in the war and was expelled from the Confederacy on March 15, 1862. Brownlow succeeded Andrew Johnson as Tennessee governor in 1865.

One of the most exciting speakers was Frederick Douglass, famous black abolitionist. His public lecture in the college chapel on January 21, 1863, was entitled "Popular Error and Unpopular Truth."[108] Douglass influenced President Lincoln's decision to enlist freed blacks in the military; and his own two sons served in the 54th Massachusetts Colored Regiment during the famous attack upon Fort Wagner, South Carolina, on July 18, 1863. Owen Lovejoy, another orator at Hillsdale College, became a leading abolitionist in Illinois after the death of his martyred brother, editor Elijah Lovejoy.[109] Elected to Congress for several terms beginning in 1856, Owen Lovejoy delivered a particularly vitriolic antislavery speech in the House in April 1860. William Lloyd Garrison, editor of *The Liberator* and abolitionist leader for three decades, spoke before a large Hillsdale audience on November 14, 1865. He described the crusade since its origin in 1833, and the *Hillsdale Standard* considered his opinions "radical to the core." Another of the many abolitionists to appear at the college was Henry Ward Beecher, Harriet Beecher Stowe's brother, who had advocated disobedience of the Fugitive Slave Act of 1850. During the Civil War, he defended the Union cause in England. Cassius Marcellus Clay, a long-time opponent of slavery who served effectively as President Lincoln's minister in St. Petersburg during much of the war, also spoke at the College.

The Alpha Kappa Phi Society hosted Hon. Schuyler Colfax, Speaker of the House of Representatives and future Vice-President of the United States, in November 1865. His topic was "Across the Continent."[110] General Oliver O. Howard, another featured speaker, held abolitionist sentiments since his years at West Point. Receiving many promotions, he took over command of the Army of the Tennessee during Sherman's Georgia campaign. On May 12, 1865, he became commissioner of the Freedmen's Bureau, which Hillsdale College actively supported. Another general to appear at the college was Lew Wallace, a scapegoat for Union failures during the first day of the battle of Shiloh. He is best remembered for *Ben Hur: A Tale of the Christ,* one of the most popular novels during the nineteenth century. After the war, Senator Sumner made a return appearance at the college, and a large audience cheered loudly when he endorsed liberty for the black race.[111] Another influential lecturer was Albion W. Tourgee, who criticized the failure of the Radical Reconstruction Acts in 1867 to prepare freedmen for citizenship. He advocated rapid reconciliation of North and South as imperative for the future of the country. His novel, *A Fool's Errand,* described the rise of the Ku Klux Klan.[112] Other speakers appearing at Hillsdale during the Civil War era were influential Senator Benjamin Wade, humorist Petroleum V. Nasby, and controversial General Benjamin F. Butler.

The spectacular news of the fall of Richmond and Petersburg reached Hillsdale on April 3. Years of fighting by Lee's superb Army of Northern Virginia were almost at an end. The church and courthouse bells pealed in Hillsdale for two hours. At 8 o'clock a burner at every window illuminated the college and presented "the most beautiful sight ever witnessed by our citizens."[113] A huge bonfire on Railroad Square ended the evening. Grief over President Lincoln's assassination soon followed the celebrations. Having experienced personal grief for much of his life, Professor Dunn courageously portrayed the national tragedy in moral terms on April 15, 1865, "Yesterday we had a vast crowd to rejoice over recent victories and the capture of

Lee and today we are all in mourning over the terrible death to Pres. Lincoln. So this world goes, but the Lord requireth."[114]

In retrospect, ideals had been much more important than adventure, excitement, the challenge of combat, and an opportunity to see a larger world in motivating Hillsdale College men during the Civil War. During those terrible days, the students fully understood that the nation, the Constitution, and the rights of blacks were under attack. Colonel Myron Baker of the 74th Indiana Volunteers told his sister less than five months before he was killed in action near Atlanta, "I am not a soldier for its horrors, nor am I here for its profits. . . . But from the first I have felt it to be my duty as one claiming that proud civic boast 'An American Freeman' to be here battling for nationality and liberty."[115]

The college community never doubted the importance of the war or of its role in it. Both the living and the dead had understood the high ideals behind the conflict. A student in 1864 explained vividly the importance of ideals such as human liberty, patriotism, and constitutionalism: "Cannon balls are mighty missiles, but ideas in the possession of a skillful writer or when hurled by the logic of an orator are mightier still. . . . An idea when properly aimed shakes the whole world from center to circumference. . . . Ideas are the great levers by which the world is moved."[116] At least 420 Hillsdale students voluntarily left their beloved college to maintain these principles. Because of heavy student volunteering, Hillsdale village was exempted from an assigned draft quota, with over 20 men to spare, as late as September 1864.[117] Western boys usually came from humble farmhouses and worked their way through college, so they already knew something of sacrifice. Monetarily poor, but rich in patriotism, courage, and devotion to duty, they were prepared well to experience years of agony, destruction, and death, followed by eventual victory. For most, there was no acclaim.

Abandoning personal ambition, the young men of Hillsdale College gained a new maturity when they placed aside their textbooks, departed from their beautiful hilltop college, and left behind their friends to march into a conflict from which many would never return. Hillsdale Mayor Asher LaFleur, whom Medal of Honor winner

Moses Luce had rescued in front of Confederate trenches, attested to student leadership during the war: "These college boys of ours with their intelligence, with their active brains and patriotic hearts went into that rank and file, and became at once the very leaven that permeated and controlled it, and by their example, by their enthusiasm and by their intelligence made that rank and file the most effective army...."[118] Many battle-hardened veterans returned to Hillsdale College after the war. The classes of 1866, 1867, and 1868 included familiar names such as Moses Luce, Henry Magee, O. A. Janes, and Washington Gardner.

For several decades after Appomattox, the college faculty and students on Decoration Day marched in procession to Oak Grove Cemetery, north of campus, to honor their Civil War dead. Fortunately, scars from the traumatic conflict could not hide permanently the fact that both sections, the Union and the Confederacy, had displayed courage beyond human understanding. In memorial exercises at Hillsdale College on May 30, 1884, Judge O. A. Janes of the Fourth Michigan admiringly described his dramatic view of Pickett's Confederate charge at Gettysburg:

> Still that long, brave and gallant line, with battle flags flying and bayonets fixed, move steadily on; they swerve not; there is no faltering, although the grape and canister, shot and shell is making sad havoc in their thinned and bleeding ranks. . . . They firmly and bravely moved forward, rapidly closing up the intervening gaps in their ranks made by the enemy's terrific fire, and with one grand charge closed with their enemy. Their brave leader in the van cries out, "Men of Virginia, give them the cold steel."[119]

Washington Gardner, enlistee at age sixteen in the 65th Ohio Infantry, Hillsdale College student after the war, and commander of the Michigan Grand Army of the Republic, summarized the reconciliation: "We come not as victors rejoicing over triumphs gained, nor as vanquished, humiliated over defeats suffered, but as messengers of peace and good will from the people in every quarter of this great land."[120] It was characteristic of national reunification that Edward Davis, great-grandson of Confederate President Jefferson Davis, later graduated with honors from the Michigan college that had symbolized abolitionism and the northern war effort. Reflecting an optimistic attitude as the largest college in Michigan, Hillsdale immediately viewed Appomattox as the beginning of a new era of academic achievement.

Endnotes

1. Speech by President George Mosher at the dedication of the Alpha Kappa Phi Civil War memorial on June 20, 1895, as quoted in *The Hillsdale Collegian* (October 11, 1895), p. 252. Hillsdale College had national significance during the Civil War, and I plan to write a monograph on the contributions of the college to the war effort in the near future.

2. Speech by Asher B. LaFleur, quoted in *The Hillsdale Collegian* (October 11, 1895), pp. 253–54.

3. Adrienne L. Hartl, "Effect of the Civil War on Kalamazoo College," in Willis Dunbar, ed., *Michigan Institutions of Higher Education in the Civil War* (Lansing, 1964), p. 40.

4. Robert Gildart, "Albion College and the Civil War," in ibid., p. 55.

5. Ann Kleimola, "Olivet College and the Civil War," in ibid., p. 83.

6. E. R. Isbell and Donald W. Disbrow, "The Michigan State Normal School and the Civil War," in ibid., p. 92.

7. Madison Kuhn, "Michigan State Agricultural College in the Civil War," in ibid., p. 106.

8. Wynand Wichers, "Holland Academy in the Civil War," in ibid., p. 123.

9. Harlan Feeman et al., *The Story of a Noble Devotion* (Adrian College, 1945), p. 27.

10. Charles P. Roland, *An American Iliad: The Story of the Civil War* (New York, 1991), p. 213.

11. President E. B. Fairfield to Ransom Dunn, September 5, 1861. Ransom Dunn Collection, MHC.

12. Henry E. Whipple to Ransom Dunn, December 8, 1862. Ransom Dunn Collection, MHC.

13. *Hillsdale Herald,* June 23, 1863.

14. Total enrollment at Yale during the Civil War dropped from 521 to 438; Harvard, from 443 to 385. Roland, *An American Iliad,* p. 213.

15. Minutes of June 16, 1862. Records of the Proceedings of the Board of Trustees of Hillsdale College, 1855 to 1869, with Proceedings of the Prudential Committee, 1855–1870. HCVPA.

16. Centennial Book Committee, Chairman Eugene Fry, *Hillsdale Area Centennial* (Hillsdale, 1969), p. 21.

17. *Michigan Almanac, 1871* (Detroit, 1871), p. 34. AKG.

18. *Detroit Advertiser and Tribune,* June 14, 1864. The trustees in 1863 reported that many valuable trees and shrubs recently had been planted to beautify the college grounds.

19. Henry E. Whipple to Ransom Dunn, September 16, 1863. Ransom Dunn Collection, MHC.

20. Henry J. King to Mrs. Frederick Fowler, November 9, 1861, in Gary and Sue Fowler, ed., *Oh Sir'll Be Home: Civil War Correspondence and History of a Union Soldier* (n.p., 1982), p. 8. MPL.

21. Wayland Dunn to his father Ransom Dunn, November 13, 1861. Francis Wayland Dunn Collection, MHC.

22. *Hillsdale Standard,* June 21, 1864.

23. D. K. Allen to Wayland Dunn, June 15, 1861. Francis Wayland Dunn Collection, MHC.

24. Don A. Hubbell to his brother, December 21, 1862. RHC. Wayne C. Mann, director of the Regional History Collections, was very helpful in providing assistance with primary materials about Hillsdale in the Civil War.

25. Don A. Hubbell to his brother, December 28, 1862. RHC.

26. *Hillsdale Collegian,* October 11, 1895, pp. 260–61.

27. Francis Wayland Dunn diary, entry for April 15, 1861. Francis Wayland Dunn Collection, MHC.

28. Wayland Dunn to his father Ransom Dunn, September 17, 1861. Francis Wayland Dunn Collection, MHC.

29. William H. Reynolds diary, entry of June 12, 1861. Reynolds diaries, MHC.

30. R. H. Pratt to Wayland Dunn, June 23, 1861. Francis Wayland Dunn Collection, MHC.

31. William C. Davis, *Battle at Bull Run* (New York, 1977), p. 36. Total membership of the old and new Fourth Michigan Infantry was 1,325. Eight officers and 115 men were killed in action, 4 officers and 50 men died from wounds, 1 officer and 95 men died of disease, and approximately 250 were discharged because of wounds.

32. Donald F. Kigar et al., *Small Arms Used by Michigan Troops in the Civil War* (Lansing, 1966), p. 14.

33. Quoted in the *Hillsdale Standard,* June 1, 1862.

34. *Hillsdale Standard,* July 5, 1864.

35. B. P. McKoon, letters of April 18 and May 1861, published in *The Amateur* (June 1861), pp. 22–23.

36. J. H. Stark to Wayland Dunn, August 7, 1861. Francis Wayland Dunn Collection, MHC.

37. M. A. Luce to Wayland Dunn, January 26, 1861. Francis Wayland Dunn Collection, MHC.

38. Wayland Dunn to his father Ransom Dunn, September 18, 1863. Francis Wayland Dunn Collection, MHC.

39. Ranson Dunn, Jr., to Ransom Dunn, September 9 and 26, October 14, 1862. Newell Ransom Dunn Collection, MHC.

40. Don A. Hubbell to his brother, October 31, 1863. RHC.

41. Wayland Dunn to his father Ransom Dunn, November 25, 1863. Francis Wayland Dunn Collection, MHC.

42. James Hawley to Wayland Dunn, August 24, 1862. Francis Wayland Dunn Collection, MHC.

43. J. H. Felch, 1860 graduate, drove horses across the Great Plains to California in 1861. He then joined the Second Massachusetts Cavalry and was wounded at Winchester, Virginia.

44. Quoted in *Hillsdale Herald,* January 7, 1862.

45. Franklin H. Bailey to his parents, April 8, 1862. Typescript, Franklin H. Bailey Collection, MHC.

46. Andrew Newton Buck to his brother and sister, July 9, 1863. Andrew Newton Buck Collection, MHC.

47. *Hillsdale Collegian,* October 11, 1895, p. 249.

48. Account by Wayland Dunn of Jerry Arnold's death, undated. Francis Wayland Dunn Collection, MHC.

49. Donald L. Smith, *The Twenty-Fourth Michigan of the Iron Brigade* (Harrisburg, 1962), p. 9.

50. *Hillsdale Herald,* October 27, 1863.

51. Speech by John Patterson to Alpha Kappa Phi, May 4, 1863. John C. Patterson Collection, MHC.

52. Wayland Dunn to his father Ransom Dunn, March 28, 1863. The receipt given to Wayland Dunn by the Adams Express Company for shipping Ransom's corpse home by railroad from Memphis is dated March 28, 1863. Francis Wayland Dunn Collection, MHC.

53. *War of the Rebellion: A Compilation of the Official Records of the Union and Confederate Armies* (Washington, 1880–1901), series I, XXXI, part II, p. 485. Hereafter these 128 volumes are referred to as OR.

54. Civil War pension papers of Francis M. Bissell. NA.

55. Will F. Peddycord, *History of the Seventy-Fourth Regiment, Indiana Volunteer Infantry* (Warsaw, Indiana, 1913), pp. 91, 93.

56. Alphonso A. Hopkins, *The Life of Clinton Bowen Fisk* (New York, 1969 reprint), p. 51.

57. Edward P. Smith, *Incidents among Shot and Shell* (New York, 1868), p. 88.

58. Fisk to President Lincoln, October 24, 1863, as quoted in Roy Basler, ed., *The Collected Works of Abraham Lincoln* (New Brunswick, NJ, 1953), VI, pp. 545–46.

59. OR, series I, XXXIV, part I, pp. 965 and 1026.

60. OR, series I, XLI, part I, p. 760.

61. Hopkins, *Life of Fisk*, p. 94.

62. Eric Foner, *Reconstruction: America's Unfinished Revolution* (New York, 1988), p. 158.

63. Letter by Fisk to General O. O. Howard, February 14, 1866, as quoted by Ira Berlin, ed., *The Black Military Experience {Freedom: A Documentary History of Emancipation, 1861-1867]* (Cambridge, 1982), Series II, p. 615.

64. Sergeant John Sweeney to General Fisk, October 8, 1865, as quoted by Berlin, ed., *ibid.*, Series II, p. 615.

65. George Roche, *A World Without Heroes: The Modern Tragedy* (Hillsdale, 1987), p. 217.

66. John Hope Franklin and Alfred A. Moss, Jr., *From Slavery to Freedom: A History of Negro Americans* (New York, 1988, sixth edition), p. 243.

67. James D. Anderson, *The Education of Blacks in the South, 1860–1935* (Chapel Hill, 1988), pp. 250–51. Until recently, Fisk University consistently was rated one of the two most outstanding private universities for blacks in the South. Two years ago, I visited Fisk University and saw how badly it had been weakened by federal funding for southern public universities. Although its debt of $9 million has been largely erased, Fisk as a private school is more expensive than public universities with tax-supported funds for racial quotas and black studies programs. Ironically, artificial integration by the state universities has failed to capture the genuine pride in black culture and identity that Fisk University represented for well over a century.

68. Hopkins, *Life of Fisk*, p. 215. The best statement of the beliefs of presidential candidate Fisk's Prohibition party is *Solid Shot: The Facts and the Arguments on the Liquor Traffic* (Springfield, Ohio, 1889).

69. John Robertson, *Michigan in the War* (Lansing, 188), p. 545. AKG.

70. Abstract of military service record for William Humphrey. SAM.

71. Wayland Dunn to his father Ransom Dunn, October 10, 1863. Francis Wayland Dunn Collection, MHC.

72. OR, series I, XLVII, p. 947.

73. Walter Beyer and Oscar Keydel, *Deeds of Valor: How America's Heroes Won the Medal of Honor* (Detroit, 1901), I, pp. 327–38.

74. Ibid., I, pp. 280–81. Sergeant William B. Rowe, who was sent on the same mission as Hadley, was captured by the Confederates and confined in Andersonville prison.

75. Alice B. Baldwin, *Memoirs of the Late Frank D. Baldwin, Major General, U.S.A.* (Los Angeles, 1929), p. 5.

76. Walter Beyer and Oscar Keydel, *Deeds of Valor*, II, pp. 180–84.

77. Civil War pension records of Francis M. Bissell, NA; Frederick D. Williams, *Michigan Soldiers in the Civil War* (Lansing, 1988), p. 34.

78. OR, series I, XXXI, part II, pp. 543–45.

79. Peddycord, *History of the Seventy-Fourth Indiana*, p. 100.

80. OR, series I, XXXI, part II, p. 244.

81. OR, series I, XXXI, part II, p. 235.

82. *The Morning Journal* (Lafayette, IN), February 26, 1894.

83. OR, series I, XXXIV, pp. 356, 359, 361.

84. Charles R. Tuttle, *General History of the State of Michigan* (Detroit, 1873), pp. 505–6. AKG.

85. Albert Hartsuff was one of three brothers who were generals. George Hartsuff became a major general in 1862 and commanded the XXIII Corps, Army of the Ohio. William Hartsuff became a general in January 1865.

86. OR, series II, VI, p. 778. General William Orme, commander of Camp Douglas, wrote to Col. William Hoffman, Commissary-General of Prisoners, "Capt. Rhines has immediate control of the prisoners."

87. OR, series I, XL, part I, pp. 572, 584–85; abstract of military service record for Levant C. Rhines, SAM.

88. Minutes of June 16, 1862, Records of the Board of Trustees of Hillsdale College, 1855 to 1969. HCVPA.

89. Report of General Robert B. Mitchell, Chief of Cavalry, September 20, 1863, in Charles E. Belknap, *History of the Michigan Organizations at Chickamauga, Chattanooga, and Missionary Ridge* (Lansing, 1899), p. 80.

90. Quoted in *Hillsdale Standard*, October 20, 1863.

91. Charles Lanman, *The Red Book of Michigan* (Detroit, 1871), p. 326.

92. *Hillsdale Collegian*, October 11, 1895, p. 261.

93. Robertson, *Michigan in the War*, p. 278.

94. OR, series I, XLIX, Part I, p. 557.

95. *Lansing Republican*, February 25, 1863, as quoted in the *Hillsdale Standard*, March 31, 1863.

96. Robert Fletcher, *A History of Oberlin College* (Oberlin, 1943), II, p. 813.

97. *Hillsdale Standard*, October 25, 1864.

98. Ben R. Cottrino to Ransom Dunn, October 13, 1861. Ransom Dunn Collection, MHC.

99. E. Root, U.S. Sanitary Commission, to M. M. Seymour, July 15, 1864. See Governor Austin Blair's appointment papers for Professor Ransom Dunn as Michigan military agent for the U.S. Sanitary Commission, July 7, 1864. Ransom Dunn Collection, MHC. Former Hillsdale student Mr. H. Pierce also worked for the U.S. Sanitary Commission.

100. *American Soldier* (Nashville, TN), July 11, 1863, as quoted in *Hillsdale Herald*, July 21, 1863.

101. *Zion's Herald*, October 14, 1869, as reprinted in *Hillsdale Herald*, October 26, 1869.

102. Eric Foner, *Free Soil, Free Labor, Free Men: The Ideology of the Republican Party before the Civil War* (Oxford, 1970), p. 105.

103. Wilmer C. Harris, *Public Life of Zachariah Chandler, 1851–1875* (Lansing, 1917), pp. 65–66.

104. DeWitt Clinton Durgin to Senator Zachariah Chandler, as reprinted in *Hillsdale Herald*, July 24, 1879.

105. James Hawley, "Sumner and Sumter," *The Amateur* (June 1860), p. 38.

106. *Hillsdale Standard*, April 15, 1862.

107. Ibid., June 3, 1862.

108. Ibid., January 20, 1863.

109. Elijah Lovejoy, an abolitionist editor from Alton, Illinois, secured weapons to protect his fourth printing press in November 1837 after opponents had destroyed the first three. A mob again attacked his press and gunned down Lovejoy. Owen Lovejoy vowed, "I shall never forsake the cause that has been sprinkled with my brother's blood."

110. *Hillsdale Standard*, October 31, 1865.

111. Ibid., November 22, 1870.

112. Richard Nelson Current, *Those Terrible Carpetbaggers* (New York, 1988), pp. 199–210.

113. *Hillsdale Standard*, April 3, 1865.

114. Ransom Dunn to Wayland Dunn, April 15, 1865. Ransom Dunn Collection, MHC.

115. Peddycord, *History of the Seventy-Fourth Indiana*, p. 98.

116. Speech by John C. Patterson to Alpha Kappa Phi, January 29, 1864. John C. Patterson Collection, MHC.

117. William H. Sherman to Edwin J. March, September 19, 1864. Edwin J. March Collection, MHC.

118. *Hillsdale Collegian*, October 11, 1895 (Alpha Memorial Number), p. 254.

119. *Hillsdale Standard,* June 10, 1884.

120. Quoted in Charles E. Belknap, *Michigan Organizations at Chickamauga, Chattanooga, and Missionary Ridge,* p. 222.

FIVE

Living the Mandate

Hillsdale College has always been open to all persons, irrespective of religious opinion, nativity, color, or sex.
— Lansing *State Republican,* December 5, 1872

Michigan Central was the first American college to prohibit all discrimination because of race, religion, or sex *as a condition of its founding.* The college opened its doors in 1844 to all students regardless of creed, nationality, color, or sex.[1] The voluntary decision by Michigan Central and Hillsdale College is significant in the history of American higher education. The fact that the first of two new buildings at Spring Arbor was a ladies' dormitory proved the founders' determination to accept women.[2] Constructed several years before the feminists' convention in 1848 at Seneca Falls, New York, the dormitory housed women free to choose any of the academic programs. Even the hub of reform around Boston offered little higher education for women until after the Civil War, but Michigan Central College on the western frontier was coeducational from its origin. The trustees reported to the Michigan Superintendent of Public Instruction in 1851 that "the ladies' course is at least fully equal to that pursued in any female college in the country." Even more important was that women from the origin of the college in 1844 could choose among the Ladies' Department, the English and Scientific Department, and the Collegiate Department.

Elizabeth D. Camp, graduating from the scientific course, received the first collegiate degree from Michigan Central in 1851. Miss Livonia E. Benedict's accomplishment was even more significant. By receiving her B.A. in 1852, she became the first female graduate with a full classical degree from a Michigan college. The 1850 catalogue listed her as teacher in languages, and the following year she was assistant principal of the Female Department.[3] After graduation, she became professor of Latin and Greek at Albion College and later helped to organize the Women's Christian Temperance Union.[4] Livonia Benedict in 1854 married Dr. William H. Perrine, former Michigan Central student and professor of natural sciences at Albion College. The Perrines served together on the Albion faculty.

Although coeducation in the United States remained rare until several decades after the Civil War, the Michigan Central College 1852 catalogue confirmed that any female could pursue a full classical course leading to the B.A. degree. Oberlin College in 1841 was the first coeducational college in the U.S. to confer a B.A. degree upon a woman, Michigan Central College the second, and Antioch College (founded in 1852) the third. "These three colleges pioneered coeducation in the United States."[5] No coeducational colleges in the East admitted women to the classical degree until after 1860.

Michigan Central College obtained a state charter in 1850 that conferred degree-granting authority. *This collegiate charter was the first in the nation to prohibit all discrimination due to race, religion, or sex.* Although the claim of being first college at anything tends to be challenged, there is no evidence of any institution prior to Michigan Central (today, Hillsdale College) in 1850 with a charter banning discrimination on the basis of all three factors: race, religion, and sex.

According to historian John R. McKivigan, the Freewill Baptists were second only to the Quakers in opposition to slavery. Michigan was admitted into the Union as a free state under the Ordinance of 1787. Because of proximity to Canada, the state became a major haven for fugitive slaves. Freewill Baptists actively supported the Michigan underground railroad network established by 1838. Students at Michigan Central College/Hillsdale College assisted fugitives on the major route of the Michigan underground railroad, which extended from Cassopolis through Climax, Battle Creek, Marshall, Albion,

Spring Arbor, Jackson, Grass Lake, Dexter, Ann Arbor, Ypsilanti, Plymouth, and Detroit into Canada. By 1860, more than 40,000 escaped slaves had crossed into Canada via the Detroit and St. Clair rivers.[6] The Freewill Baptists in the state were in the minority on the antislavery issue, however. Michigan voters in 1850 rejected a proposal to extend voting rights to black men by 32,026 votes to 12,840. Daniel McBride Graham, Oberlin graduate and first president of Michigan Central, served on the executive committee of the American and Foreign Anti-Slavery Society from 1853 to 1855.[7]

After relocation to Hillsdale, the college voluntarily continued to oppose any discrimination. At a meeting on March 22, 1855, Hillsdale College was organized as the first Michigan private college under the new general incorporation statute of that year. The newly adopted Articles of Association clearly stated that the object of the college was "to furnish to all persons who wish, irrespective of nationality, color, or sex, a literary and scientific education as comprehensive and thorough as is usually pursued in other colleges in this country, and to combine with this, such moral and social instruction as will best develop the minds and improve the hearts of the pupils." (Details about the Articles of Association and the organizational meetings are found in Chapter 3.) Edmund Fairfield, Ransom Dunn, and other college leaders immediately persuaded not only the town but the entire county to oppose slavery and to support the Free Soilers politically. Hillsdale College trustees and professors helped to organize the antislavery Republican party at Jackson in 1854; and they are largely responsible for Hillsdale County becoming a leader in the Republican ranks of Michigan by the 1856 election.

Hillsdale College unquestionably was a leading advocate of abolitionism. Evidence of the number of black men and women attending the college during the antebellum era is lacking, because Hillsdale never designated students by race. Although enrolling fewer black students than Oberlin, Hillsdale was one of the first of a relatively few northern colleges to promote racial integration of higher education. An undergraduate wrote in 1857 that hearing a lecturer speak about the cursed institution of slavery was "enough to make us shudder and cause freemen to awake."[8]

The best evidence of Hillsdale's strong abolitionist position was enthusiastic support for the Civil War. Governor Blair and Senator Chandler, the two major political leaders of Michigan, and close friends of Hillsdale College, put constant pressure on the Lincoln administration to end slavery. Evidence in Chapter 4 confirms the extraordinary roles of Hillsdale students and leaders during the war years. The Hillsdale College soldiers' most unique characteristic, distinguishing them from other troops, was genuine concern for the plight of southern blacks. Benjamin Comstock, 12th Wisconsin Volunteers, described the condition of blacks in Missouri and Kansas: "The more I have seen of slavery, the greater has been my detestation and abhorrence of it. . . . I have talked with slaves by the wayside and in their lowly cabins, and never yet have I found one contented, one that loved his master, nor one that did not pant for freedom."[9]

Hearing of President Lincoln's Preliminary Emancipation Proclamation, Ransom Dunn, Jr., wrote to his father, "Will the first of January [1863] witness a consummation for freedom? When will this war end?"[10] Wayland Dunn even considered rescuing fifty or sixty refugees who were hiding in the Mississippi swamps, but getting a pass for such an expedition was impossible. After seeing many blacks in Georgia, Wayland believed that their biggest need was education and that revival work would do no good.[11] Another Hillsdale student, Captain Joseph McKnight of the Fifth Wisconsin Battery, described the Emancipation Proclamation as the "climax of the development of a settled policy, alike beneficial to the government and humanity."[12]

Many Hillsdale troops expressed concern about the high percentage of proslavery Union soldiers. Reid Mitchell, author of a recent excellent study of the common soldier, claims that the Union army would have been extremely small had it recruited only abolitionists.[13] A Hillsdale College recruit charged that General William Rosecrans' army "fulminates against the abolitionists. I talk a little John Brown to them in as mild a way as I know how. . . . It is a matter of curiosity to see the intense prejudice against the blacks."[14] Another Hillsdale soldier, Sergeant William Bouton of the Second Missouri Cavalry, complained that he "nowhere heard more bitter denunciation of an 'abolition crusade,' than in the army. Three-fourths of all the army I think would today say, let slavery alone in this contest. . . . I have been frequently surprised at hearing men of intelligence, who ought to know better, acknowledge the same right to property in man that they do in cattle. . . . "[15] Major Myron Baker of the 74th Indiana Volunteers informed his sister that the army was "opposed alike to the 'Copperhead' [sic] and the abolitionists."[16]

Hillsdale College supported blacks through various freedmen's agencies during the war. Chaplain N. Woodworth of the 31st Wisconsin hoped that "the Freedmen's Aid Society that makes Hillsdale a center, will make this place [Atlanta, Ga.] a field of labor just as soon as possible. . . . I have had charge of a church and a colored congregation since we came to this place."[17] E. O. C. Bartholomew of Hillsdale College was chief clerk of the Department of Freedmen and Refugees.

Also important were Hillsdale students who became officers in black regiments. Negro troops, mustered directly into federal service, were led by officers chosen under the authority of the United States.[18] Wayland Dunn wrote to his father during the Georgia campaign on September 14, 1864, that a former Hillsdale student had just become lieutenant in a colored regiment. Sergeant Cornelius Hadley, Medal of Honor recipient, was honorably discharged in June 1864, to accept a commission with U. S. Colored Troops, and Lieutenant Weller Bishopp commanded Company B of the 5th U.S. Colored Heavy Artillery. Lieutenant Franklin Bailey led Company B of the 137th U.S. Colored Troops,[19] recruited from refugees in Mississippi, Alabama, and Georgia. Alvin J. Wilber was captain in the 42nd U.S. Colored Infantry; and Lieutenant R. E. Whipple, son of a Hillsdale professor, served in the 6th U.S. Colored Cavalry. A formal report to Secretary of War Stanton on January 2, 1865, described the 6th Colored Cavalry's victory over the last remnant of General John Hunt Morgan's famous raiders at Marion, Arkansas: "The negroes charged over open ground, and did not fire a gun until within thirty yards of the rebels. This is the first time that any of these men were under fire."[20]

The role of Hillsdale College women during the Civil War also was outstanding. Most female college students, including soldiers' wives, continued their academic work. Because many women had attended Hillsdale since 1844, total college enrollment in the war did not decline drastically despite the high rate of male enlistments. Hillsdale in 1864 enrolled 584 students, more than the annual average since 1855. The women's decision to remain on campus did not preclude assisting the war effort, however. Activities such as writing letters, sewing soldiers' clothing, making bandages, and providing moral support for their loved ones were extremely beneficial. Major Joseph McKnight of the Fifth Wisconsin Battery, who served almost four years in the war, agreed that his wife should remain at Hillsdale College. He wanted her to benefit from the social associations and mental challenges that higher education provided.

A remarkable woman during the war was Mary Barnum, who married Captain James Hawley on July 29, 1863. Less than two months later, on September 20, 1863, her husband was killed at Chickamauga. Mary Hawley immediately became an army nurse and spent her widow's pension of twenty dollars per month to buy medical supplies for the United States Sanitary Commission. She explained, "I intend to get an education—but country and sick soldiers first. Wounded men we do not always have with us, but Hillsdale College we do." The *Chicago Tribune* paid high tribute to Mary Hawley in an article entitled "Nobly Done at Hillsdale, Mich." The reporter's concluding statement was: "Surely the republic need never despair while such pure devotion to the Union kindles the fires of patriotism upon her altars."[21]

Mary E. Blackmar, whose pioneering family had moved to Moscow Township in 1831 and owned an inn on the Chicago Military Road, northeast of Hillsdale, was another remarkable woman. After attending Hillsdale College in the late 1850s, Miss Blackmar became a medical student and chose to do field work as a military nurse, instead of the required year of training in a regular hospital. Although she could not meet the age requirement of thirty years, Miss Blackmar became an exception and served as a field nurse at age twenty-one. In 1864 she was assigned to City Point, the largest Union field hospital of the war with capacity for 10,000 patients. The complex, a merger of five corps hospitals, contained 90 pavilions and 324 hospital tents.[22]

During heavy fighting around Petersburg, Blackmar was in charge of the large Confederate ward near the front lines. Unexpectedly, tall and sorrowful President Lincoln, accompanied by General Grant with his ever-present cigar, approached the prisoners' quarters at City Point. The war-weary leader stated, "I wish to go in here alone." In her reminiscences, Miss Blackmar graphically described President Lincoln:

> He went at once to a bedside, and reverently leaned over almost double so low were the cots, and stroked the soldier's head, and with tears streaming down his face he said in a sort of sweet anguish, "Oh, my man, why did you do it?" The boy in gray said, or rather stammered weakly, almost in a whisper, "I went because my state went." President Lincoln went from one bedside to another and touched each forehead gently. . . . [23]

Mary Blackmar graduated in 1867 with a class of ten from the Woman's [sic] Medical College in Philadelphia, the first medical college for women in the world.[24] The commencement program listed her thesis as aural surgery. Dr. Blackmar served in the New York Infirmary Hospital for Women and Children, operated by Emily and Elizabeth Blackwell, the most outstanding pioneer women physicians in the United States.[25] (In 1849, Dr. Elizabeth Blackwell became the first American woman to earn an M.D.) One of four Hillsdale College female students to become physicians in the 1860s, Dr. Blackmar did research on hookworm and diabetes and practiced medicine until 1911.

After Appomattox, abolitionist Hillsdale College supported earlier rhetoric by providing assistance for freedmen. Freewill Baptists and Quakers were the two denominations most involved in freedmen's work. Ronald Butchart recently concluded that evangelical religion was more important than abolitionism in motivating white teachers of blacks.[26] An instructor at Fisk University thanked Hillsdale College on February 10, 1868, for sharing materials:

Everything is just what we needed. . . . It is a source of comfort and strength to us in our labors for this lowly people, that we have warm friends in the North who are praying for us and our cause. . . . Were it not that we felt that we were borne often and earnestly to the throne of heavenly grace by our dear friends in the North, our hearts would certainly fail.[27]

At a special church service at Hillsdale in April 1868, a collection of over $80 was raised for freedmen's relief. A. H. Chase, treasurer of the Freedmen's Mission Society, delivered the sermon.[28]

Hillsdale students willingly taught freedmen after the war. The most famous alumnus contributing to black education was General Clinton Bowen Fisk. He became assistant commissioner of the Freedmen's Bureau for Kentucky and Tennessee during Reconstruction and opened his Fisk School for Freedmen at Nashville in 1866. An article in the *Hillsdale College Herald* of November 27, 1890, refers to Hillsdale students who worked among the "contrabands in the South." Sarah V. Douglass, '63, taught with her husband Thomas Jay Slayton, '62, for the Northwestern Freedmen's Aid Commission at Goodrich Landing, Louisiana, from 1864 to 1865. Francis Judson Douglass attended Hillsdale College in the late 1850s and graduated from Chicago Theological Seminary in 1869. He served from 1859 to 1865 with the American Missionary Association, one of the most influential groups supporting black education. Dr. F. P. Woodbury became secretary of the A.M.A. Luthera I. Wilson, '72, taught for the A.M.A. in Kentucky, 1865–66; at Gallatin, Tennessee, 1866–67; and at Tullahoma, Tennessee, 1867–68. During this entire period she was supported by Freewill Baptists. She later taught for the American Baptist Free Mission Society at Cairo, 1870–71.

LeVant V. Dodge, '72, was professor of Greek at Berea College beginning in 1874; he probably worked with black students. Bruce S. Hunting of the class of 1873 also taught at Berea College as principal of the preparatory department. Eugene C. Bartholomew, who graduated from Hillsdale in 1861, was Superintendent of Education in Texas after the war. Phillip C. Tolford, '63, worked for the A.M.A. in Virginia, 1864–65, and at Cairo, Illinois, 1865–73. For several

years he was principal of the colored mission school at Cairo. Hillsdale
students who taught for the A.M.A. at Cairo included Mary E. Curtis,
'60, 1864–67; Wellington Joy; and the Reverend and Mrs. H. H.
Keyes. The *Hillsdale Standard* of February 25, 1896, referred to Matilda Blackman, who entered Hillsdale College in 1861. After marriage to Mr. W. B. Randolph, she taught for the A.M.A. at Lexing-
ton, Kentucky, at Montgomery, Alabama, and at Artesia, Mississippi. Mrs. Randolph's work included five years at the state normal
school for blacks at Jefferson City, Missouri. In *Plantation Pictures:
Colored Views,* she described blacks living in the South.[29]

During Reconstruction, 1865 to 1877, enrollment of blacks at
Hillsdale College increased. The Hillsdale Theological Society admitted S. H. Jones, a black student who enrolled in 1869. Jones' excellent oratory attracted large crowds from the college and the town,
with no hint of prejudice. The University of Michigan, meanwhile,
accepted its first black in 1868.

The number of black students at Hillsdale continued to increase
in the last quarter of the nineteenth century, although the black
population of Michigan remained small. Because the college refused
to specify race on any records, an estimate of the larger number of
black students is impossible. Many of them came to Hillsdale College
from the border South. In 1876, for example, only 140 Negro children were born in Michigan.[30] Even by the early twentieth century,
only two Negro families lived in Hillsdale city, in addition to black
college students.[31] Of all Michigan counties, Hillsdale as late as 1930
had the highest percentage of white Anglo-Saxons and the lowest ratio
of immigrants of the first and second generations.[32]

The *Hillsdale Herald* proudly observed in April 1886, that "the
colored students at Hillsdale College are associated with the whites
in all school work; they attend the same classes, are members of the
same literary societies, and are treated with the same consideration
and courtesy by professors." Jared M. Arter, who as a slave near
Harper's Ferry had witnessed John Brown's raid, typified the equal
education received by blacks at Hillsdale. Entering college in 1882,
he enrolled in the classical course and earned high academic rank. A
meeting of blacks in Hillsdale elected Arter delegate to the state

convention of colored citizens at Battle Creek on March 25, 1884. The purpose of the convention was to organize northern black citizens in helping fellow southerners to secure political and civil rights.[33] Graduating from Hillsdale in 1885, Arter was described as "a worthy man, an earnest scholar, a gentleman everywhere, and a cool-headed, deep thinker."[34] He used his commencement address to urge blacks "to push off from the dark background and inhospitable shores of the past toward a future of nobler manhood; that industry shall displace indolence; providence, improvidence; intelligence, ignorance; virtue, vice."[35] Arter later graduated from the Chicago Theological Seminary, taught at the Virginia Seminary, and served as principal of the public schools of Hagerstown, Maryland.

Bernard Tyrrell, born a slave, was another outstanding black student at Hillsdale. He earned his way through college by performing manual labor, including sawing firewood. While working outside in cold weather, Tyrrell suffered severe frostbite. He spoke at the annual anniversary of the Theadelphic Society in June 1886, about the responsibility of the press: "When the Reform Press has swept fair Columbia clean with the broom of intelligent reform, the black man, covered with the stripes of two and a half centuries, will not be driven from the ballot box and found murdered upon his couch, and the worthy, industrious 'darkey,' the 'nigger,' not be driven from public hotels, restaurants, respectable railroad cars, and even isolated from the house of the one common God." A local editor observed that Tyrrell held the attention and sympathy of his listeners throughout the speech, which was frequently interrupted by applause.[36]

Tyrrell lectured on "The New South" at the Hillsdale Presbyterian church on November 10, 1887. The audience, perhaps the largest ever crowded together in the beautiful building, "seemed to hang upon the very words of the eloquent young son of Africa."[37] A convention of Michigan blacks met at Jackson on April 25, 1888, to adopt resolutions endorsing the Republican party. This organization became the Michigan Protective League, and Tyrell represented the second congressional district. He received his classical degree in 1888. In his oration on "The American Idea, Its Tendency and Result" at the college commencement program, Bernard Tyrrell concluded that "it is a long distance from the slave hut to the college; it is a longer distance to universal equality."[38] After receiving a degree from the Yale Divinity School in 1893, Tyrrell taught theology at the Virginia Seminary in Lynchburg, Virginia. He explained to President J. W. Mauck on May 6, 1904, that "the greater the obstruction, the more need have we of well prepared men for the undertakings of life."

Booker T. Washington, president of the Tuskeegee Normal Institute, spoke to a large Hillsdale audience on "The Negro Problem in the South" on January 7, 1897. The local reporter claimed that a listener could seldom hear a lecture of more value and interest. Washington urged the black race to work out their own salvation, with leaders to teach thriftier and more advanced ways of living. He argued that the keys to improving the condition of American blacks were "efficiency and ability, especially in practical living." Without being sacrilegious, Washington claimed that Negroes should not take literally their song, "Give Me Jesus and You Can Have the Rest." No longer should blacks be willing to sing of heavenly mansions while they lived in one-room log huts.[39]

When varsity teams appeared in the 1890s, blacks gained a prominent role in Hillsdale athletics. Aaron S. Jennings, '94, played left end on the 1893 M.I.A.A. championship football team; Robert Porter Sims was a member of the 1895 squad. (Nate Johnson, a black student, became Hillsdale's first athlete to win a national small college championship by claiming two titles, the outdoor 100 meters and the indoor 60-yard dash.)

Joseph L. Manus, a full-blooded Cherokee from the Indian Territory, was attending a Presbyterian mission school when a former resident of Grand Rapids described the advantages of Hillsdale College. Manus entered the classical program in September of 1891. A participant in wrestling and track, he played left guard on the Hillsdale football team in 1893–94. When Oklahoma was admitted as a state, Manus, '95, was elected to its first legislature.

Female students, like racial minorities, continued to shape a pioneering role at Hillsdale after the Civil War. Many women entered Hillsdale in an era when coeducation in the liberal arts colleges remained uncommon. The new women's institutions, while segregated, exerted an increasing influence by the 1880s. These colleges included Mount Holyoke (founded in 1836 but not a full-fledged college until the 1880s), Vassar (1865), Wells (1868), Wellesley (1870), Smith (1871), Bryn Mawr (1880), Goucher (1885), etc. The first coed at the University of Michigan, Madelon L. Stockwell, was admitted in 1870.[40]

Large attendance at Hillsdale College, even during the Civil War years, was partially due to the many women attracted by its nondiscriminatory policy. Female students, except for city residents, were required to room at the college. Perhaps the best account of Hillsdale's coeducational role was by Sophia Jex Blake, who travelled from England in 1865 and 1866 to visit American colleges admitting women. According to recent scholars, Miss Blake later became the leading pioneer for women physicians in Europe. Founder of the London School of Medicine for Women in 1874, Dr. Blake was the first female doctor in Scotland.[41] Her book about higher education in the United States, *A Visit to Some American Schools and Colleges*, focused particularly on Hillsdale, Oberlin, and Antioch. Miss Blake lived for a week in the women's dormitory at Hillsdale and wrote a detailed description of campus life.

Women at Hillsdale had proved themselves academically, and Miss Blake conceded that few ladies in England pursued as thorough a course of study as offered at Hillsdale. The professor of mathematics told her that he could not distinguish which sex, male or female, had written an examination; the classics professor also found equal work by the two sexes. On a lighter note, Miss Blake observed that student roughness at Hillsdale was less than at other colleges, with no spitting in class! The English visitor's endorsements were all the more remarkable because instruction and culture at Hillsdale College developed in an environment of cattle and sheep grazing near Manning Street.[42]

Hillsdale College maintained Victorian regulations longer than most colleges, and as late as the 1890s students were prohibited from attending a local dance school. Double staircases extended to the chapel on the second floor of the main part of the building; women used one, and men the other. Particularly intimidating in enforcing social rules was "Mother Peterson," matron of the dining hall. As chaperones, the Lady Principal and teachers who lodged in dormitories ate their meals with students in the college dining room. Pupils regularly joined the faculty table.

Miss Blake believed that Hillsdale students lived a healthier life than those at Oberlin and most other schools. The Prudential Committee in 1868 voted to improve the ladies' accommodations by building a water tank on the fourth floor of the east wing. Three years later, the trustees ordered a privacy screen of boards constructed in front of the outbuilding behind the ladies' hall. A women's gymnastics class was organized to provide physical activity.

The women's literary societies maintained excellent standards. Their outstanding lecture series included Mary Livermore, famous Civil War nurse, who spoke on "Wendell Phillips and His Times." Student Lilian Kirkwood described Livermore's presentation in 1886 as the "most inspiring and grandest lecture I ever heard."[43] Susan B. Anthony, president of the National American Woman Suffrage Association, in 1893 appeared at the first college in the nation to be founded specifically on the principle of equal education for women. By the late nineteenth century, the Germanae Sodales Society had over 600 members, past and present. The sisters publicly debated such issues as *"Resolved,* that women are as intellectual as men." One of the Germanae was the first female to address the New York assembly at Albany on woman's suffrage.

Approximately 40 percent of Hillsdale College graduates in the nineteenth century were women. An 1876 alumna claimed that Hillsdale women "never forget home is their richest kingdom—motherhood their holiest crown; that their virtues never elsewhere shine so bright as by their own hearthstones."[44] Although most alumnae committed themselves to marriage and raising children,[45] Hillsdale women's careers ranged from authors of textbooks to physicians. The most popular profession was teaching. Eighty alumnae became instructors, and four held professorships. (For example, Mignon Kern, '88, taught French at DePauw University.) There is a strong evidence to suggest that Miss May Preston, '78, was the first American woman to earn a Ph.D.[46] Alumnae included three medical missionaries. Dr. Mary H. Fulton, '74, headed a mission hospital at Kwang Sai and trained women physicians in China for thirty-four years. Dr. Nellie Phillips and Shirley H. Smith, '90, both served as medical missionaries in India. Nettie Dunn, '82, worked at Lahore, India, with her missionary husband, the Reverend Walter J. Clark. Mary Garard, '78, a graduate of the Theological School, became pastor of the Free Baptist church at Pittsford. Ellen Cross Copp, '73, Lady Principal at Hillsdale College, received her divinity degree in 1890 and became an ordained Freewill Baptist minister in 1895. Viola Augir, '81, was manager with the Mutual Life Insurance Company of New York. Cynthia J. Simpson, '85, moved to Arvada, Colorado, and defined herself as a "capitalist." Mary E. Powell, one of George Gardner's students from 1879 to 1883, today is recognized as one of the finest early artists in Michigan.[47] Rose Hartwick Thorpe gained wide recognition for her poetry.

A friend described Hattie Magee, one of the first Hillsdale coeds to receive an M.D., as "a woman's righter under the grandiose style."[48] Dr. Loretta Mann Hammond, who entered Hillsdale in 1859, probably was the first female doctor in California. President James Calder willingly lectured on "Women in China."[49] An ally of Hillsdale's support for equal education of women was Mrs. Nannette B. E. Gardner, active worker in the women's suffrage movement and abolitionism. Mrs. Gardner hired Sojourner Truth, a famous ex-slave in Battle Creek who had been active in the underground railroad, as nurse to her daughter Sarah. Following the death of her second husband, Mrs. Gardner moved to Hillsdale for her two children to attend college.[50] Detroit newspapers reported that she was the first Michigan woman to cast a political vote. Meanwhile, most colleges and universities did not admit women until the 1870s or later, and they consciously or unconsciously placed females in the role of outsiders.[51]

Hillsdale coeds played croquet during the Civil War years, but a stronger athletic program emerged later in the century. Chapter 8 contains information about one of the earliest women's gymnasiums in the West, which was installed on the third floor of East Hall in 1884. The Dickerson Gymnasium, built in 1885, provided improved facilities for women's and men's physical education. Hillsdale constructed tennis courts on both the west and east sides of the central campus, and the M.I.A.A. tournament in 1896 was among the first women's intercollegiate competitions in the nation.[52] Zoe Smith of Hillsdale claimed the first M.I.A.A. women's tennis singles title, with additional wins in 1897 and 1899. Hillsdale women also won the first five M.I.A.A. tennis doubles championships from 1896 through 1900. Professors commented that almost all the ladies practiced on the tennis courts during the spring term and benefitted from exercising in the open air.

Hillsdale coeds organized campus basketball teams in the 1890s, and women's baths and lockers were installed in the gymnasium in 1899. On April 18 of the same year, the women's varsity team hosted a Jackson club in the first exhibition of its kind in the history of Hillsdale athletics. Hillsdale and Albion waged the first intercollegiate competition between women's basketball teams in Michigan on February 12, 1900.[53] The *New Collegian* reported in November 1900, that "Hillsdale girls have won more intercollegiate honors since they have had a place in athletics than any other college."[54]

The Board of Trustees made a significant decision in 1892 that promoted the unique role of women at Hillsdale College. The trustees created a commission of ladies to complete the endowment of the Lady Principal's chair. This organization was the origin of the Hillsdale College Board of Women Commissioners, a highly capable group that controlled its own work and reported to the college officers at its pleasure. The ladies held their organizational meeting on March 2, 1893, and elected as president Mrs. Helen M. Gougar, of Lafayette, Indiana. The thirty-five board members promptly decided to raise $50,000 to endow two professorships for women, and they pledged to promote the interests of the college in every way possible, beginning with improvements to the chapel.[55]

Two Women Commissioners (President Gougar and Miss Laura De Merritte, of Dover, New Hampshire) were elected to the Board of Trustees in June 1893.[56] Hillsdale could claim another "first"—the first Michigan college to elect a female trustee. Frances Willard, president of the National Christian Temperance Union and well-known organizer of the women's suffrage movement, in 1894 declined an invitation to speak to the Women Commissioners because of her scheduled trip to England. She expressed a sincere interest in Hillsdale College: "Some of its earliest professors were valued friends of my father and mother, and we used often to talk of the college when we lived in the old home in Wisconsin; and, but for my father's new denominational proclivities, I should very likely have enjoyed the advantage of being a student at Hillsdale."[57]

The Michigan Woman's Missionary Society in 1894 adopted a resolution complimenting Hillsdale College for electing two female trustees and for the Women Commissioners' successful efforts in raising endowment money.[58] The college trustees in 1896 requested the Women Commissioners to "lead in the work of completing the endowment of the chair of Lady Principal and promote the interests of the college in every way possible." A permanent sponsor of the college, the Women Commissioners in the 1890s began a tradition of giving large contributions annually, including the refurbishing of East Hall and the provision of scholarships. For a century, the Women Commissioners have continued to demonstrate their dedication to Hillsdale College.

A leader in admitting blacks and women to classical higher education in the nineteenth century, Hillsdale College was equally successful in implementing the founding fathers' principle of religious integration. As the largest private college in Michigan, Hillsdale remained nonsectarian. Students, faculty, and administrators of all denominations—Baptists, Episcopalians, Presbyterians, Catholics, Congregationalists, Methodists, Unitarians, the Church of God, Jews—were welcomed. Few if any Freewill Baptist students graduated from other church colleges, except Hillsdale's sister school, Bates College in Maine. Thousands of students from other denominations, however, attended Hillsdale College during the nineteenth century. Joseph Mauck, professor of classical languages in the early 1880s, asserted that the Christian college appealed widely to most denominations. Over 400 clergy and missionaries who graduated from Hillsdale by 1900 primarily served the following denominations: Freewill Baptist, Baptist, Episcopalian, Presbyterian, Congregational, Methodist, Free Methodist, and Unitarian.

Since 1844, the pioneer Freewill Baptist college voluntarily rejected all segregation based on race, sex, or religion. The founders and the faculty, eager to offer an inexpensive higher education to all serious students, fully supported the historic antidiscriminatory clause of their 1850 college charter.

Endnotes

1. An act (by the Michigan legislature) to incorporate the Michigan Central College at Spring Arbor, March 19, 1845, in *System of Public Instruction and Primary School Law of Michigan* (Lansing, 1852), p. 500. Act No. 34 of the Laws of the Legislature of Michigan of 1846 recognized the right of Michigan Central College to admit students "irrespective of nationality, creed, color, or sex." See also Article 3 of the Articles of Association of Hillsdale College, approved by the Board of Trustees on February 9, 1855, HCVPA; *Michigan Baptist* (May 1923); Lansing *Republican,* December 5, 1872; and *Hillsdale Standard,* August 25, 1874.

2. The first women's dormitory at Michigan Central College was still intact in the early 1940s. Mead W. Killion, "A History of Spring Arbor Seminary and Junior College," M.A. thesis, University of Michigan, 1941. JPL.

3. Oberlin College claims that the first female faculty member in the United States was Rebecca Mann Pennell, who taught classes in geography and natural history in 1853, although Livonia Benedict taught languages part-time at Michigan Central in 1850. Incidentally, the Moses Benedict who is buried in the cemetery next to the site of the old Michigan Central campus in Spring Arbor may be Livonia's father.

4. Robert Gildart, *Albion College, 1835-1960* (Albion, 1961), p. 59. Mrs. Livonia Benedict Perrine listed all the graduates from Michigan Central College before removal to Hillsdale: 1851, Elizabeth D. Camp (scientific); 1852, Joseph Andrews (scientific), Harriet Benedict (scientific), Livonia Benedict (classical), Laura Hayes (scientific), Julia Woodman (scientific), Sarah Woodman (scientific), Jane Tripp (scientific), and Abigail Tripp (scientific); and 1853, William Perrine (classical), Levant Rhines (classical), Walter Watkins (classical), and James Stewart (scientific). According to her

handwritten list, eight of the thirteen graduates were women. Livonia Benedict Perrine, undated list of graduates from Michigan Central College.
Michigan Central College Collection, MHC.

5. Willis F. Dunbar, *The Michigan Record in Higher Education* (Detroit,
1963), p. 97. Oberlin College maintained close ties with the abolitionist
Freewill Baptists at Hillsdale. Daniel Graham, first president at Spring
Arbor, and Henry Whipple, longtime professor at Hillsdale, were Oberlin
graduates. Charles Henry Churchill, graduate of Dartmouth, taught Latin
at Hillsdale for five years before becoming mathematics professor at Oberlin.
Robert S. Fletcher, *A History of Oberlin College* (Oberlin, 1943), I, p. 256;
II, p. 692.

6. Charles L. Blockson, *The Underground Railroad* (New York 1989), p.
176.

7. John R. McKivigan, *The War Against Proslavery Religion: Abolitionism and
the Northern Churches, 1830–1865* (Ithaca, NY, 1984), pp. 28, 210.

8. William H. Reynolds diary entry for April 30, 1857. William H.
Reynolds Collection, MHC. The Census of 1860 recorded only 6,779 blacks
in a Michigan population of 751,110.

9. Letter by Benjamin B. Comstock, n.d., in *The Amateur* (June 1862), p.
44. Comstock died at Humbolt, Kentucky, on July 17, 1862.

10. Ransom Dunn, Jr., to Ransom Dunn, October 13, 1862. Newell Ransom Dunn Collection, MHC.

11. Wayland Dunn to his father Ransom Dunn, January 8, 1863; Wayland
Dunn to his father Ransom Dunn, May 30, 1864. Francis Wayland Dunn
Collection, MHC.

12. Joseph McKnight to Ransom Dunn, February 23, 1863. Ransom Dunn
Collection, MHC.

13. Reid Mitchell, *Civil War Soldiers* (New York 1988), p. 131. As an
undergraduate at Hillsdale College, Mitchell submitted a paper on Robert
Toombs and Alexander H. Stephens in my honors course. Currently on the
history faculty of Princeton University, he has expanded the pioneering work
on the Civil War common soldier by Bell Irvin Wiley and James I. Robertson, Jr.

14. Ransom Dunn, Jr., to Ransom Dunn, October 18, 1862. Newell Ransom Dunn Collection, MHC.

15. Letter by William Bouton, n.d., in *The Amateur* (June 1862), p. 46.

16. Captain Myron Baker to his sister, March 19, 1863, as quoted by Will F. Peddycord, *History of the Seventy-Fourth Regiment, Indiana Volunteer Infantry* (Warsaw, IN, 1913), p. 95.

17. Chaplain N. Woodworth to Ransom Dunn, November 2, 1864. Ransom Dunn Collection, MHC.

18. Dudley T. Cornish, *The Sable Arm: Black Troops in the Union Army, 1861–1865* (Lawrence, KS, 1987), p. 131.

19. Abstract of Cornelius Hadley's military service record. SAM.

20. OR, series I, XLV, part II, pp. 494–95.

21. Article from the *Chicago Tribune*, as quoted in *Hillsdale Standard*, April 19, 1864.

22. George W. Adams, *Doctors in Blue: The Medical History of the Union Army in the Civil War* (Dayton, OH, 1985), p. 103. A photograph of part of the general hospital at City Point on the James River is reproduced in *The Photographic History of the Civil War* (Secaucus, NJ, 1987), IV, p. 281.

23. Adelaide W. Smith, *Reminiscences of an Army Nurse during the Civil War* (New York, 1911), p. 232.

24. Margaret Jerrido, staff member of the Archives and Special Collections on Women in Medicine, Philadelphia, provided valuable material about Dr. Mary E. Blackmar. Correspondence of May 1, 1989.

25. James M. McPherson, *Battle Cry of Freedom: The Civil War Era* (New York, 1988), p. 480. Ruth J. Abram, ed., *Send Us a Lady Physician: Women Doctors in America, 1835-1920* (New York, 1985) provides excellent information about the pioneering role of the Woman's Medical College in Pennsylvania.

26. Ronald E. Butchart, "Recruits to the 'Army of Civilization': Gender, Race, Class, and the Freedmen's Teachers, 1861–1875," p. 12. Paper delivered at the 1990 annual meeting of the Organization of American Historians.

27. Letter by Lydia B. Lee, as quoted in *Hillsdale Standard*, March 3, 1868.

28. George A. Slayton to Delia Slayton, April 12, 1868. HC. Hillsdale graduates who became ministers in the South included the following: George Bisby, '82, Baptist clergyman in Cuthbert, Georgia; Greenleaf Jones, clergyman at Grand Lake, Arkansas, in the 1870s; James Kirbye, clergyman in Charleston, South Carolina, in the 1890s; Albert Marshall, '73, city missionary in St. Louis, Missouri; Charles Minor (a black), clergyman in Magnolia, South Carolina, in the 1890s; and Judson Palmer, '77, clergyman in Galveston, Texas.

29. Mrs. Matilda Randolph, with her experience teaching blacks in the South, referred to "the discipline of school-life, rapid advance in refinement and self control, and the readiness with which . . . Christian sentiments [were] inculcated at the Institute." A black student told her, "After I came here I began to see that there was no difference between the bright and dark to the teachers, and that helped me to understand what you were always trying to teach us—that God is no respecter of persons, but had made of one blood all the nations of the earth, and that in Christ there was neither black nor white, bond nor free, male nor female, but that he was alike the Great Elder Brother of all mankind." *Plantation Pictures: Colored Views,* pp. 121, 125. Ronald E. Butchart of the Department of Education at SUNY College at Cortland is doing valuable research on freedmen's teachers from 1861 to 1875. He and I have exchanged information about Hillsdale College students who taught freedmen, and Dr. Butchart generously provided some of the facts included here.

30. Students during and after Reconstruction came to Hillsdale College from southern locations including the following: Gadsden, Alabama; Shelby, Alabama; Pomona, Florida; Cairo, Illinois (4); Cordyon, Kentucky; Ford's Ferry, Kentucky; Fulton, Kentucky (2); Mindon, Louisiana; Shreveport, Louisiana (2); Bayfield, Missouri; DeSoto, Missouri (2); Laddonia, Missouri; Manchester, Missouri; New Madrid, Missouri; Newburg, Missouri; Potosi, Missouri; St. Louis, Missouri (7); Charleston, South Carolina; Taylor, Texas; St. Augustine, Florida; Peach's Grove, Tennessee; Gordo, Texas; Abingdon, Virginia; Alexander, Virginia; Berryville, Virginia; Earlysville, Albemarle County, Virgina; McGaheysville, Virginia; Speedwell, Wythe County, Virginia; Charleston, West Virginia; and Harper's Ferry, West Virginia.

31. Willfred O. Mauck, "Dear Hearts and Gentle People," (n.d., n.p.), II,

p. 1. Manuscript loaned by Mrs. Charles Buchanan. Lon Pennock, local historian, has shared with me his memories of Frank Smith, head of a black family in Hillsdale during the early twentieth century. Smith, who had moved to Hillsdale from the South, was a meticulous trash collector. He once told a dowager to keep her unsanitary garbage can so clean that she could place it under the dining room table! In his spare time, Smith trained championship horses. He appreciated the people of Hillsdale and left a bouquet for everybody in town who died. As a boy, Pennock saw Frank Smith's house on fire. Unfortunately, two local men were named Frank Smith, and the firemen went to the wrong building. As two horses pulling a fire wagon finally arrived, the burning house already had collapsed.

32. *Tenth Annual Report Relating to the Registry and Return of Births, Marriages, and Deaths, in Michigan for the Year 1876* (Lansing, 1881), pp. 22, 81. AKG. George N. Fuller, *Michigan: A Centennial History of the State and Its People* (Chicago, 1939), II, p. 303.

33. *Hillsdale Standard*, March 25, 1884.

34. *The Reunion*, June 10, 1885.

35. *The Advance*, March 31, 1886.

36. *Hillsdale Standard*, June 15, 1886.

37. *Hillsdale Herald*, November 10, 1887.

38. Ibid., June 28, 1888.

39. *Hillsdale Standard*, January 12, 1897.

40. F. Clever Bald, *Michigan in Four Centuries* (New York, 1954), p. 472; Martha M. Bigelow, "Michigan: Pioneer in Education," Michigan Historical Collections Bulletin No. 7 (June, 1955), pp. 14–15.

41. Beatrice S. Levin, *Women and Medicine* (Metuchen, NJ, 1980), pp. 85–92.

42. Sophia Jex Blake, *A Visit to Some American Schools and Colleges* (London, 1867), pp. 68–93.

43. Lilian Kirkwood diary, August 12, 1885 to December 31, 1886, entry for November 10, 1886. Loan from Dr. Lilian Rick.

44. *Hillsdale Collegian*, June 28, 1895.

45. Julia Reed Shattuck, '60, speech at 1885 Germanae Sodales reunion, in *Hillsdale Standard,* June 23, 1885.

46. *Addenda to Memorabilia of the Class of 1887,* #5 (Hillsdale, 1944), p. 49; *Hillsdale Herald,* July 10, 1890. May Preston's son, Dr. Preston Slosson, became a distinguished professor of history at the University of Michigan. Hillsdale College awarded him an honorary doctor of laws degree in 1944, when he delivered the commencement address. Also, Dr. Perry Miller, highly respected professor of American intellectual history at Harvard University and now deceased, told me that his grandmother was a Hillsdale alumna.

47. *Early Michigan Paintings: Kresge Art Center, Michigan State University, East Lansing* (Michigan State University, 1976), p. 98.

48. Wayland Dunn diary, entry of February 16, 1869. Francis Wayland Dunn Collection, MHC. Hattie Magee, '68, and her brother Henry, '67, came to Hillsdale College from Meadville, Pennsylvania. Both pursued very successful careers in Chicago, where the former was a physician and the latter an attorney.

49. George A. Slayton to Nettie Henderson, October 4, 1870. HC.

50. Nannette B. E. Gardner Collection, MHC.

51. Helen Horowitz, *Campus Life: Undergraduate Cultures from the End of the Eighteenth Century to the Present* (Chicago, 1988), p. 17.

52. Thomas L. Renner, ed., *Celebrating a Century of the Student Athlete: The 100 Year History of the Michigan Intercollegiate Athletic Association* (M.I.A.A., 1988), p. 29.

53. Willis F. Dunbar, *The Michigan Record in Higher Education* (Detroit, 1963), p. 187.

54. *New Collegian,* November 28, 1900.

55. *Hillsdale Standard,* March 14, 1893.

56. Ibid., June 20, 1893.

57. *Hillsdale Collegian,* June 22, 1894.

58. Ibid., December 14, 1894.

Photographs
and
Illustrations

Figure 1. Sketch of Michigan Central College at Spring Arbor, 1845. Spring Arbor Historical Committee, *Spring Arbor Township, 1830–1980*

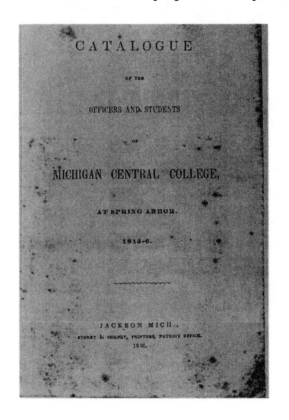

Figure 2. Title page of first Michigan Central College catalogue, 1845–46. MHC

Figure 3. Austin Blair: Michigan Central College professor and Michigan Civil War governor. Carte de visite, SAM

Figure 4. Edward Everett: president of Harvard College and benefactor of Michigan Central College. Crayon drawing, ca. 1850, by R. M. Staigg in Paul Frothingham, *Edward Everett: Orator*

Figure 5. Edmund B. Fairfield: president of Hillsdale College, 1848–69. 1864 carte de visite, HC, donated by Jean Darling

Figure 6. Ransom Dunn: the "Grand Old Man" of Hillsdale College. 1864 carte de visite, HC, donated by Jean Darling

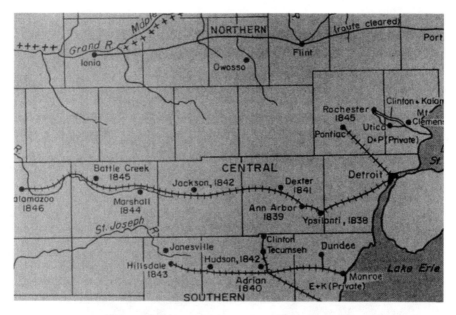

Figure 7. Map of Michigan Southern Railroad locating Hillsdale as railhead in 1843. Drawing in Robert Parks, *Democracy's Railroads: Public Enterprise in Jacksonian Michigan*

Figure 8. President James A. Garfield, who gained his first formal education at Geauga Seminary, which became part of Hillsdale College in 1854. President James Garfield Library, Lawnfield, Mentor, Ohio

Figure 9. View of the Hillsdale business district, 1866. Postcard, AKG

Figure 10. Hillsdale village and College Hill, ca. 1856. Photograph, HC

Figure 11. Hillsdale College, ca. 1865. Photograph, HC

Figure 12. Sketch of Hillsdale College before the 1874 fire. 1872 Hillsdale College catalogue, HC

Figure 13. Sgt. Moses A. Luce: one of three Hillsdale students to win the Congressional Medal of Honor in the Civil War. Carte de visite, ca. 1866, HC

Figure 14. Major Levant C. Rhines: one of several Hillsdale regimental commanders killed in the Civil War. Photograph, SAM

Figure 15. General William Humphrey: participant in 54 Civil War battles. Photograph, MHI

Figure 16. Major General Clinton B. Fisk: Civil War commander of the district of North Missouri. Photograph, MHI

Figure 17. Ensign Charles V. Gridley: Civil War naval officer and Spanish-American War hero. Photograph, MHI

Figure 18. Abolitionist Frederick Douglass, one of many famous speakers at Hillsdale College.

Figure 19. Senator Zachariah Chandler: benefactor of Hillsdale College and prominent Radical Republican. Photograph by Mathew Brady, SAM

Figure 20. Julia Moore: principal of the Hillsdale College Ladies' Department, 1864–65 and 1867–70. Undated carte de visite, HC

Figure 21. Hattie Magee, '68: one of several early Hillsdale alumnae to earn an M.D. degree. Carte de visite, HC

Figure 22. Mary Blackmar: Hillsdale student and Civil War nurse who became an M.D. Adelaide W. Smith, *Reminiscences of an Army Nurse during the Civil War*

Figure 23. Leaders of the "Great Rebellion" in 1866. Photograph, HC

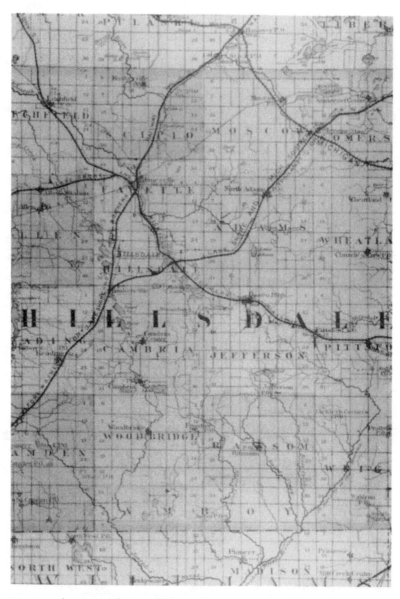

Figure 24. 1873–74 map of Hillsdale County locating six railroad routes through Hillsdale. Original lithograph by William Tackabury, AKG

HILLSDALE COLLEGE.

Figure 25. Architect's plan for new campus following fire of March 6, 1874. Sketch, HC

Figure 26. The new Hillsdale campus, 1879. Photograph, SAM

Figure 27. Knowlton Hall immediately after construction in 1875. Photograph, MHC

Figure 28. Alpha Kappa Phi hall before the 1874 fire. Photograph, HC

Figure 29. May Gardner: Hillsdale College student in late 1860s. Carte de visite, HC

Figure 30. Franklin H. Bailey: Hillsdale alumnus, professor, and scientist. Photograph, MHC

Figure 31. Professor D. M. Fisk and family. Photograph by Carson, Hillsdale, Michigan, AKG

Figure 32. Senior men of the class of 1875 planting trees on campus. Photograph, MHC

Figure 33. ATΩ's J. M. Davis and A. E. Ewing, 1888. Photograph, HC

Figure 34. Bernard Tyrrell: former slave, graduate of Hillsdale College and the Yale Divinity School. *Manual of the Theadelphic Literary Society*, Hillsdale, 1900

Figure 35. Senior class in front of fountain, 1886. Photograph, HC

Figure 36. Senior preparatory students in front of Worthing Hall, 1885. Photograph, HC

Figure 37. The "Gypsy Girls," ca. 1890, a theatrical group. Photograph, HC, donated by Frances Green

Figure 38. General Frank D. Baldwin: winner of two Congressional Medals of Honor. RHC

Figure 39. Jared M. Arter: Hillsdale College graduate and principal of the public schools in Hagerstown, Maryland. *Manual of the Theadelphic Literary Society*, AKG

Figure 40. Hillsdale four-man crew: national champions in 1879, 1880, and 1881. Sketch in *Harper's Weekly*, June 10, 1882

Figure 41. 1892 football team. Photograph, HC

Figure 42. Hillsdale women, including college coeds, at picnic lunch at Baw Beese Lake, ca. 1896. Photograph, AKG

Figure 43. Art class on front campus, late Victorian era. Photograph, HC

❦ SIX ❦

Leadership in Higher Education

> . . . you will find in each country [England and the United States] abundant courtesy, fairness, and toleration. That there is no deficiency of these qualities in America, I, at least, must bear grateful witness; and nowhere did I find their presence more prominent than among the Professors and Teachers of Hillsdale [College].
> —English visitor Sophia Jex Blake, 1866
> (first female physician in Scotland)

The end of military strife by the spring of 1865 enabled Hillsdale College to concentrate solely on educational improvement for the first time since its founding. Survival on the frontier, relocation from Spring Arbor, abolitionism, political issues focusing on the new Republican party, and wartime sacrifice had drained some of the new institution's resources. Alumnus Wallace Heckman, who became legal counsel and business manager for the University of Chicago, believed that institutions (like individuals, nations, and issues) surviving early crises were prepared for future greatness. Hillsdale College withstood the tests of the 1840s, 1850s, and 1860s because Christian leaders shaped the institution through sacrifice, plain habits, and generosity. Faculty and students went forth from Hillsdale to voice their convictions against antebellum slavery. At Hillsdale, young men eagerly closed their books to enter the smoke of conflict. The main bequest of the Freewill Baptist institution was character in education, and alumnus Heckman believed that men and women from colleges like Hillsdale were the nation's best security: "A school is not a gigantic intellectual Bessemer stamp into whose crushing grooves all ingots of individuality shall be shoved and molded to come forth exact likenesses."[1]

With an excellent location on major railroads, Hillsdale College by the end of the Civil War was ready to use its advantages—freedom from indebtedness, willingness of a strong faculty to accept modest compensation, and outstanding financial management—to attain higher academic standards. Lorenzo P. Reynolds' diligence as secretary and treasurer for nearly fourteen years was partially responsible for the excellent financial administration. President Daniel Graham reported to the State Superintendent of Public Instruction on December 5, 1872, that "through the judicious management of its finances, the college has never lost a dollar of its endowment, and is wholly free from the embarrassment of indebtedness."[2] The college proudly advertised that no other American institution offered such fine facilities for a liberal arts education at so low a cost.

For decades the business record of Hillsdale College bore favorable comparison with the soundest American banks and investment companies. In contrast, Kalamazoo College had such pressing monetary problems that the trustees passed a resolution, later rescinded, to close the college for at least a year.[3] President Daniel M. Graham recognized in 1872 that the success of Hillsdale as a strong college would depend largely upon endowment. Freewill Baptists planned to establish only a few colleges but to support them adequately.[4] College authorities accordingly sought an endowment of many small gifts rather than a few large contributions, because it "secured each individual interest and . . . a broad Christian sympathy, which gives growth and power."[5] Some gifts, such as books for the library, were not monetary. Senator Chandler gave the college a complete set of the *Congressional Globe,* and Representative Henry Waldron contributed Civil War histories and all then-current congressional reports.

A correspondent for the *Inter-Ocean* of Chicago analyzed Hillsdale's position in 1872: "The college, under its present management, has enjoyed a high degree of prosperity. During the present year just closed $27,000 has been added to its endowment fund, which now amounts to $150,000."[6] The Alumni Association was organized in the spring of 1865, and a membership of almost 300 by 1872 contributed financial support for the chair of logic and belles lettres. The trustees announced at their 1873 meeting that endowment had increased another $10,000 to $160,000. It was by such consistent financial improvement that Hillsdale became a pacesetter as the largest private college in Michigan. The *Gazetteer of the St. Joseph Valley* in 1867 classified Hillsdale as "a large and esteemed institution." A local editor in late 1866 expressed his opinion that the college ranked among the best educational institutions in the United States.[7] Sophia Jex Blake, an English observer visiting Hillsdale in 1866, thought that the books used and the work assigned were more thorough than at Oberlin, and that the educational quality differed little from that of Yale College.[8] Another writer affirmed in 1871 that the prospects of the college were never more optimistic and that "the interests of this institution are so deeply planted in the affections of the people of this city and of its alumni, and its reputation as a seat of learning is so rapidly spreading, that its future will no doubt realize the most sanguine expectations of its friends."[9]

Average annual attendance in all departments between 1865 and 1870 was 582; between 1870 and 1875, 652. According to statistics from the 1871 *Michigan Almanac,* Hillsdale College had a total of 694 students and 16 instructors. In the same year, Adrian College had an enrollment of 154; Albion College, 217; Kalamazoo College, 165; and Olivet College, 231. The University of Michigan had 495 undergraduates, in addition to 290 students in the Law School and 310 students in the Medical School. The most accurate evaluations of Michigan colleges are the annual reports to the State Superintendent of Public Instruction. In 1872, Hillsdale College recorded a year of marked prosperity: "The number of students in attendance is large, and all matters connected with the College are such as indicate the vigorous condition of its various departments. . . . Valuable additions have been made to the library and apparatus of the College." Total enrollment was 606. In the same year, Olivet College reported a total of 307, and Kalamazoo College 247.[10] As late as 1892, Kalamazoo College had only 40 students at the collegiate level and 125 in the preparatory school.[11]

The Lansing *Republican* in 1872 declared that Hillsdale had improved until "it stands [except for the state university] at the head of all institutions of learning in this state, both in point of numbers and thoroughness of instruction." Another leading Michigan newspaper agreed that Hillsdale occupied "the honorable position of being next in point of numbers and thoroughness of instruction to the State University, and at present and prospectively gives promise of a grand position in the future."[12] The *Michigan Teacher* affirmed that "among the numerous institutions of learning that have sprung into existence since the West was opened to the enterprise of the American people, few can point to a better record than the college founded by the Free Baptists in Michigan and now located in Hillsdale."[13]

The class of 1870 illustrated general characteristics of the student body. Of thirty graduates, twenty-one were gentlemen and nine were ladies. Eleven had pursued the classical course, twelve the scientific course, and seven the ladies' course. Their home states were Michigan, 12; Ohio, 8; New York, 3; Indiana, 2, Illinois, 2; Iowa, 1; Minnesota, 1; and Connecticut, 1. Median age was 24 years, and the majority of the class relied on their own income and spent vacations doing manual labor. Chosen careers were law, 9; theology, 6; farming, 3; writing, 1; teaching, 1; and medicine, 1. Political preferences were Republicans, 17; Democrats, 3; and Prohibition party, 1. On the woman suffrage issue, 3 favored, 12 opposed, and 6 were indifferent. Seven of the class served in the Civil War, and four had been severely wounded.[14]

To promote camaraderie, many classes adopted hats. The senior men of 1870 chose the "silk plug," the juniors picked a broad-rimmed straw hat, and the senior girls adopted a class bonnet. Upperclass students intercepted the sophomore boys, who had chosen pasteboard bandboxes, on their way to town. In the physical contest that followed, it was proved that a man could not fight well and protect his hat at the same time!

Besides having the highest enrollments of all Michigan private colleges, Hillsdale College was riding a crest of academic progress. The faculty informed the trustees in 1868 that more students had joined Hillsdale classes during the previous two years than left to go elsewhere; it was "a reputable thing to carry a diploma bearing the seal of Hillsdale College."[15] In his 1873 history of Michigan, Charles Tuttle referred to Hillsdale's "brilliant reputation."[16] Applicants for the bachelor of arts program were admitted to the freshman class only after satisfactory examination in the following fields: Latin grammar, Latin composition, Caesar, Cicero, Sallust, Greek grammar, Xenophon, Greek prose composition, Greek Testament, algebra, English grammar, and ancient and modern geography.[17] Will Carleton, an 1869 graduate, studied Cicero, Latin grammar, and Greek grammar during the fall of 1865 to prepare for the collegiate classical curriculum. Candidates for admission to Yale were examined in similar fields: Cicero's orations, Sallust's histories, Latin grammar and prosody, Greek Testament, Greek grammar, English grammar, arithmetic, and geography.

According to the 1872 Hillsdale catalogue, the freshman year of the classical curriculum included Herodotus, Greek prose composition, Homer's *Iliad,* geometry, Livy, and Roman history. Listed as sophomore courses were Horace, trigonometry, Tacitus, Thucydides, Juvenal or Plautus, Demosthenes, and natural philosophy. Among the junior studies were Plato's *Apologia,* Greek testament, chemistry, logic, French grammar, zoology, rhetoric, astronomy, physiology, geology, and Racine's *Fasquelle.* The senior classical curriculum included mental philosophy, evidence of Christianity, Hebrew [optional], history of civilization, English literature, moral philosophy, and the American Constitution. Seniors were required to take political economy, an important part of the curriculum ever since outstanding scholar Amasa Walker had taught at Spring Arbor. The textbook, Arthur L. Perry's *Elements of Political Economy,* strongly endorsed Adam Smith.[18] Some classes were very small; only three students, for example, studied Juvenal's poetry in 1871.[19] Speaking to the new Alumni Association, John C. Patterson described the college as "the first in the state to grapple with the question and to solve the problem of co-education. . . . There is no room for drones among the students, alumni, or faculty. So long as the institution lives up to its instincts and traditions it must have an active existence."[20]

Hillsdale College in 1870 established the earliest theological school to grant degrees in Michigan, and the first four students graduated in 1873. The Freewill Baptists previously had lacked a seminary for their preachers in the West. A fourth course, the theological, now was added to the classical major, Ladies' Department, and scientific course with which the college had started. The three-year theological program included Hebrew and Greek, unlike the two-year option. Faculty included Ransom Dunn as professor of Biblical theology, D. M. Graham as professor of church history, and H. E. Whipple as professor of sacred rhetoric. Joining the new department was Professor J. J. Butler, author of *Butler's Theology,* who accepted the chair of Hebrew language and literature.

The college catalogue specified that "those in good standing, of any denomination, and giving evidence of a call to the ministry, may be admitted to the Theological Course without charge for tuition." Not only was tuition free for theological students, but no room rent was charged in the second and third years of study. Tuition also was free for those in other collegiate departments who were preparing for the ministry. Another financial benefit was income paid by regional churches to theological students who served as interim preachers. Professor Dunn feared that the Theological School, with limited income, might be absorbed by Bates College. To the contrary, the department successfully pursued a broad religious policy and attracted ministerial candidates from many denominations. As early as the fall of 1866, students organized the Theological Society as predecessor to the Theadelphic literary society, which broadened its base to accept members from any department.

The trustees' agreement to transform an independent commercial school into an integral part of the college also expanded the curriculum. Charles P. Griffin and Alexander C. Rideout opened the Commercial College, or Union Business Institute, in downtown Hillsdale on September 26, 1866. Two days later, the business college building collapsed and killed two men and a woman.[21] Located in the commercial block across from the courthouse, the enterprise later survived several fires. By 1869, a total of 584 students had attended the commercial college.[22] The president of Wheaton College claimed that Rideout "owns and administers one of the best and most thorough business colleges I have ever known."[23] In August 1870, the business school moved from its previous location to become a self-supporting department paying revenue to the college. Commercial students received all college privileges. Hillsdale College now offered five courses: classical, ladies', scientific, theological, and commercial.

Within a year, enrollment in the business department had increased to 217 students, with an average attendance of 225 from 1870 to 1878. The curriculum included commercial, real and personal property, telegraphy, and penmanship classes. The bookkeeping course examined forty sets of stock and partnership books, with accounting forms for single and double entry. Instruction included bookkeeping for the following fields: wholesale and retail merchandising, joint stock business, banking, railroading, steamboating, manufacturing, jobbing, brokerage, and exchange. The local newspaper editor stated that "for purposes of a commercial education Hillsdale College has no superior, and for instruction in telegraphy no equal west of the Allegheny mountains."[24] Students had access to the telegraph line from college hill to the downtown business area. Also, they received training in the Hillsdale Western Union office, with connections to cities and large towns 300 miles away. The telegraphy course covered magnetism, systems of telegraphy, insulation, circuits, conduction, induction, aerial telegraph, submarine telegraph, frictional electricity, and galvanic electricity. Before coming to Hillsdale, Professor Warren A. Drake had taught five years at Oberlin College, where he succeeded P. H. Spencer, founder of the Spencerian system of penmanship.[25] Alexander C. Rideout, head of the business faculty, previously was professor of telegraphy and commercial law at Oberlin College.

For twenty-one years ending in 1869, President Edmund Fairfield provided leadership in achieving academic excellence. Like Ransom Dunn, he overcame many personal losses without complaint.

Student Franklin Bailey observed in his diary on March 24, 1866, that "today President Fairfield buried his little crippled daughter 12 years old. She died yesterday."

The college faculty after the Civil War included talented and hardworking professors, "some of the ripest scholars of the age."[26] They held undergraduate and graduate degrees from institutions such as Oberlin, Denison, Bowdoin, Bates, Dartmouth, Union, Brown, Hamilton, and the University of Pennsylvania. Many had studied in European universities. On Thursday afternoon, a member of the Hillsdale faculty sometimes presented an all-campus lecture on a literary, moral, or scientific topic. These faculty lectures, which instructed, entertained, and motivated the student body, were extremely popular. Professor Dunn, for example, spoke on the "History of the College." During the decade following the Civil War, Hillsdale College had an average of twenty professors when most small colleges had ten or less. Albion College, for example, was in serious financial condition and had only six instructors in 1870.[27]

Spencer J. Fowler, mathematics professor from 1857 until his death in 1875, endeared himself to the community, the college, and the church as a man, a teacher, and a Christian.[28] George McMillan was professor of Latin and Greek for sixteen years before moving to the new University of Nebraska. Hiram Collier, Hillsdale alumnus, taught natural sciences from 1864 until 1871 and later became professor of physics at the University of Nebraska. Melville W. Chase, who succeeded Fenelon B. Rice in 1869 as head of the music department, was responsible for classes in vocal and instrumental music, a choral society, church music, and a series of public concerts. Admiring students each contributed fifty cents to present him a watch in 1887. Chase remained active as instructor and musician at Hillsdale College for fifty-four years. Alvah Graves, instructor of vocal music and Chase's assistant later in the century, published *The Voice, in Conversation, Speech, and Song.*

A native German, George B. Gardner, was head of the art department from 1868 to 1900, which offered a four-year course including drawing, perspective, sketching, oil painting, and art history. He previously had traveled widely in Europe and the United States and had lived on a plantation in the antebellum South to learn about slave life. A well-known landscape painter of the native or vernacular school, Gardner showed his work at the Detroit Art Exhibit in 1878. Sotheby Parke Bernet, Inc., New York, offered for sale his 1857 "The Mountain Meadows Massacre" in 1967; and the Detroit Institute of Arts recently exhibited his "West Street from the Campus of Hillsdale College, 1873."[29]

Perhaps the most outstanding young instructor was Daniel M. Fisk, who came to Hillsdale to teach chemistry and natural history in 1872. Fisk broadly defined natural history to include botany, zoology, geology, and physiology. Under his direction, the science department developed a valuable herbarium, a collection of New England, Michigan, California, Alpine, and European dried plants. The college also maintained an outstanding museum of natural history with specimens in geology, ornithology, entomology, and botany. Believing that laboratory investigations were the best method of studying nature, Fisk introduced Hillsdale students to biological experimentation. In 1883 he created the Harrington Laboratory, probably the first in the state, by partitioning the fourth floor of East Hall into seven rooms equipped with microscopes and dissecting tables. Scientific laboratory work in most American colleges at this time was confined to a few experiments performed by the professor in front of his class.

Another exceptional young teacher was John S. Copp, who accepted the chair of ecclesiastical history in 1872. At the age of eighteen, Copp had enlisted in the Union army but was discharged with a severe wound after eighteen months. With his arm in a sling, he entered Hillsdale College in 1864. Following graduation, he completed the theological course at Andover Seminary in 1872 and returned to teach at his alma mater. Weakened by disease contracted during the war, Copp continued teaching classes at his home until unable to leave his bed. Four years later, in 1896, he died at Hillsdale.

Low salaries posed a difficulty for the most dedicated teachers. Outstanding professors, including Whipple, Fowler, and McMillan, were paid the unchanging maximum of $900 in 1867. By 1882, $900 remained the top salary for the best instructors, such as D. M. Fisk, A. E. Haynes, and J. W. Mauck. From 1855 to 1900, the average salary increased about $100. At every commencement, some graduates left campus with starting positions at higher salaries than their professors. Wayland Dunn, beloved professor of belles lettres, confided in his diary, "I would be glad to give up my teaching. I can make more money elsewhere. . . . In another ten years there is a chance that the salary may get up to 1200 or more."[30]

President James Calder's address at the inauguration of Daniel McBride Graham on October 5, 1871, contained some evidence of faculty unrest. Following his brief introduction of the new president, Calder took a "dig at the obnoxious members of the faculty."[31] There were few cases of faculty indiscretion, but the most sensational involved Henry E. Whipple, professor of rhetoric and belles lettres since the Spring Arbor era. Wayland Dunn wrote in his diary on May 1, 1871, that Whipple "had confessed to immoralities with Mrs. Bayless & sent in his resignation. There have been rumors of this thing for some two years but it is not certain how long the affair has lasted. Some woman who was stopping at Mrs. B.'s made the discovery [of adultery] and the charges. The Faculty had the thing under consideration last winter but Prof. W. denied it and they, excepting [President] Calder, thought him innocent. The Pres. believed him guilty and told him he ought to leave. . . . The professor seems crushed by the consciousness of the disgrace. . . . It is a personal matter and can not tell against the school." Student George A. Slayton told his sister that Professor Whipple confessed that the reason for his leaving was a "violation of the seventh commandment, and the *cause* of his resignation is deeply lamented by all."[32] Slayton later referred to the Whipple affair as "our late and grievous embarrassment."[33] The professor moved to California, but six years after his personal tragedy he still suffered humiliation and sorrow. Whipple described his life as "inexpressibly painful."[34]

The *Chicago Evening Journal* on February 15, 1868, published false accusations against Professor Spencer Fowler that caused immediate sensationalism. Emma Burt, a prostitute living in Chicago, claimed that Fowler had seduced her when she was a student at Hillsdale College. President Fairfield and Professor Fowler immediately went to Chicago and confronted the young woman. Miss Burt admitted that she had never before seen either Professor Fowler or President Fairfield and that she had never attended Hillsdale College. She confessed only to have visited Hillsdale and boarded at a disreputable location near the railroad depot. The *Chicago Evening Journal* promptly issued a retraction, apologized, and hastened "to correct, as far as possible, the injustice done to that excellent institution. . . . We heartily regret that the *Journal* has been made the vehicle for giving publicity to so gross and outrageous a scandal upon an institution of learning that stands high for its morality as well as its educational character." The *Chicago Tribune* reported that nothing in the affair reflected upon the good name of Hillsdale College or anyone connected with it.[35]

Another false accusation involved Lorenzo P. Reynolds, college secretary and treasurer. Newspapers in Chicago, Toledo, Detroit, and Jackson in early 1874 covered the incident, which involved Lewis A. Clark, whom Reynolds had employed to carry college mail to the post office. Reynolds discovered that articles from his office were missing and suspected Clark, who carried a key. To obtain evidence, on January 15, 1874, Reynolds left a new pocket knife in his office over the lunch hour, when the mail was picked up. Clark admitted taking the missing knife but denied tampering with the mail. A police officer suspended charges when Clark promised future good conduct. The next day, Clark filed exaggerated claims of oppressive conduct against Reynolds. He also accused Reynolds of sending for a police officer without first conferring with the faculty.[36] Although the incident seems innocent enough in retrospect, the honor of Lorenzo Reynolds and Lewis Clark was on the line for a few days.

By 1880, fewer than two percent of Americans between the ages of eighteen and twenty-one had received any higher education, and the figure had varied little since 1800.[37] Hillsdale, however, continued to increase enrollment and remained the largest private college in Michigan in the post-Civil War era. In local and regional publications, the college advertised the availability of scholarships for all incoming students. Tuition fees were low, and financial assistance reduced the cost of college education even more. In effect, Hillsdale College boldly offered what was essentially free tuition. Most students relied on manual labor to meet remaining college expenses, and Hillsdale in a unique sense became the "home of self-supporting youth."[38] President Graham reported to the State Superintendent of Public Instruction in 1871 that students "who are compelled to support themselves find such facilities for doing so in Hillsdale, or its immediate vicinity, so that no diligent and economical person need despair of securing an education."

The kitchen steward supervised the only outside help hired by the college, and students themselves provided all other manual labor. The fee for board averaged $3 per week. No Monday classes were held, so that the young ladies could clean their rooms, wash clothing in the kitchen, and sew and mend their wardrobes. Many coeds later gained distinguished social status, but at Hillsdale College "labor and self-reliance were not only honorable but popular."[39] It was not unusual for Orville Whitney to write to his family in Susquehanna County, Pennsylvania, that his clothes were in poor condition, that he needed a whole suit, and that he might be able to get by until the end of the spring term. His expenses included $3.25 a week for board, literary society fee of $1.75, and $3 for laundry.[40] Whitney, surviving financial challenges, graduated with his class in 1875.

Franklin H. Bailey, who fought in the Civil War and became an officer in the 137th U.S. Colored Troops, also demonstrated self-sufficiency. Entering Hillsdale in 1866 with $3.31 in his pocket, he worked manually to pay his relatively low costs. Bailey split wood for Edmund Fairfield, fixed the pump in the cistern behind the College, and helped to repair the road north of the College to Oak Grove Cemetery for the funeral procession of the president's twelve-year old daughter. After his freshman year in 1870, Bailey proudly announced that he had not missed, been tardy to, or made a failure in any class, so in fact he had made a good recitation every time in every course.

George Slayton, who began working his way through college by digging potatoes the first week he arrived in Hillsdale, was another student dependent upon manual labor. In the afternoons when his classes were over, Slayton cut firewood with a bucksaw for fifteen cents an hour. During an entire summer of farm work he usually earned about $75. He plowed ground for wheat, hoed corn and potatoes, harvested grapes in vineyards, sheared sheep, put up hay, built a stone wall, did janitorial work at the college, helped at the post office, and was steward of a boarding club. Like most students, Slayton took two years to complete the preparatory course before becoming a classical freshman. He supported himself by manual work at the college for six years.

Slayton also earned $300 by teaching two two-month winter terms in rural schools. He then signed another contract to teach four months at Moscow, on the Chicago Military Road east of Jonesville, during the unseasonably cold fall and winter of 1869–70. The snow froze apples on the trees in early October and never disappeared until about April 1. Slayton occasionally visited friends at Hillsdale on weekends by taking the Moscow stagecoach after school on Friday afternoon and by walking back Sunday afternoon through deep snow. When a relative died in Orleans, located northwest of Hillsdale in Ionia County, Slayton made the return trip by a combination of horse carriage, train, stagecoach, and walking (i.e., horse carriage to Marshall, train from Marshall to Albion, stagecoach to Jonesville, and walking to Hillsdale). For recreation, Slayton attended the Hillsdale County fair. Paying a round trip fare of one dollar, he also accompanied about fifty college students by train to the Michigan state fair at Jackson. While there, he visited the penitentiary. Slayton also took an excursion to the Capitol in Lansing to observe both legislative houses in session.[41]

During the fall of 1870, Slayton became ill from a bilious attack but resumed his studies after five days.[42] He assured his father that summer earnings should meet all expenses for the fall term, because he did not expect to buy any clothing except a pair of shirts.[43] In his junior year, he used the winter term to teach four months at Grattan for $160. He returned to college in the spring to study German, Greek, and geology. In spite of earning money, Slayton occasionally requested funds from his family "to meet present obligations and cancel expenses for the remainder of the present term."[44] Once he implored his father for assistance "to allow me to finish my course with my present class. . . . Besides, this seems only justly due to your son, myself, as you are well aware of the time when I endangered my health and life even, for these very resources for the purposes for which I am now using them."[45] Due to financial troubles, Slayton was refused admission to classes in the winter term of his senior year until he could settle his college bill.[46]

During his last year as a student, Slayton earned income by reporting the literary societies' contests to the Detroit and Hillsdale newspapers, but his most satisfying experience that year was the "more intimate acquaintance and companionship with my classmate Abbie Dunn [daughter of Professor Dunn]." He also was chairman of the committee of arrangements for his own commencement in 1872. Suffering typhoid in the summer following graduation, Slayton remained in his college room during recovery. His first full-time job as teacher began at Quincy in the fall, with a salary of $90 per month for nine months. Slayton eventually married Abbie Dunn; and on the fiftieth anniversary of their graduation they gave the college fourteen acres of land, later developed by Dr. Bertram Barber and his students into the outstanding Slayton Arboretum.

Hillsdale students' characteristics in the post-Civil War era included a pioneering background, middle-class origins, experience at manual labor, Christian faith, a strong desire for higher education, reliance on personal merit, and strong physical and mental endurance. Their enterprise, when shaped by the vision and dedication of the Hillsdale faculty, produced outstanding alumni. Many became teachers, ministers, missionaries, superintendents of schools, physicians, judges, lawyers, businessmen, and politicians.

William C. Ringenberg, in his 1970 Ph.D. dissertation entitled "The Protestant College on the Michigan Frontier," confirms the success of Hillsdale's graduates. His article on "The Vocations of the Alumni of the Early Michigan Denominational Colleges" in *Michigan History* (September 1980) is exceptionally well documented. He specifically lists fifteen outstanding former students from Michigan church colleges in the mid-nineteenth century. Of that number, ten came from Hillsdale College: two generals (Clinton B. Fisk and Frank

Baldwin); a naval officer (Charles Gridley); two authors (Harvey Fuller and Will Carleton); an astronomer (William Payne); a medical doctor (Loretta Hammond); and three millionaires (Austin Mitchell, William Mitchell, and Lewis Emery, Jr.).

Harvey A. Fuller, class of 1868, was one of Hillsdale's most courageous students. After attending the New York Institution for the Blind, Fuller traveled to Hillsdale to pursue a higher education. President Fairfield personally welcomed the blind student and introduced him to professors. Fuller gained his information "by having the students read their lessons to me, and by listening to recitations and oral exercises. . . . I found no difficulty in obtaining all the reading I needed, and their interest in my welfare was more apparent when I began to take an active part in the recitations."[47] Membership in the Amphictyon Society provided him many benefits. Fuller proudly stated that his alma mater had the "honorable position of being next in point of numbers and thoroughness of instruction to the State University." After graduation, he made a career of lecturing and writing throughout the United States. John Greenleaf Whittier, who earlier had been perhaps the best-known literary figure in the abolitionist movement, in 1890 complimented Fuller's literary ability and wrote, "I can in some sort understand thy trial, for my sight is so impaired that I cannot write or read much." Oliver Wendell Holmes also gained pleasure from Fuller's poetry.[48]

The moral strength of the hilltop college impressed many observers. One writer remarked that the college offered facilities "quite equal, if not superior, to any furnished in Michigan, unless it be the state university at Ann Arbor; and, when we consider the moral and religious influence that have pervaded the college . . . even that great institution, sustained as it is by state appropriation, does not surpass Hillsdale College."[49] Evidence of moral standards at the small college included the popularity of temperance meetings. A student observed in 1873 that "temperance has become an issue here in Hillsdale."[50] Senior Will Carleton delivered his popular poem on temperance, "Lost and Reclaimed," to the local Methodist Church. The blind Harvey A. Fuller presented an impressive speech on "Tobacco" to the

Theological Society. He claimed that the evil weed, proceeding from the Devil, caused deterioration to the human physical and moral condition. Why make a chimney of one's own nose?

Another student boasted to his parents that he got up to study at five a.m., had not smoked a cigar for almost three months, and drank no tea and only one morning cup of coffee to soak his crackers. He never sat with women at the dining table and scarcely spoke to any females except the women who did his washing and sewing. The student concluded his exaggerated self-examination by claiming that "this restraint I do not deem necessary for my health or enjoyment, but think it a good thing to aid in the mastery of my numerous school duties."[51]

The first Hillsdale College chapel service was held on November 6, 1855. Two weeks later on November 21, the Hillsdale First Free-will Baptist Church was organized at the college chapel. Two college students, A. Wix Munger and William J. Lindsley, were among the first eight charter members signing the church's articles of association on November 24, 1855.[52] The Home Mission Society of the national denomination endorsed the Hillsdale church and reported that "hundreds of scholars from different parts of the country have gone there to obtain an education . . . and the prospects of the institution are reported to be encouraging."

Although the First Freewill Baptist Church of Hillsdale had only twenty members, within a year sixty-five additional persons joined. Pastor Henry E. Whipple headed the congregation growing from many conversions and baptisms. Services originally were held in the chapel, a room 60 by 60 feet on the second floor of the large college building. At one end of the sanctuary was a small organ gallery. Approximately 300 students attended weekly Bible lessons,[53] which English observer Sophia Jex Blake described as much quieter than those at Oberlin: "At Hillsdale the whole tone seemed to me in this respect much more healthy. The desire was evident that a religious feeling should pervade the College, but we heard nothing of revivals, and the students did not seem oppressed by the kind of religious melancholy that one regretted [at Oberlin]."[54] Two years after leaving the Hillsdale campus, James C. Thomas reflected in 1868: "I can

almost hear the old College bell summoning together those who re-
vered the name of God and who were wont to gather in and around
that old College chapel, where we and they were accustomed to listen
to such wholesome instruction. . . . "[55]

H. M. Ford, born in Hillsdale and a member of the class of
1879, described how as a boy he had heard Fairfield, Dunn, and
Whipple preach:

> It was a question whether Dunn or Fairfield was the greater preacher.
> They were so different they could hardly be compared. Dunn was chain
> lightning, a cyclone, a torrent carrying all before him. His oratory at
> times was awe-inspiring, like standing before Niagara. Fairfield was
> like a modern four hundred-ton locomotive sweeping majestically
> along without much noise and every part synchronized and working
> with absolute precision and drawing a half mile load. His thought
> moved with majesty; he was the scholar, his presence and manner were
> impressive and held his listeners captive to the end. He was orator,
> preacher, poet, and actor all in one. . . . Henry Whipple was also
> one-time pastor, large, dark, slow, deep-chested, and deep-voiced and
> an unusual reader. When he read scripture or a hymn you felt it was
> the first time you had really heard it. His voice was like low thunder
> but musical and rich.[56]

From 1855 to 1871 only members of the college faculty or staff
filled the pulpit of the Hillsdale First Freewill Baptist Church. Professors serving as pastor included Ransom Dunn from 1857 to 1859,
1863 to 1870, and 1879 to 1883; Edmund Fairfield from 1859 to
1863; and James B. Calder from 1870 to 1871. By March 29, 1865,
the trustees voted to raise funds for their own building. The church
experienced its first great revival in 1866, when 155 new members
joined. Construction of the Hillsdale First Freewill Baptist Church
(now referred to as the College Baptist Church) began on March 10,
1867. The structure at North Manning and Fayette on College Hill
was dedicated on January 5, 1868, and its physical size made it one
of the largest churches in the West. An impressive crowd of almost a
thousand people attended the church dedication. Dr. Ransom Dunn,
in his happiest and most inspired mood, preached the sermon.

The new facility relieved overcrowding in the college chapel. More important, the college maintained its close connection with the First Freewill Baptist Church. Students were required to attend a daily prayer service in the old chapel, in addition to public worship at church twice on Sunday. Attendance at the Sunday afternoon service in the College Baptist Church was mandatory, but in the morning or evening each student had the option of attending another church with faculty approval. (Incidentally, on December 23, 1871, the students from their classrooms watched a heavy gale blow down the high tower at the southeast corner of the church.) College faculty continued to serve at low pay as minister of the First Freewill Baptist Church. President DeWitt Clinton Durgin, who preached in the late 1870s and early 1880s, made an imposing appearance with his white beard and height of six feet and four inches. His pay was never over $10 per Sunday, but he was "a splendid preacher and drew great crowds to hear him."[57] For twelve years in the 1880s and 1890s, Dr. A. T. Salley, professor of sacred literature at the college, was pastor of the College Baptist Church. H. M. Ford regarded Salley as "the most beloved, the most popular, the most successful" of all ministers at the college church.[58] Another faculty member to assist the church was Professor Melville W. Chase, organist for fifty-five consecutive years. Many college students attended the services, and most of the twenty-seven foreign missionaries from the College Baptist Church were Hillsdale graduates.

The college students continued to enjoy pranks and minor misconduct. They could request written exemption from some of the social rules. As a nineteen-year-old student in 1871, future college president Joseph W. Mauck wrote the following humorous satire on the tribulations of obtaining a faculty exemption: "Prof. Dunn absent. Prof. Collier refers to senior members of faculty. Prof. Rideout thinks he is not sufficiently connected with literary department to grant request. Prof. Drake, Prof. Chase, Prof. Gardner . . . and numerous other instructors consider themselves invested with too limited power. The 'polished and polite professor,' McMillan gives a verbal permission. This final success only tends to show that it is with some degree of reason that it has been said: 'If at first you don't succeed, try again.' Yes, try again."[59]

Less responsible was student Calvin Abbott, who wrote on October 9, 1873, to a friend in Pulaski that he liked school pretty well. He had just returned from the county fair, and it was a "damned hard fair, too." Discussing the opposite sex, Calvin had heard that "the girls were a raising the devil around home. Well, never mind. There are four darned pretty ones just a little ways from where I room and they are old business, too . . . but I don't paddle my own canoe as we did last summer. I have to keep pretty straight. I have six weeks to stay yet and thank God it ain't any longer."[60] Abraham H. Whitaker, severely wounded in the charge against Fort McAllister during Sherman's Georgia campaign, studied at Hillsdale College for four years after the Civil War. Baptized by President Fairfield in 1866, Whitaker was expelled when he broke the college rule prohibiting student marriages. Students already married, incidentally, were readily admitted to Hillsdale College. Unperturbed by his dismissal, Whitaker pursued a successful preaching and temperance career in Ohio, Wisconsin, Kansas, and Michigan.[61] Emily Ames, '73, wrote of another youth similarly expelled.[62] In 1869, the trustees decided for the first time to collect $3 from each male renting a room in the west wing. The fees were necessary to repair student damages to individual bedrooms and to the halls and stairways.

Amid the active temperance crusade at Hillsdale, a favorite student song was "There Is a Tavern in the Town." Another popular tune was "Meerschaum Pipe," and the college men enjoyed their rare opportunities to smoke a pipe or a cigar. In an act of carelessness in March 1870, a student living on College Hill almost burned down his rooming house. Leaving for class, he left his bed too near a defective stove with a broken door. A hot coal fell on the floor, and dense smoke soon poured out of his window. Not knowing that it was more smoke than fire, students carried pails of water to the upper rooms and threw out chairs, lamps, clocks, books, and valuable furniture. A local reporter summarized the lively incident, "But lo! there is no fire!"[63] Neither was there insurance.

More disruptive than acts of carelessness were student pranks. John Hallack, entering Hillsdale College in 1866 after service in the war, earned money by doing college janitorial work. His assignment brought him into frequent conflict with imaginative students whose midnight feats included rolling loaded barrels down the stairway, hiding pigs and chickens in the college chapel, throwing stoves down the hall, and blocking the stairs to the chapel with a farm wagon broken apart into sections. College students celebrated April first in imaginative ways; some sewed knives and forks to table clothes in the dining room and nearly sawed the legs off tutors' chairs.

Five outstanding literary societies were among the strongest assets of postwar Hillsdale College. Three were for men—Amphictyon, Alpha Kappa Phi, and Theological, and two for women—Ladies' Literary Union and the Germanae Sodales. Although associated with the college, they organized under a state statute and maintained an independent existence. The societies, beginning with the Eunomians and the Philogrammatians at Michigan Central College, offered students opportunities for self-improvement that complemented classroom work. Excellent writing and public speaking skills resulted. With seriousness of purpose, Hillsdale literary societies into the early twentieth century prepared students for public service, long after most colleges adopted the fraternity system as a more popular substitute. Literary societies at Williams College disappeared by the 1850s, and even traditional southern colleges and universities abandoned their valuable student organizations decades earlier than Hillsdale.

The Alpha Kappa Phi society, founded on October 6, 1857, was an immediate success, and the members' high spirit soon was termed the "Alpha fire." The Alphas held their first public meeting on March 1, 1858, in the college chapel. Members returning from the Civil War in 1864 and 1865 gave the society new vigor. The Amphictyon society held its first official meeting on December 21, 1857, although some business sessions occurred earlier. After dedicating their hall on August 18, 1858, the Amphictyons incorporated under state law in June 1859.

Kentucky abolitionist Cassius M. Clay and Congressman Joshua R. Giddings, Abraham Lincoln's friend who had fought renewal of the gag rule, soon became honorary Amphictyon members. Hon. John Bright, M.P., one of the most active European supporters of the Union during the American Civil War, accepted membership.

The Amphictyons' motto was "Inveniam viam aut faciam" ("I will find a way"). These words were an heroic Roman commander's reply when he was told that the enemy's works could not be taken. The societies encouraged close friendship, and a former Amphictyon described his feeling: "I am ever proud of that institution and look back to it with greater emotion than to any other association to which I have ever been connected."[64] In the fall of 1868, senior William Steward became ill, returned home to Wheatland, and died of typhoid. His Amphictyon brothers and the entire senior class attended the funeral fourteen miles from Hillsdale. Each brother draped his society badge with dark cloth and wore a black ribbon around his left arm. Another member honored by the Amphictyons was C. C. Smith, killed by the Ku Klux Klan when en route for Austin, Texas, as state senator-elect. The concluding verse from Theadelphic G. C. Alborn's "A Reverie" describes the bond among literary society members:

> Friends' happy faces once again I see,
> As real now as e'er they were to me
> > In College Hall.
> Now scattered each his separate way,
> My brothers still; and I devoutly pray,
> > God bless them all.
> And may we meet once more in realms above,
> Where all is peace and righteousness and love,
> > And joys ne'er pall.[65]

The Ladies' Debating Club was formed at Hillsdale in the spring of 1856 because the faculty prohibited the association of both sexes in the same society. By December 1857, with fifty-four sisters, the name of the club was changed to the Ladies' Literary Union. After the society's membership increased to 145 women in 1862, the college trustees allowed the L.L.U. to have a meeting room on the first floor of East Hall. Decorations included a carved book case the length of the west wall, and French windows on the north side of the room. The L.L.U. held annual oratorical contests beginning in 1868. The Germanae Sodales, organized by Julia Reed and Eliza Cole in the spring of 1858, also had their meeting room on the first floor of East Hall. Incorporated by the state as a lyceum in 1864, the society adopted the motto "per aspera ad astra" ("through struggles to the stars"). In 1870 the Germanae Sodales held their first annual public oratorical contest. According to faculty records, Oberlin College was reluctant as late as 1874 to let women give public orations.[66]

Each of the five societies held a weekly program. From nine to twelve exercises (including eulogies, debates, discussions, papers, speeches, impromptus, orations, essays, biographies, and extempores) were given at each meeting. Emily Ames, '72, commented after her speech to the L.L.U. that it was "more embarrassing to speak without any paper." In addition to speeches, programs featured performances by the best talent from the music department. For more than half a century, each society held exercises on Monday evenings and public programs twice annually. The societies followed the example of the Amphictyons, who in October of 1867 began printing attractive small programs on colored cardboard for their weekly meetings. The trustees continued to provide each society with its own room.

Probably the only extravagance at Hillsdale College in the nineteenth century was the decoration of these magnificent society rooms, which contained armchairs, carved bookcases for libraries, oil paintings, carpeting, sculpture, chandeliers, a melodeon, a rosewood piano, an organ, and other luxuries. The Alpha Kappa Phi "little chapel" was beautifully paneled. Draperies covered three large windows, and two brass chandeliers illuminated the elegant Brussels carpet. On a raised rostrum were seats and marble-top tables for the society officers. On the wall above the president's chair was a crescent with the A.K.P. motto upon a blue silk curtain. Bronze busts of Daniel Webster and Henry Clay were placed on either side of the crescent. A life-sized portrait of Lieutenant Theodore S. Mead of the 27th Michigan, killed at Petersburg, was a generous gift from H. L. Hall of Hillsdale. The eastern side of the hall was lined with library cases. Comfortable chairs for the audience had writing desks.

The Amphictyon society room on the first floor of the west wing of the college had frescoes on the walls and ceilings. To the rear of the platform was a bust of George Washington. One wall was ornamented with a full-length figure of the Goddess of Poetry. Oil paintings lined a side wall. The members raised funds for these elaborate decorations.[67] In 1868 alumnus A. N. Buck, a cavalry officer during the Civil War, gave the society 103 expensive carved black walnut, upholstered chairs. The ladies' societies in the late 1870s moved to the third story of the new Fine Arts Hall, where their rooms contained such elegant furnishings as a grand piano, tables, carpeting, an oil painting, plush chairs, frescoed walls, and chandeliers.

To a large extent, public speaking as promoted by the societies was the measure of collegiate training in the nineteenth century. Orville Whitney complained in 1873 that he had worked four weeks preparing an oration that was still unfinished. His previous society speech, entitled "The Calling of Life," had been judged the best of the evening.[68] The experience provided by societies was the major reason why Hillsdale students competed so well in oratorical contests against other colleges.

A local reporter in 1871 wrote favorably of recent lecturers such as Charles Sumner and Wendell Phillips but claimed that the college itself had produced equally outstanding speakers. Henry W. Magee of the class of 1867, who addressed the Alphas, was an excellent "lecturer of home manufacture" capable of holding his own with famous statesmen.[69] Graduates from no other college won so many prizes for composition and delivery at the University of Michigan as did Hillsdale students. Furthermore, the societies strongly encouraged moral purpose in their members. J. C. Thomas, a former Amphictyon living in Walnut Fork, Iowa, wrote in 1868 that he was "most happy to learn than the religious interest still is paramount and that those [society] meetings which in times ago were so productive of good, still go on performing their offices of love and mental regeneration."[70] A.K.P. purchased eight pews to seat fifty in the front gallery of the new College Baptist Church.

General C. J. Dickerson praised Hillsdale's societies: "In the short space of ten years, your College has been established and endowed, and can now boast of literary societies that would do credit to many of the older institutions of the East. The spirit of the great West, that spirit which sweeps away the forest and causes villages and cities to spring up as suddenly as the flowers of the tropics, has characterized all your undertakings."[71] A local reporter believed that Hillsdale College could boast perhaps of the best literary societies in the West.[72] After commencement exercises, a Hillsdale editor stated in 1867 that the literary societies held first rank among all such institutions in the state. He proudly claimed that "no star spreads a brighter sheen over the literary firmament of the West than our own favorite institution—Hillsdale College."[73] In addition to the literary societies, a student musical organization called the Beethoven Society performed at commencements and similar events. Members contributed their proceeds from concerts in 1867 toward the purchase of an organ for the new College Baptist Church.[74] Another musical organization was the brass band that Will Carleton helped to organize.[75]

The "Great Rebellion," an unfortunate controversy involving the literary societies, began in early May of 1866, when the faculty passed a rule forbidding them to admit anyone of the opposite sex without a pass signed by the president of the college or a faculty member.[76] Without exception, the societies regarded this control as an invasion of their chartered rights and refused to submit to the new regulation. Many members requested honorable dismissal from the college but were refused. The faculty even placed injunctions on the property of students preparing to transfer to other colleges. At this point, a majority of the student body rose in open rebellion and deserted classrooms. President Fairfield arbitrarily dismissed approximately twenty-five student leaders. Early one Sunday morning a large poster that read "TURN OUT PRESIDENT FAIRFIELD" was placed over the pulpit in the chapel.

Franklin Bailey, who attended a society meeting while most members were in rebellion, wrote in his diary on November 18 that "last night the college steps, doors, and halls were covered with advertisements, put up by the rebel students called G.O. 2568 [a general order supposedly from President Fairfield]. My books all thrown from the back window into the mud, had clothes strewn all over the ground, were picked up by the faculty, which held a meeting nearly all night trying to find the burglars." At the treasurer's office, Bailey retrieved his personal belongings that had been tossed by rebellious students into a large mud puddle when they "renovated" his dormitory room. Bailey's loyalty to the administration had precipitated student retaliation. A week later, Bailey assisted the college authorities by doing picket duty until 3 a.m.[77]

The faculty finally amended the offensive rule and reached a compromise acceptable to both sides. All students who had been expelled received general amnesty. Unfortunately, the truce was short, and the rule was reinstated during the summer vacation of 1866. Returning for the fall term, society officers resigned and closed their meeting rooms. The Alpha Kappa Phis appointed a committee empowered to dispose of their property. Many students would have left, except for strong emotional ties to the college. Wayland Dunn described the continuing conflict on November 22, 1866: "There was another disturbance at Hillsdale. . . . The theologs were admitting ladies without tickets claiming that they did not come under the regulation. . . . Father [Professor Ransom Dunn] and the President are going to be opposed on this matter. Good many of the students are leaving & a bad state of things generally."[78] Wayland Dunn's prediction of disagreement between his father and President Fairfield was accurate.

Professor Dunn championed the Theological Society and willingly signed all requests to invite women to meetings. He even approved female visitors for an entire term and endorsed invitations before they were filled out. Professor Dunn ultimately allowed members to issue and sign their own invitations! President Fairfield, meanwhile, argued that only he was authorized to sign invitations. The conflict finally was resolved in a faculty meeting, where Ransom Dunn claimed the right to sign invitations for the society in his department. A unanimous vote supported Dunn, and Fairfield threw out the objectionable rule.[79] By the spring term of 1867, the faculty made adequate concessions, and the societies immediately reorganized.

The "Great Rebellion" of 1866–67 at Hillsdale College was an exception in the entire history of the institution. Student uprisings were not uncommon in American higher education in the nineteenth century, however, as young men even rioted against college presidents and faculty.[80] For example, students protested at Kalamazoo College in November 1863 when popular President J. A. B. Stone and his wife, an instructor, resigned. The Baptist State Convention had opposed the Stones' liberal ideas. Between 120 and 150 students denounced the resignations and submitted a petition for reinstatement of the Stones, which was denied. The protesters at first were threatened with expulsion, but the trustees changed the wording to honorable dismissal. At this point, most students left Kalamazoo College.[81]

Civil War veterans were an important student group at postwar Hillsdale College. One returning soldier was Wayland Dunn, who came home on November 12, 1864, after service with the First U.S. Cavalry, Alabama Volunteers. It seemed like old times as he visited former classmates. On Monday morning he promptly went downtown to choose cloth for a new suit, and in the evening he attended the Amphictyon meeting to see his brothers.[82] In the following spring, Dunn was visiting in Chicago when news came of President Lincoln's assassination. Wayland wrote in his diary that "the feeling in the city is genuine sorrow, not tokens of respect. Men cry and curse. Have not seen a man laugh today. The streets are hung in black, and places of business are closed." Dunn viewed Lincoln's funeral procession on May 1 and described the slain president: "The skin was somewhat discolored but the features were natural and more an expression of kindness than I had expected to see."

Veteran George A. Slayton, entering Hillsdale in the fall of 1866, found "many lately returned soldiers from the Civil War, many who expected as I did to work to help themselves with their school expenses. Some of the best and brightest students we had were of those who had been in the army, either going from the college to the war, or having come to college for the first time after having had service in the army. . . . A considerable number of the graduates of the college from the classes from 1865 to 1873 were men who had been in army service during the Civil War."[83] For example, the thirty-four members in the class of 1868 included eleven who had served in the war, with six wounded.[84]

On April 5, 1870, the students, including many veterans, held a memorial service for Major General George H. Thomas in the college chapel. After the speeches, students who had returned from the war adopted the following resolution: "That we have heard, with profound sensibility, of the sudden and comparatively early death of Major General George H. Thomas, who bore so conspicuous and glorious a part in the great struggle of our national existence . . . *Resolved,* That the uprising millions of those who so lately groveled in bondage, should hold in everlasting remembrance, the name of this departed hero. . . . "[85] In 1868 the first annual Decoration Day (now Memorial Day or Veterans' Day) gave an opportunity to students, faculty, and townspeople to mark the graves of fallen Hillsdale students. At 10:30 a.m., a large crowd gathered in front of the courthouse square. When the procession passed the campus, students and faculty joined the march to Oak Grove Cemetery. Participants in the ceremony spoke from a stand built at the cemetery. Will Carleton's "Cover Them Over" was read at Hillsdale in 1870 and soon became an extremely popular poem on Decoration Day throughout much of the United States. A portion of the poem follows:

> Oh how they gleamed at the Nation's first cry!
> Oh how they streamed when they bade you good-by!
> Oh how they glowed in the battle's fierce flame!
> Oh how they paled when the Death Angel came!
> Cover them over, yes, cover them over,
> Parent, and husband, and brother, and lover
> Kiss in your hearts those dead heroes of ours,
> And cover them over with beautiful flowers!

Another feature of college life was student athletics, because sports in general, and baseball in particular, started coming into their own in the 1860s. Williams and Amherst probably played the first intercollegiate baseball game on July 1, 1859, but college baseball in the West was in its infancy when Hillsdale College fielded a club on May 26, 1868. As early as 1860, baseball was the "principle [sic] game" at Hillsdale,[86] and many returning veterans had learned the sport during the Civil War. The college club at first played teams from towns in the vicinity. On October 6, 1868, students defeated the Reading club at the Hillsdale fairgrounds by 45 to 39 in a game taking three hours. Emerson, Hillsdale catcher and leadoff batter, scored nine runs and made no outs! Calling themselves the Praktikoi Club, the relatively inexperienced Hillsdale athletes traveled to the University Grounds in May 1870, to defeat the state champion Ann Arbor city club by 29 to 28 before a large crowd.[87] The baseball players probably wore cherry and gold, the earliest Hillsdale College colors. On June 6, 1874, the Praktikois defeated Albion College by 31 to 10 in an away game called at the close of the fifth inning by request of the Albions. Hillsdale on the same day defeated Eaton Rapids, 5 to 1, in a contest that ended when the umpire ruled that the losing pitcher had used an illegal motion.[88]

The baseball clubs representing Hillsdale were some of the earliest in the state. The State Agricultural College (now Michigan State University) had a team in 1865, but interest in the sport there declined greatly by the early 1880s; Kalamazoo College fielded a baseball club by 1880. Hillsdale women, meanwhile, largely confined their athletic interests to croquet and gymnastics, but their opportunities would expand greatly later in the century. Coed Lillian Steward in 1871 wrote that she stopped on the college croquet ground to see friends "playing lots of sport."[89]

The most significant social event of the academic year was commencement week. Each literary society held an oratorical contest during the ceremonies, and titles of winning speeches in the decade following the Civil War included "Eternal Vigilance the Price of Liberty," "Elements of Success," "The Index of Manhood," "Governing Ideas," "Universal Economy," "The Hard Side of It," "Christian Heroes," "Individual Effort," "Struggles," and "Power of Action." Books, including Milton's works, Rollin's *Ancient History,* Dante's *Divine Comedy,* and Hase's *Church History,* were given as prizes. When fourteen years old, H. M. Ford in 1867 "sat in the west gallery [of the old college chapel] . . .and listened and was thrilled over Henry Magee's graduating oration, as with a flourish of arms and the toss of his long brown hair, he declared he had come to college without a dollar, had gone through, and was going out without a dollar."[90] In addition to other festivities, the Beethoven Society performed an annual concert of instrumental and vocal music.

A student wrote in June of 1870 that "the various exercises pertaining to the closing weeks of school, such as the society anniversaries, reunions, examinations, &c. all passed quite pleasantly. . . . First, each of the five societies held an anniversary. . . . Thursday, each of the graduates before receiving a diploma either spoke an oration or read an essay. . . . The class consisted of thirty members and although we met at the church at nine in the morning and only had 1 1/2 hours recess for dinner, the exercises were not completed until 5:30 p.m. . . . most of us are now somewhat weary."[91] Commencement ceremonies were held in the new College Baptist Church, usually filled to overflowing. In 1868 the first table supper for the senior class was held at Mr. Vineyard's home on Hillsdale Street. The large rooms of the residence were brilliantly lighted, and forty-two persons sat down to an excellent supper at nine p.m. and adjourned by eleven. The seniors' reaction was that "we can conceive of nothing that will make the memory of a student's life more pleasant to recall, or that will tend more to unite the bonds of class associations, than meetings like this."[92] The seniors' final banquet in the college dining hall was attended by trustees, administrators, faculty, alumni, and invited guests.

Political interest and support for the Republican party remained important at Hillsdale College after the Civil War. In the 1868 campaign, Auditor General William Humphrey, a student at Michigan Central College before achieving fame as brigade commander in the Civil War, urged the Hillsdale community to secure by the ballot what they had won by the bullet.[93] "Waving the bloody shirt" (i.e., attacking the Democratic party for disloyalty to the Union) was not common at the college, however. President Fairfield and Professor Whipple, in March 1868, provided political support for a local resolution favoring a vote of impeachment against President Andrew Johnson by the House of Representatives.[94] Senator Zachariah Chandler, benefactor of Hillsdale College and advocate of impeachment in the fall of 1867, influenced Fairfield's thinking.[95]

Students and faculty also expressed interest in campus politics. George Slayton, for example, commented about the resignation of President James Calder in 1871: "We are going to lose the president of the college soon, he goes to Pa. to take charge of a smaller institution with larger pay. However it is not a loss to H.C. as probably the position will not be filled by a less competent man. It would seem difficult to do that. He is, to use a vulgar expression, 'played out' here and his departure will be hailed with joy by all classes."[96] Formerly a missionary in China, Calder, as president of Hillsdale, had to face unfortunate contrasts between himself and his predecessor, the esteemed and popular Fairfield. Calder understandably returned to his native state to become successful president of the "smaller institution," Pennsylvania State College, that became Pennsylvania State University.

Relations between town and gown remained positive. As Professor Ransom Dunn observed, the community appreciated the college for many reasons, including economic prosperity. After the Civil War, the college may have been indirectly responsible for at least half the steady growth of the community, which had few major manufacturing enterprises and business interests. Maps of the city of Hillsdale in the 1872 *Atlas of Hillsdale County Michigan* reveal a substantial increase in housing construction.[97] The few town-and-gown controversies focused on relatively insignificant issues. For example, college officials protested the location of large stockyards at the base of Manning Street, the grand avenue between college hill and the downtown business district. During delays of up to fifteen minutes caused by heavy train traffic, pedestrians could not avoid the stench of hogs and cattle near the depot. City leaders were urged to open Manning Street through the railroad grounds and to remove the stockyards and depots to another location.[98] In spite of such minor controversies, the community and the college recognized their mutual dependence.

With the continuing prosperity of Hillsdale College, the trustees began plans to enlarge substantially the original brick structure, which was 262 feet in length and four stories high exclusive of the lower level. The trustees also hoped to build additional structures. But tragedy suddenly struck the ambitious western college. At one o'clock in the morning of March 6, 1874, fire broke out in the majestic domed building that had housed the institution for almost two decades. Within hours, only the east wing remained. Determined to triumph even in this, their tragic hour, the members of Alpha Kappa Phi clasped hands and sang their society song over the smoking ruins of the great hall. The crisis of physical destruction would test severely the character and fortitude of the entire college family.

Endnotes

1. Wallace Heckman, "Character in Education," *The Reunion* (June 17, 1885), p. 99.

2. *Thirty-Sixth Annual Report of the Superintendent of Public Instruction of the State of Michigan* (Lansing, 1872), p. 233.

3. Arnold Mulder, *The Kalamazoo College Story* (Kalamazoo, 1958), p. 12.

4. *Hillsdale Standard*, February 13, 1872.

5. Ibid., June 25, 1872.

6. Quoted in *Hillsdale Standard*, July 2, 1872.

7. *Hillsdale Standard*, December 18, 1866.

8. Sophia Jex Blake, *A Visit to Some American Schools and Colleges* (London, 1867), p. 83.

9. *Hillsdale Standard*, May 9, 1871.

10. *Thirty-Sixth Annual Report of the Superintendent of Public Instruction*, pp. 27–29, 230.

11. Mulder, *Kalamazoo College*, p. 15.

12. *Michigan Teacher*, quoted in *Hillsdale Standard*, May 16, 1876.

13. Quoted in *Hillsdale Standard*, May 16, 1876.

14. *Hillsdale Standard*, June 7, 1870.

15. Faculty report to trustees on June 15, 1868. Records of the Proceedings of the Board of Trustees of Hillsdale College, 1855 to 1969. HCVPA.

16. Charles R. Tuttle, *General History of the State of Michigan* (Detroit, 1837), p. 623.

17. *Seventeenth Annual Catalogue of Hillsdale College* (Lansing, 1872), p. 22.

18. Hillsdale student Julian A. Palmer's copy of Perry's *Elements of Political Economy* (New York, 1871) is in my collection of more than a hundred books and pamphlets relating to nineteenth-century Hillsdale College.

19. L. V. Dodge to George A. Slayton, January 22, 1871. HC.

20. John C. Patterson speech to Hillsdale College Alumni Association, 1880. Manuscript, John C. Patterson Collection, MHC. Patterson wrote in an autograph book when he graduated from Albany University Law School in 1865, "I wish popularity, but it is that popularity which follows, not that which is run after."

21. Franklin H. Bailey diary, entry for September 28, 1866. Franklin H. Bailey Collection, MHC.

22. *Hillsdale Standard*, April 27, 1869.

23. Quoted in *Hillsdale Standard*, April 13, 1869.

24. *Hillsdale Standard*, May 16, 1876.

25. *Portrait and Biographical Album of Hillsdale County, Mich.* (Chicago, 1888), p. 545.

26. Quoted in *Hillsdale Standard*, December 10, 1872.

27. Robert Gildart, *Albion College, 1835-1960* (Albion, 1961), p. 88.

28. *Hillsdale Standard*, May 16, 1876.

29. *Early Michigan Paintings: Kresge Art Center, Michigan State University, East Lansing* (Michigan State University, 1976), p. 56; James W. Tottis, Department of American Art, The Detroit Institute of Arts, to author, March 9, 1989. Mr. Vernon Stevens of Hillsdale owns Gardner's 1869 oil painting of Baw Beese Lake as seen from the site of the present power station.

30. Wayland Dunn diary, entry of November 21, 1871. Francis Wayland Dunn Collection, MHC. An outstanding young professor, Wayland Dunn developed tuberculosis and endured intense physical pain preceding his death in 1874. The loss of his sons Ranson Dunn, Jr., and Wayland was one of a

long series of crises than Ransom Dunn faced throughout his career at Hillsdale College.

31. Ibid., October 5, 1871.

32. George A. Slayton to Nettie Henderson, April 20, 1871. HC.

33. Ibid., May 8, 1871. HC.

34. H. E. Whipple to Penfield [no first name], March 27, 1877. Ransom Dunn Collection, MHC.

35. Reprinted in *Hillsdale Standard*, February 25, 1868.

36. *Hillsdale Standard*, February 24, 1874.

37. Ibid., pp. 4–5.

38. *Hillsdale College: A Sketch of Its History, Scope and Advantages* (Hillsdale, n.d.), p. 3. This college pamphlet does not provide the author's name.

39. John C. Patterson, "History of Hillsdale College," *Collections of the Pioneer Society of the State of Michigan*, VI (1907), p. 158.

40. Orville Whitney to family, April 15, 1873. Loaned to author by Margo Shidaker, Sarasota, Florida.

41. George A. Slayton to Nettie Henderson, March 19, 1871. HC.

42. George A. Slayton to his father William Slayton, October 11, 1870. HC.

43. Ibid., September 18, 1870.

44. Ibid., January 15, 1869.

45. Ibid., September 18, 1870.

46. Ibid., December 8, 1871.

47. Harvey A. Fuller, *Where Dark Shadows Play* (Milwaukee, 1890), p. 103.

48. Ibid., pp. 123–24.

49. *Michigan Teacher*, quoted in *Hillsdale Standard*, May 16, 1876.

50. Orville Whitney to family, April 15, 1873. Loaned to author by Margo Shidaker, Sarasota, Florida. The temperance movement opposed the drink-

ing sprees that characterized the American frontier. Average annual consumption of liquor around 1830 was seventeen gallons per adult male. Michigan in 1853 passed a prohibition law, which was held unconstitutional the next year.

51. George A. Slayton to parents, March 27, 1871. HC.

52. Windsor H. Roberts, *A History of the College Baptist Church, 1855–1955* (n.p., n.d.), 7. AKG.

53. *Twenty-Second Annual Report of the Freewill Baptist Home Mission Society* (Dover, NH, 1856), p. 17.

54. Blake, *A Visit to Some American Colleges*, p.74.

55. J. C. Thomas to George A. Slayton, April 12, 1868. HC.

56. Henry M. Ford, "Some Reminiscences of the College Church and Its Pastors" (June 10, 1934), pp. 2–3. Manuscript, HC.

57. Ibid., p. 6.

58. Ibid.

59. Joseph W. Mauck to Sophia Randolph, December 9, 1871. Gift of Mrs. Marie E. Davis, North Adams,Michigan. AKG.

60. Calvin Abbott to James Fisher, October 9, 1873. Calvin Abbott letter, MHC.

61. *Manual of the Theadelphic Literary Society of Hillsdale College* (Hillsdale, 1900), p. 81.

62. Emily Ames to Sophia Randolph, n.d. Gift of Mrs. Marie E. Davis, North Adams, Michigan. AKG.

63. *Hillsdale Standard*, March 22, 1870.

64. J. C. Thomas to George A. Slayton, April 12, 1868. HC.

65. *Manual of the Theadelphic Society*, p. 194.

66. Frances J. Hosford, *Father Shipherd's Magna Charta: A Century of Coeducation in Oberlin College* (Boston, 1937), pp. 104–5.

67. *History of the Amphictyon Society of Hillsdale College* (Hillsdale, 1890), pp. 22–25. Unfortunately, none of the original society rooms remain. Most

were destroyed by the campus fire in 1874. With the construction of the new campus, the Theological Society met in the south hall on the second floor of Knowlton Hall; the Alpha Kappa Phi Society in the north hall on the third floor of Knowlton; the Amphictyons in the south hall on the third floor of Knowlton; the Ladies' Literary Union in the south hall on the third floor of the Fine Arts Hall; and the Germanae Sodales in the north hall on the third floor of the Fine Arts Hall.

68. Orville Whitney to family, April 15, 1873. Loaned to author by Margo Shidaker, Sarasota, Florida.

69. *Hillsdale Standard*, January 12, 1871.

70. J. C. Thomas to George A. Slayton, February 23, 1868. HC.

71. Quoted in *Hillsdale Standard*, November 7, 1865.

72. *Hillsdale Standard*, November 28, 1865.

73. Ibid., June 18, 1867.

74. Ibid., June 11, 1867.

75. Jerome A. Fallon, "The Will Carleton Poorhouse" (Hillsdale, 1989), p. 12.

76. *History of the Alpha Kappa Phi Society of Hillsdale College* (Hillsdale, 1890), p. 11.

77. Franklin H. Bailey diary, entries for November 18 and 23, 1866. Franklin H. Bailey Collection, MHC.

78. Wayland Dunn diary, entry for November 22, 1866. Francis Wayland Dunn Collection, MHC.

79. *Manual of the Theadelphic Society*, p. 15.

80. Horowitz, *Campus Life*, p. 11.

81. Mulder, *Kalamazoo College*, p. 13; Judson LeRoy Day, Jr., "The Baptists of Michigan and the Civil War" (Lansing, 1965), pp. 16–20.

82. Wayland Dunn diary, entries of November 12, 13, and 14, 1864. Francis Wayland Dunn Collection, MHC.

83. George A. Slayton autobiography, pp. 2–3. Handwritten manuscript, MHC.

84. *Hillsdale Standard,* June 9, 1868.

85. Ibid., April 12, 1870.

86. Journal of Ransom Dunn, Jr., entry for May 11, 1860. Newell Ransom Dunn Collection, MHC.

87. *Hillsdale Standard,* May 17, 1870.

88. Ibid., June 9, 1874.

89. Lillian Steward to friend, October 1, 1871. Gift of Mrs. Marie E. Davis, North Adams, Michigan. AKG.

90. After serving four years in the Civil War, Henry W. Magee graduated from Hillsdale College and studied law at the University of Michigan. Before settling down to a career in law, Magee set out on foot to seek adventure. He hunted buffalo with Buffalo Bill and took part in the ceremonies at Promontory, Utah, that marked the completion of the first transcontinental railroad on May 10, 1869. Magee then shipped as a sailor to Hong Kong and Calcutta, and he witnessed the dedication of the Suez Canal. Ready to begin the practice of law in 1871, Magee became one of the leading corporate attorneys in Chicago. Wayland Dunn wrote in his diary on October 12, 1871, that Henry Magee was instrumental in saving an entire block on Michigan Avenue during the Chicago fire several days earlier. "All of his papers were burned. No money left except what they had in their pockets." Francis Wayland Dunn Collection, MHC.

91. George A. Slayton to Nettie Henderson, June 20, 1870. HC.

92. *Hillsdale Standard,* June 9, 1868.

93. Ibid., September 29, 1868.

94. Ibid., March 3, 1868.

95. Wilmer C. Harris, *Public Life of Zachariah Chandler, 1851–1875* (Lansing, 1917), p. 98.

96. George A. Slayton to his father, William Slayton, March 27, 1871. HC.

97. *Atlas of Hillsdale County Michigan* (Philadelphia, 1872), pp. 52–61. AKG.

98. *Hillsdale Standard,* December 10, 1872.

SEVEN

Destruction and Recovery

> The shock of so destructive a fire just following a financial panic
> [of 1873] which involved the whole country put the college to
> the severest test of its life. Never again can there come a time
> when its destiny will hang so dangerously poised as through this
> trying period.
>
> —Lorenzo P. Reynolds, secretary-treasurer,
> Hillsdale College, September 1, 1874

Almost twenty-one years after the cornerstone of the majestic building
was placed on July 4, 1853, the most serious fire in Hillsdale College
history began on campus at one o'clock on Friday morning, March 6,
1874. Excessive heat awakened two male students, rooming on the
third floor of the west wing. The floor almost burned their feet as
they ran to wake up other inhabitants. Students alerted the city by
ringing the college bell until 1:30 a.m. This was the same bell that
had called the college community to class and to chapel thousands of
times. The bell finally was melted by intense heat about an hour after
the students used it to sound the fire alarm. Fortunately, the winter
term was over and most students already had returned home, when
the fire broke out from a front window on the third story in the center
of the west wing and soon poured out of the fourth floor windows.

The flames almost reached the cupola before a fire engine arrived.
The city lacked steam fire engines, and the two hand-operated machines were totally inadequate, although they reputedly pumped the

college cistern dry.[1] Less than a year before, Hillsdale treasurer L. P. Reynolds ironically had endorsed Rowley's Force Pump in use at the college well, which was over seventy feet deep: "It is particularly worthy on account of its utility in the use of hose for throwing water in case of fire." The heavy wooden cornice connecting West Hall with the central building provided a pathway for the spreading fire. Rain and a strong east wind momentarily blew some flames away, and adequate fire-fighting equipment probably could have saved most of the magnificent structure. The scene became particularly agonizing as flames reached the classic dome. Students and firemen, on the roof of the east wing and from the ground, tried in vain to stop the advancing fire. Almost trapped on the burning west roof, a young lad from town courageously fought the flames. He was Clarence Terwilliger, who later became captain of Hillsdale's national championship crew team.

Darkness turned to daylight as flames lit up the surrounding area for miles. The front campus was littered with piles of books, chairs, carpets, paintings, pianos, and literary society furnishings rescued by students, faculty, and local citizens. Some valuable scientific instruments from the first floor, including the telescope and the air pump, were saved. The college library and the secretary-treasurer's papers also were rescued. However, the valuable natural history collection, with specimens illustrating botany, entomology, geology, and ornithology, was lost. The costly telegraphic apparatus, bolted to the floor, could not be moved. Not all the curiosity seekers offered assistance, even when firemen called for their help; the sheriff removed some of them. Meanwhile, coeds carried furniture from the east wing. Within two hours from the time the fire was discovered, the west and central wings were in ruins.[2]

Fortunately, the fire met an obstacle. Mr. Hugh Cook discovered a brick basement wall that divided the center section (the chapel) from the east wing, with only one door as an opening. The fire would have spread rapidly through the east wing, but volunteers hurriedly carried bricks from the burned structure for Cook, Dr. J. L. Mills, and G. M. Troy to close the opening. With trowel and mortar, the three men hurriedly constructed a barrier, and the fire diminished. By four a.m., the blaze was under control after three hours of devastation. Some spectators exclaimed, "Thank God, a part of the noble old building is saved!"[3] More importantly, no lives had been lost. The origin of the fire in one of the upper floors, probably the third, never was proved. However, more than a hundred wood stoves in one building presented an obvious hazard.

The college carried total insurance of $40,000, distributed among different companies. No single policy exceeded $5,000; and even the most prestigious companies, such as Aetna and Hartford, took several months to pay full compensation. Other carriers were Firemen's Fund, German American, Westchester, Michigan State, Humboldt, Black River, Continental, and Girard. Loss of the destroyed wings was more than three-fourths of the total value of the original building.

The task facing Hillsdale College seemed impossible, but determination to continue was immediate. On the morning of the fire, treasurer Reynolds established his office in a vacant store across the street from the ruins. Franklin H. Bailey, a Hillsdale graduate teaching at Wheatland, walked to North Adams after school and took the 9:30 p.m. train to Hillsdale on Friday, March 6. He found the college in ruins, with blackened remains still smoking. Bailey stayed in Hillsdale to help on Saturday, and he heard "the talk of the faculty about next term's school & about rebuilding."[4] On the day of the fire, the professors had agreed to resume classes in the spring term as scheduled. Reports about the college fire, telegraphed across the nation, confirmed that operations would not be interrupted. Activities were transferred to East Hall, the College Baptist Church, professors' homes, and rented rooms.

College leaders, optimistic about constructing a new facility, wasted no time in self-pity. The Prudential Committee of the trustees voted at 2 p.m. on the day of the fire to open the spring term with no interruption.[5] The college motto became "We must build again." The question was not *whether* to rebuild, only *when,* and the pressures of the 1873 financial panic never restrained the trustees. On March 6 President Daniel Graham called a trustees' meeting for March 31 "to consider measures for the rebuilding of the College Buildings which were destroyed by fire this morning."[6] The positive attitude at Hillsdale was unusual, because a fire that destroyed a western college's only building in the nineteenth century usually killed any incentive to replace it.[7] A student publication only a month after the fire envisioned new goals:

> There is an honorable and glorious mission before Hillsdale College, yet to be fulfilled; and if, out of these ashes, and from these broken, crumbling walls, there shall arise a nobler spirit of self-sacrifice and devotion to our alma mater that shall find expression in deeds for her welfare and shall be consummated in the erection of more sightly and convenient halls for her home, the seeming disaster may yet prove a blessing in disguise.[8]

As knowledge of the Hillsdale disaster spread, donors from New England to the West began sending gifts of $1 to $100. Senator Zachariah Chandler pledged $1,000. Even with donations and insurance money, however, college officials could not hope "to replace . . . the buildings without great additional expense, much less enlarge our plans, and erect more commodious and beautiful structures, such as the increasing wants of the college have long demanded."[9] According to Detroit newspapers, the senior class displayed confidence in the future of their alma mater by placing a large memorial on the campus soon after the fire. A conglomerate rock weighing fourteen tons, the boulder with glacial marks and specimens of agate had been discovered in Wheatland Township. Seniors used sixteen horses to pull their memorial by a specially made sled to the campus.[10] Two months after the fire, a student publication stated with pride that "as an institution of learning Hillsdale College may well compare with any other in the West, and in regard to literary societies we acknowledge no superior in America."[11]

Although the greatest single calamity ever to confront the college in the nineteenth century, the fire provided an opportunity for necessary expansion. G. S. Bradley, a former tutor at the college, wrote that "in the long run the fire will prove a blessing. Such an event has aroused the sympathies of the whole West."[12] Some advocates favored one large building with a grandiose appearance, while others proposed several detached structures. A controversial debate followed. The trustees' final vote on the issue was a tie, and President Graham cast the decisive ballot to construct a series of buildings. The faculty endorsed the decision not to replace the solitary structure that for twenty years had contained everything—chapel, classrooms, administrative offices, and dormitories for women and men. Students for years had regarded the back rooms of the original building as gloomy and unhealthy, and some space in the basement and on the fourth floor never was used. Hillsdale authorities pointed out that colleges such as Yale, Bowdoin, Williams, Union, Harvard, Brown, and Cornell had constructed multiple rather than central buildings. Amherst College, like Hillsdale, built separate structures after fire destroyed the major building.

Elijah E. Myers, architect of the new state Capitol at Lansing, advised, "Since your people are so nearly released from the old they would be very foolish to go back to it."[13] The five separate buildings of the master plan improved ventilation and natural lighting, and they substantially reduced insurance costs. The fire that would gut Knowlton Hall on February 25, 1910, was contained successfully. Many friends confidently stated that Hillsdale College would come out of the misfortune in a stronger position. Some alumni, of course, found it difficult to accept the new campus design. John C. Patterson, speaking to the Alumni Association in 1880, admitted that "the modern beauty and the symmetrical proportion of the new home cannot in the hearts of the ancients fully compensate for the memories of the old." Patterson also characterized the old and the new faculty: "The finished scholarship and the brilliant talents of the present instructors cannot observe our grateful recollections of the pioneer faculty, who amid chaotic difficulties inspired hopes, disciplined minds, and developed energies and created impulses that move us yet."

Signed in June, the original contract with Richards and Mickle of Jackson for rebuilding the college was slightly less than $45,000. The cost of $27,157.18 for Central Hall was an impressive amount to be raised during the 1873 financial panic, but the cornerstone was laid on August 18, 1874. A speakers' platform for the occasion was placed on the first floor of the central structure under construction.

Celebrities included ex-Governor Austin Blair, Governor J. J. Bagley, ex-President E. B. Fairfield, President Angell of the University of Michigan, the presidents of Oberlin, Adrian, Albion, Kalamazoo, and Olivet colleges, and alumnus General Jasper Packard. Professor Ransom Dunn delivered a magnificent speech on the history and mission of the college to the crowd of 5,000. He confirmed that the purpose of the institution was to develop the mental and moral powers of young people, and he disclaimed sectarianism altogether. He dismissed state universities as incapable of providing the higher moral components of an education. Dunn dramatically pointed out that "intellectual power alone, without conscience, is of little comparative value to the world. The mission of this school is . . . to make better men, better lawyers, better ministers, and better members of society generally."

Congressman Henry Waldron then defined the independence of the proud college that had maintained itself for thirty years. He pointed out that:

> without aid from the state, nor having a powerful denomination to give it support, its managers have been so schooled that this very lack has given energy and self-reliance. . . . Hillsdale College from its very beginning has been radically and fundamentally right. Open to all from its very founding, it has furnished equal privileges to young ladies and gentlemen.

Dr. W. H. Perrine of Albion College, former student at Michigan Central College, proclaimed that Christian education was founded on the principle of human liberty. College authorities then deposited the Bible from the original 1853 structure in the new cornerstone, and they also enclosed a prayer: "May all needed aid and blessing come to the College until its mission is complete, and then may a blessing be reserved for all those who have served or sacrificed for it."[14] As he had done at the 1853 ceremony, Professor Dunn delivered the consecrating prayer.

The old college bell had melted in the fire, and the trustees wanted a replacement loud enough to be heard clearly downtown. The

Octavous Jones & Company Troy Bell Foundry of Troy, New York, one of the foundries on the Hudson River that had manufactured cannon for the Union artillery in the Civil War, cast a bell specifically for the college. Made from the finest brands of Lake Superior copper and East India tin, the bell costing $1,001.36 had a diameter of 50 inches and weighed 2551 pounds. Abbie Slayton wrote to her husband on March 7, 1875, that the college bell had arrived the day before. She thought that it was "about the size of the church bell, fully as large. I guess they did not put it up, for we did not hear it any."[15] By March 23 the bell was in place in the dome atop the tower. George M. Stevens of Boston built the clock to accompany the new bell.

The *American Artisan* of New York City published an article entitled "The New Clock for Hillsdale College," with an engraving of the superior mechanism.[16] The clock was one of the largest yet made, with four dials, each eight feet in diameter. The pendulum, nine feet in length, weighed a hundred pounds. The wheels and bearings were constructed of hard brass, and the pinions of steel. The total weight of the clock was about a thousand pounds, and winding required ten minutes every eighth day.[17] The bell and clock together were regarded as superior to any others in Michigan, except those in Detroit City Hall. The heavy weight over time caused the tower with its 12 by 12 inch wooden beams to lean, and the bell had to be removed from the tower in 1956. Steel beams were installed to prevent further structural damage.

A year after the 1874 fire, Central Hall, and Knowlton Hall to the west, were opened for classes on September 1. Central Hall, already was completed, contained the president's and the dean's offices, recitation rooms, chapel, business office, social room, college printing office, and library with separate reading rooms for men and women. The college formerly had seven separate libraries, including those of the literary societies; their consolidation was a major improvement. Knowlton Hall, although ready for classes, still required additions to the literary society halls.

The walls of the east structure (the Fine Arts Building) had reached the second floor by September, and much additional work was completed in the winter. The local editor recognized that the town was heavily indebted to the college officials for "their pluck and energy in so soon recovering from their misfortune."[18] The architectural firm, Breeze & Smith of Detroit, claimed that the new plan had many advantages over the old. Better lighting and ventilation probably were the most important improvements. When the contractors turned the structures over to the building committee, not a single crack in the interior plastering caused by settling could be found. The bricks had been brought directly from the kiln, and the handsome woodwork was superior.

A writer for the *Inter-Ocean* of Chicago, viewing the surrounding countryside from the deck of the new dome 150 feet high, saw the landscape in every direction for about fifteen miles.[19] The reporter spontaneously exclaimed, "What a happy thought it was, locating a college on that hill, the Parnassus of southern Michigan."[20] Until the early twentieth century, college officials allowed the public to use the tower as a popular lookout and requested visitors to sign a register before climbing to the top.

Costing $10,725.99, Knowlton Hall to the west was named in honor of college trustee Ebenezer Knowlton of Montville, Maine, who had died a year earlier in 1874. Elected to the Maine legislature in 1845, he served a term beginning in 1855 in the U. S. House of Representatives. Preferring to remain active in the ministry, Knowlton declined the nomination for governor of Maine. He wrote, "I would rather see one young man in my congregation soundly converted to Christ than to have any office in the gift of man."[21] Knowlton also declined an appointment as foreign minister by President Grant. Trustee of both Colby College and Bates College, Knowlton worked as missionary to the freedmen after the Civil War.

The new building bearing Knowlton's name contained lecture rooms, laboratories, and three elegant society halls. Scientific materials included telescopes, numerous microscopes, and chemical instruments. The Department of Chemistry, which had lost all its supplies in the fire, within two years was equipped better than ever before. Knowlton Hall also contained the museum of natural history, which was rebuilt with specimens from donors including Wabash College,

Brown University, and trustee Frederick Fowler of Reading. By 1878 the museum was more valuable than before the fire. Professor Fisk arranged the various specimens in cases, with precise classification and numbering. L. P. Reynolds, college secretary-treasurer, hoped that the new museum would some day equal the best of any western college. The Theological Society on September 6, 1875, held the first meeting in their new room, 28 x 46 feet, on the south side of the second floor of newly constructed Knowlton Hall. So attractive and spacious was the new meeting place that society members seemed to forget the loss of their original hall. The Alpha Kappa Phi Society room, on the third floor of Knowlton, contained a piano, seating arranged in tiers, stuccoed walls, and a silver and glass chandelier. Above the president's chair were portraits of "Our Heroic Dead," the Alpha Kappa Phi members killed in the Civil War. The stage and auditorium had elegant carpeting. On the opposite side of the third floor was the Amphictyons' meeting room.

The Fine Arts Hall, completed in 1876 at a cost of $10,318.00, contained lecture rooms, recitation rooms, the art gallery, a studio, the music room, Beethoven Hall, and two rooms on the third floor for the ladies' literary societies. The Ladies' Literary Union hall contained a piano and tables salvaged from the fire; and new carpeting, inside blinds over the windows, an oil painting, and seventy-five plush chairs were added. The hall later was frescoed, and a chandelier was installed. Griffin Hall, the fourth building of the master plan, was completed in 1877 for the commercial department and gentlemen's dormitories. Construction began after President Durgin announced that $13,000 dollars had been raised. The hall was named for Professor Charles P. Griffin, founder of the commercial department of Hillsdale College, benefactor, and general manager of the Universal Life Insurance Company of New York. The sale of tuition scholarships raised much of the money for Griffin Hall; of the first $5,000 secured, Hillsdale citizens contributed $3,500. The *New York Mail* reported that no other commercial department in the nation had such a magnificent building and facilities.[22]

Opened for students in the fall term of 1877, Griffin Hall contained twenty-seven suites of dormitory rooms. Each suite was furnished with spring beds, a stove, chairs, a table, and a washstand. Students provided their bedding and carpet, and the cost for room rental and boarding at the college was $2.60 weekly. Griffin Hall also held offices, lecture and recitation rooms, and facilities for the commercial and telegraphic department. Professor Rideout, who had been awarded an honorary doctor of laws degree from Muskingum College a year before, taught courses in political economy, commercial law, shorthand, telegraphy, and electrical engineering. The popular program soon attracted students from all over the country. To raise money for renting telephones on the new college line, Professor Rideout lectured at Underwood's Opera House in June 1878, on "The Telegraph, Telephone and Phonograph." He demonstrated the technology of the trans-Atlantic cable, and members of the audience used a telephone connected to a line strung between the college and the opera house.

The original campus plan included the replacement of East Hall with a new structure, Garfield Hall. This projected memorial to the American president who had begun his formal studies at Geauga Seminary (which merged with Hillsdale College in 1854) lacked practicality. The most important reason for not constructing Garfield Hall was that the five existing buildings provided ample space during the 1880s and 1890s. East Hall, structurally sound and functional, contained parlors in addition to study and sleeping rooms for fifty ladies. The college dining hall, kitchen, and ladies' reading room were located on the first floor. Excellent biological laboratories were located on the fourth floor of East. Like all the college buildings, East Hall was lighted by gas. College Hall (Central Hall today) contained twelve major rooms, including the president's office, the treasurer's office, mathematics and Latin classrooms, library and reading room, and chapel. Griffin Hall (later Worthing Hall) had two major classrooms for the Commercial School. Knowlton Hall provided six public rooms: three men's literary society halls, chemistry laboratory, museum, and Hebrew classroom. The Fine Arts Hall held nine public rooms, including two ladies' literary society halls and classrooms for art, vocal and instrumental music, physical science, Greek, and French.

By October of 1874, Hillsdale College had recovered sufficiently to host its new president, DeWitt Clinton Durgin, in grand style. President E. B. Fairfield had departed in 1869 to become chancellor of the University of Nebraska, James Calder resigned after two years to accept the presidency of Pennsylvania State College, and his successor Daniel Graham filled only a two-year term. President Durgin now would provide consistent leadership for the next twelve years.[23] The faculty and students gave the new president and his family a memorable reception on October 23, 1874, and local citizens joined in crowding the college parlors. As the evening proceeded, Professor Dunn officially greeted Durgin with hospitality and a call to action:

> We welcome you to our hills and dales that are filled with beauty and the good things of earth; we welcome you to our pleasant city . . . we welcome you to this institution of learning, with all of its past and future honors; we welcome you to the honored alumni of this college; we welcome you to the toil and labor of all the workers that are here trying to mold minds for usefulness; we welcome you to the public sympathy of true friends and we welcome you to our homes and to our hearts.

Speaking for the alumni, Will Carleton observed:

> As citizens we are proud of our college and of its reputation. . . . The property of Hillsdale has been increased in value more than all the cost, and four or five thousand young men and women have had their intellects improved and have gone out into the world and made it better for having been to Hillsdale College. The boy has become of age and we are giving him a new suit of clothes and we expect his manhood will be as honorable as his boyhood.

President Durgin replied that he saw before him noble young men and women whom no New England college could surpass, and that he eagerly desired to work with them.[24]

According to a *Detroit Post* reporter in early 1876 Hillsdale College had returned fully to a prosperous and flourishing condition following the fire. The college "has greater strength, more real life and vital energy, enlarged resources and capacity, and stands upon a stronger, surer, and better foundation than at any time heretofore in its history."[25] The *Morning Star* of Dover, New Hampshire, suggested that there was no question about permanent success at Hillsdale College, "with a faculty holding the confidence of the West as it does, and with the enterprising management that has presided over its affairs during the past year or two."[26] The Michigan Freewill Baptist yearly meeting at Grand Ledge in June 1877, unanimously passed the following resolution: "We have cause for devout gratitude to God for the success which has attended Hillsdale College, and hereby express our ardent desire for its prosperity."[27] College supporters had proved their ability to turn bad luck into good fortune. A major factor behind the recovery was the Board of Trustees' decision not to plunge into debt by rebuilding too quickly. The institution chose to expand only after it had acquired the necessary funding.

The college frequently had demonstrated financial expertise even before the fire. President Daniel Graham in 1872 told the Michigan Superintendent of Public Instruction what had been true for decades: "Through the judicious management of its finances, the College has never lost a dollar of its endowment, and is wholly free from the embarrassment of indebtedness." Lorenzo P. Reynolds, elected secretary-treasurer of the college in 1862, was an excellent financial manager. His father, a founder of Michigan Central College, had donated a farm of eighty acres to support the school at Spring Arbor. After the 1874 fire, Lorenzo Reynolds played a major role in raising endowment and in planning the new campus.[28]

The *Michigan Teacher* claimed in May 1876 that among the numerous institutions established since the West was opened, "Few can point to a better record than the college founded by the Free Baptists in Michigan and now located at Hillsdale. . . . "[29] An evaluation of all private educational institutions in the United States in 1879 ranked Hillsdale College twelfth,[30] as the remarkable resurgence of the small college from disaster continued. Senator Zachariah Chandler expressed appreciation to President DeWitt Clinton Durgin for his honorary degree of doctor of laws from Hillsdale College in 1879: "I . . . desire to assure the trustees of your college that the priceless gift at their hands will be ever held in highest remembrance. Such an honor, though unmerited, will but serve to urge me to greater effort in serving my fellow-countrymen."[31]

The literary societies were among the strongest college supporters after the great fire. They helped to retain the student body, when physical ruins pointed to an era of inconvenience. *The Crescent,* a monthly student publication begun in 1874, claimed that the literary societies more than anything else bound the best students to Hillsdale College and insured their return after the fire.[32] As the societies renewed their programs, the local press boasted that oratorical contests at Hillsdale College "can beat the world."

The *Detroit Post* reported that delegates from Hillsdale, Albion, and Olivet met at Hillsdale in October 1875, to plan the first Michigan intercollegiate oratorical contest. A permanent organization resulted, and Kalamazoo College soon joined, although Adrian College at first was excluded.[33] A special train carried a hundred people from Hillsdale to attend the first contest at Albion in February 1876. Hillsdale College hosted the second annual state oratorical contest in February 1877. Dr. Kendall Brooks, president of Kalamazoo College, arrived with his students by train, and the reception committee included President Durgin, several professors, and officials of the Amphictyon Society. A special train with 250 people from Albion arrived later. After a social gathering in the East Hall parlors, dinner was served at 6 p.m. The contest itself was held in the decorated Hillsdale College Baptist Church, filled to capacity. The speakers were superior, and the large audience showed enthusiasm and appreciation. Top prize went to Hutson Coleman of Kalamazoo College.[34]

In December 1877, Hillsdale College decided to select two participants annually, one gentleman and one lady, through an intersociety contest among the five literary societies at Underwood's Opera House. The winners then represented Hillsdale at the yearly intercollegiate competition. In the 1879 competition, for example, Miss Lou Pierce of Hillsdale won first prize for essays, and V. K. VanDeventer of Hillsdale came in a close second in the oratorical contest.

Although the size of the Hillsdale student body decreased slightly after the 1874 fire, within two years enrollment had returned to its former level. During the 1870–75 period, average annual attendance in all Hillsdale departments was 652, the highest in Michigan. Because public schools in the state were taking over some preparatory work, Hillsdale College could give less and less instruction in subjects such as grammar, algebra, and geography, and an increasingly higher percentage of the student body was enrolled in collegiate courses. By 1877, 20 percent of the students pursued the classical course for the full seven years, and the total number of liberal arts students steadily increased. Examinations for promotion, required before a student could pass to a higher level, became more demanding. Twice as much Latin was assigned in the preparatory program as earlier. A Hillsdale official estimated in 1877 that every classical student completing the full preparatory and collegiate programs received 4,200 hours of class contact with instructors.

As a young instructor, Joseph W. Mauck wrote on March 4, 1878, that the past term had been orderly, busy, and profitable, with an increase in the thoroughness of academic work. Mauck believed that the progress was due primarily to the students' high caliber, and he indicated that "no outbreak of any kind has occurred, so far as we know, which is a record seldom reached."[35] Undergraduates continued to be rural, religious, and conscientious. A college guest commented in 1879, "They are polite down here at Hillsdale. I'll send my daughter here this winter." A local student, born in a log house one mile east of Hillsdale, delivered the commencement oration in 1879. He emphasized that it was a mistake to suppose that "the student of the West is wholly ignorant of the brawny work of the world. This may be true elsewhere, but a vast majority of our students have taken compulsory studies in the world's university before ever entering a western college. . . . The worthy man is the self-made man, and only as he is self-made has he honor."

To attract students with modest incomes, Hillsdale continued to keep expenses low. A young man, entering college for the first time in 1879 with no scholarship and choosing the higher rates for board and room, paid a maximum of $154.50 for three terms. This total included incidentals such as visiting home (one-way distance of 180 miles) by train twice a year, firewood, books, and laundry fees.

The annual cost could be cut to $95.50 by getting a scholarship, returning for the second year, rooming in Griffin Hall, and boarding for only $1.50 per week. Total expenses for Hillsdale students attending three terms averaged less than $100 a year. Because most students earned money by manual labor, the average total cost of $30 a term was reduced to practically nothing. The self-sufficient students, upon leaving Hillsdale College, maintained a tradition of public service. As before, alumni and nongraduates in the late 1870s were primarily teachers, professors, clergymen, missionaries, lawyers, judges, physicians, merchants, and politicians. By 1879 Hillsdale graduates included eighty-two teachers and college professors, eighty attorneys, fifty-eight clergymen, twelve physicians, five editors, three authors, and forty-six businessmen.

Although the students were disciplined and accustomed to manual labor, Lady Principal Mary Phillips set down harsh standards for incoming females in the fall of 1877. While willing to admit the widespread popularity of euchre, she urged every woman to focus all her time and attention upon studies and school duties. A student "should have nothing to do with general society. She cannot afford it."[36] Principal Phillips was upset by seeing college girls going to parties until one or two o'clock in the morning. She thought that they looked jaded when they came to class the next day.

Social misbehavior and pranks never could be avoided entirely. The local newspaper reported an incident that took place on a Saturday evening in June 1876. About 11:30, students walked downtown for ice cream following the Alpha Kappa Phi literary meeting. Passing the Michigan Southern railroad depot, they were challenged by "a gang of five city bloods." John F. Bates, weighing 217 pounds and enrolled in the classical preparatory program, stepped out and demanded satisfaction (i.e., western version of the Old South's honor code). According to the local press, "The five bloods responded, and the fray as reported by the bystanders, was short but interesting. Twice were the five sent to grass on the depot platform, by the prep alone. . . . The bloods have gone into dry-dock for repairs, while Bates resumed studies Monday morning as usual. The only damage he sustained being a pair of shirt sleeves, stained with the blood of his victims."[37] Besides holding their own against the townies, the students delighted in giving shivarees to newly married students. (Theological students were allowed to marry, unlike the others!) The local newspaper reported on June 5, 1877, that many college students had "visited the premises of Mr. Joel Hill, who had recently married, to give him a tin pan entertainment, which resulted, as usual in such cases, in personal squabbles, and called out many residents of that vicinity to witness the affair. A few arrests were made."[38]

Although baseball was the earliest club sport at Hillsdale, the first national fame in athletics came from an unusual source, a four-oared crew composed of former students.[39] Training without a coach on Baw Beese Lake, the four young men never had used a four-oared shell until May 1, 1879. Through superb physical conditioning, they won the National American Amateur Rowing Championships for three consecutive years, 1879, 1880, and 1881. Clarence W. Terwilliger, captain at the bow position, was only 5'7" and weighed 149 pounds. The tallest member of the crew was 5'11." Their first major victory was at the Northwestern Regatta at Toledo in 1879, and the *Toledo Blade* observed: "That a crew from the oak openings of Hillsdale County should take the prizes of the four-oared race in the Northwestern regatta on the Maumee astonished the old water ducks of the association." Rowing was a major national sport in the late Victorian years, and the urban press continued to be amazed by the success of the unknown crew from southern Michigan.

The Hillsdale crew won their first national championship at the Saratoga Regatta in July 1879. The *Chicago Tribune* described the determined Hillsdale athletes in the first heat as having a "long, sweeping, and powerful" stroke, and the same newspaper viewed the final heat of the four-oared championship as "a terrific race from the start, which eclipsed any similar struggle ever seen in this country." The *New York World* reported that "the great surprise of the day has been the victory of the Hillsdale four, of Michigan. Perhaps it will be necessary to inform our readers that Hillsdale is a town, village, or something, of Michigan. It must be, at all events, on water. One would be inclined to infer from the performance of four of its inhabitants this morning, that it is a sort of small Venice." Hillsdale won the mile and a half contest in 8:32, the best time on record.

Hundreds gathered at the Hillsdale train depot to greet the returning athletes, who were driven in an open carriage during a long procession. Community businessmen closed their stores on the afternoon of July 14 to promote the grand reception. Smith's Hotel served the crew dinner, and a large crowd gathered to shake their hands. Flags and banners of the crew's colors, blue and white, decorated the downtown streets. (The oarsmen wearing royal blue and white established the college colors, although many Hillsdale athletic teams wore aquamarine for another decade.) Fireworks and band music filled the evening hours. A Hillsdale reporter with local pride pointed out that the crewmen were sons of some of the oldest local settlers, and that "all have received a good education from our school and Hillsdale College."[40] The community later gave a reception for the crew at Underwood's Opera House, with guests from Detroit, Lansing, Coldwater, etc. At this occasion Will Carleton first read his popular poem dedicated to "Our Four in a Row."

The champion oarsmen of America continued for three years to win every race in sight. As late as the summer of 1882, they remained unbeaten. They took first place at Toledo, Saratoga, and Hillsdale in 1879, and at New Orleans, Moline, and Philadelphia in 1880. The *New Orleans Picayune* accurately described the Hillsdale crew as "the brawny lads from Michigan," who relied on sheer strength rather than style. The fame of the local oarsmen brought much attention to Hillsdale College and city. A New Orleans reporter described Hillsdale as the "site of one of the largest denominational colleges in the West." *Harper's Weekly* on June 10, 1882, published a sketch of the crew.

A race against the Thames rowing club in England on September 15, 1882, finally broke the winning streak. Leading for two miles, the Hillsdales were four lengths ahead when double disaster struck—a broken seat slide and a snapped rudder wire. The Englishmen pulled ahead to win but later described the Hillsdales as the fastest crew they had ever seen. The *New York Herald* reported that "by one of those unavoidable accidents which will happen at the most inopportune moment, the Hillsdale crew have been robbed of the honor of coming in first in the race against the Thames crew." The English oarsmen refused to give Hillsdale a repeat race, but the Americans' reputation remained high after losing their chance for a world championship.[41] When President Theodore Roosevelt visited Hillsdale on May 31, 1907, he recalled the "great impression made upon me" by the local crew more than twenty-five years earlier.

In the years after the fire, strong cooperation with local residents continued. The town, with a population of 3,541, considered the college a community institution. Residents of Hillsdale County (31,705 population) contributed $75,000 for buildings and endowment, and the college in turn provided cultural and educational benefits. For example, at the county fair the college presented a natural history exhibit with scientific apparatus and three hundred specimens of minerals. An anonymous citizen stated in 1877, "I do feel that the interests of our beautiful city and of Hillsdale College *are* and *ought* to be *one*. It is the folly of ignorance to deny that a good institution of learning in any place is at once an honor and a blessing to the community."[42]

Hillsdale College not only recovered from the disastrous fire of 1874 but quickly cancelled the rebuilding debt and increased the endowment. Academic quality, excellent literary societies, and sound financial management put Hillsdale in good standing when contrasted with the 356 American colleges and universities reported in 1876 by the United States Bureau of Education. John Patterson informed the Alumni Association in 1880 that "we cannot now anticipate the growth or compass the possibilities of the college. We are now combined under auspicious skies. At this seat of learning, on this day, shall its scholars, its scientists, its artists, its artisans, its jurists, its orators, its poets, its statesmen" gather to learn what is accomplished in science, in art, in literature, in philosophy, in statesmanship, in learning, and in all that concerns the moral or intellectual world. Over 13,000 students had received instruction by 1880, and enrollment increased rapidly to 815 in 1881. The next decade would indeed be a golden age for Hillsdale College.

Endnotes

1. The first Hillsdale fire department, Neptune Fire Engine Company No. 1, had an elaborate constitution and uniforms but no engines! A working department, established in the 1850s, did not purchase an efficient steam fire engine until the late 1870s. *Hillsdale Area Centennial, 1869–1969* (Hillsdale, 1969), p. 63.

2. *Hillsdale Standard,* March 10, 1874.

3. "Our Great Loss," *The Crescent* (April 1874), p. 10.

4. Franklin H. Bailey diary, entries for March 6 and 7, 1874. Franklin H. Bailey Collection, MHC.

5. Prudential Committee minutes of March 6, 1874. Records of the Proceedings of the Board of Trustees of Hillsdale College from June 13, 1870, to September 18, 1883, with Proceedings of the Prudential Committee, June 20, 1870, to June 3, 1884. HCVPA.

6. Ibid., Board of Trustees' minutes of March 31, 1874.

7. Richard A. Bartlett, *The New Country: A Social History of the American Frontier, 1776–1890* (Oxford, 1974), p. 395.

8. *The Crescent* (April 1874), p. 11.

9. Ibid.

10. *Hillsdale Standard,* April 21, 1874. The 1874 memorial, or "sugar-loaf" rock, remains today at its original location on the front campus. The classes of 1869, 1873, and 1875 also placed permanent stone memorials on the campus. Other senior gifts included groves of trees, the 1886 fountain, and various tablets.

11. *The Crescent* (May 1874), p. 53.

12. Quoted in *Hillsdale Standard,* June 2, 1874.

13. Quoted in *Hillsdale Standard,* May 5, 1874. Elijah E. Myers, noted American architect, designed the Michigan State Capitol which was completed in 1879. The Renaissance Revival building in Lansing recently has undergone extensive restoration.

14. *Hillsdale Standard,* August 25, 1874.

15. Abbie Slayton to George Slayton, March 7, 1875. HC. The plaque next to the "Victory Bell" today erroneously cites 1874 as the year when the bell was placed in the new tower. The Central Hall cornerstone was not even laid until August 1874, and the bell was cast in 1875.

16. Quoted in *Hillsdale Standard,* October 5, 1875.

17. Merl Brodock, beloved custodian for many years in Central Hall, was the last person who regularly climbed 135 steps to wind the tower clock. His hand crank is preserved today in the College Archives. Brodock wound the clock for the last time in August 1959; beginning in 1960, the mechanism was powered by electricity.

18. *Hillsdale Standard,* August 24, 1875.

19. The majestic tower was struck by lightning on August 7, 1942, and the gilded ball on top was blown off in a storm in 1943. Many pranks have involved the tower. Fraternity men frequently took the clapper out of the bell, and sometimes in the middle of the night the bell was rung to signal a "dorm raid."

20. Quoted in *Hillsdale Standard,* October 5, 1875.

21. Quoted in *Hillsdale Standard,* January 4, 1876.

22. Quoted in *Hillsdale Standard,* February 29, 1876.

23. DeWitt Clinton Durgin, a native of New Hampshire, was the son of Captain Francis Durgin, a veteran of the War of 1812. The third Hillsdale College president whose father had fought in the War of 1812, Durgin continued the New England traditions of the institution's early leaders.

24. *Hillsdale Standard,* October 27, 1874.

25. Quoted in *Hillsdale Standard,* February 1, 1876.

26. *Hillsdale Standard,* December 14, 1875.

27. Ibid., June 12, 1877.

28. Following his service to Hillsdale College, Lorenzo Reynolds built up the best insurance agency in Hillsdale County. He was severely injured in 1879, when fire during the night demolished the block in downtown Hillsdale where his office was located. Reynolds ran a mile to his office and

tried to save some records, but an explosion threw him from the second story to the street. More dead than alive, he survived the accident but never recovered fully.

29. Quoted in *Hillsdale Standard,* May 16, 1876.

30. *Hillsdale Herald,* October 23, 1879.

31. Senator Zachariah Chandler to President DeWitt Clinton Durgin, June 23, 1879. Reproduced in *Hillsdale Herald,* July 24, 1879.

32. *The Crescent* (May 1874), p. 53. The weekly *Herald* in 1878 replaced the monthly *Crescent* as the Hillsdale College student publication. The *Collegian* in turn replaced the *Herald,* and Hillsdale College accurately claims to have the oldest student newspaper in Michigan.

33. *Hillsdale Standard,* October 26, 1875.

34. Ibid., February 13, 1877.

35. Quoted in *Hillsdale Standard,* March 12, 1878.

36. Quoted in *Hillsdale Standard,* October 16, 1877.

37. *Hillsdale Standard,* June 13, 1876.

38. Ibid., June 5, 1877.

39. Elon Reynolds, ed., *Compendium of History and Biography of Hillsdale County, Michigan* (Chicago, 1903), p. 448, claims that Clarence Terwilliger assisted in "organizing the first rowing ream of the college, and this for three years subsequently held the championship of the United States." Contemporary sources, however, indicate that the team was formed after the four students left Hillsdale College. Captain Terwilliger, Lou F. Beckhardt, T. D. Wilson, and E. B. Van Valkenburg were the original crew.

40. *Hillsdale Standard,* July 15, 1879. I have read the Jackson and Hillsdale newspapers from 1844 to 1900, and the editors' thorough knowledge of their communities was remarkable.

41. The four-oared Columbia University crew, which defeated Hertford College in the finals on the Thames on July 5, 1878, scored the first American victory at the Henley Regatta.

42. *Hillsdale Standard,* June 5, 1877.

❧EIGHT❧

A Golden Era

In these times when there are such inducements to surcharge the college curriculum with modern subjects, we think it very creditable that this college [Hillsdale College] should maintain its integrity with respect to the humanities. So far as we could observe, there prevailed in the college a sincere and well-directed effort to educate rather than to instruct. . . .

—State Board of Visitors' report
October 14, 1882

In the 1880s Hillsdale College was consistently ranked as the strongest and most prominent denominational college in Michigan. It had more students, a stronger endowment, and better buildings and equipment than any educational institution in the state, except the University of Michigan.[1] An enrollment of 816 students in 1881 was barely surpassed by any of the state universities in the Old Northwest.[2] The college proudly announced in 1883 the largest enrollment of its entire history. The nonsectarian college attracted students and faculty of all denominations—Baptists, Episcopalians, Presbyterians, Catholics, Congregationalists, Methodists, etc. An acquaintance of Hillsdale College stated that "so far as I know no Free [Will] Baptist student has graduated from any other denominational college in the state, while scores of Methodist, Presbyterian, Episcopal, and Baptist students are among the alumni of Hillsdale."[3]

Academically, the college advanced by establishing the following newly endowed chairs: Burr professorship for pastoral and systematic theology; Marks professorship for ecclesiastical history; Alumni professorship for logic and belles lettres; Fowler professorship for mathematics; and Marks professorship for Latin. Former trustee S. F. Smith contributed 480 acres of Nebraska land worth $10,000 to endow an additional chair in 1885. The family of Congressman Henry Waldron, a generous college benefactor who died in 1880, contributed $15,000 as the largest single endowment gift. A Rutgers graduate, Waldron had come to Michigan in 1837 to make preliminary surveys for the Michigan Southern Railroad. Director of the Michigan Southern Railroad and trustee of Hillsdale College since its founding, he was elected to Congress in 1854 and served three consecutive terms. Again elected to the House of Representatives in 1870, 1872, and 1874, Waldron served a total of six terms. He was the first president of the Second National Bank of Hillsdale. His brother, Charles N. Waldron, his widow, Mrs. Caroline M. Waldron, and his sister, Mrs. Mary E. Waterman, each contributed $5,000 toward the college endowment shortly after his death.[4] The sum compared favorably with the largest recent gifts to Vassar of $2,500; to Bowdoin, $15,000; and to Harvard, $25,000. In addition to endowments, the college received other gifts in the 1880s. Mrs. Grace Chandler, for example, in 1881 donated a life-sized oil painting by Detroit artist Lew T. Ives of her husband, the late Senator Zachariah Chandler.

Unlike many institutions, Hillsdale obtained little revenue from tuition and fees. As in earlier years, the college received few large gifts and relied primarily upon contributions under $100 from Freewill Baptists, friends in the community, and alumni. Dr. D. D. Ball in 1887 declared that Hillsdale College's accomplishments with small means formed "a chapter of history which ought to thrill our young men with courage, and move them to mighty endeavor."[5] For years the college received essentially no tuition, and all fees in the fall term of 1881 would not have paid for the firewood burned that winter! In financial terms, the college was poor even in years of prominence. Income from a total endowment under $140,000 effectively paid most costs for educating students in 1885! A student publication accurately described Hillsdale as "a piece of practical philanthropy." The *Free*

Baptist observed in 1888 that "in the item of expense, Hillsdale College has stood almost without a competitor; and it has held out to the poor but ambitious seeker ... the opportunity to successfully compete with the more favored child of fortune." Annual tax support for the University of Michigan exceeded the total endowment of Hillsdale College.

Hillsdale's success in providing an outstanding education in the 1880s for more than 800 students annually was a tribute to dedicated faculty, excellent fiscal administration, and emphasis of moral over material values. In his 1885 report to the State Superintendent of Public Instruction, Ransom Dunn reaffirmed that the college was free of debt.[6] Yet Dunn frequently reminded the local community that financial and material assets were "only investments in the supreme work of mental and moral culture." He claimed that Hillsdale College accomplished more in providing sound education and moral standards, in proportion to its means, than other schools.[7] Judge O. A. Janes, elected secretary-treasurer of Hillsdale College in 1884, deserved much credit for superior financial management in the late 1880s.[8]

The *Hillsdale Herald* praised the positive effects of common interests between the town and the college; little if any antagonism existed between the two groups.[9] A *Chicago Herald* reporter observed that "Hillsdale dotes on three things—her Republicanism, her college and herself."[10] A *Cleveland Plain Dealer* writer observed in 1885 that Hillsdale, with a population of 5,000, was the best place to escape labor troubles and the hard times of modernization. Visiting the Michigan town, he asked why there were not more factories. Residents replied, "We don't want them. Our sky is never dimmed with coal smoke, nor our peace disturbed with labor troubles. We have all around us the richest agricultural district in the state. . . . No one has hard times except the saloonists." The *Plain Dealer* claimed that "a prosperous college furnishes the town with a mild, refined sort of excitement. Its pure air and pure morals are attracting men of wealth who desire to live in a pleasant city with good educational facilities." The college received strong local support for maintaining its position "in the front rank of western educational institutions." Although the college received $29,940.82 from insurance claims after the 1874 fire, county residents contributed an additional $75,000 for construction and endowment.[11] This amount exceeded all outside gifts during the 1874 to 1890 era.

The college and community prospered also from the location on six railroads with excellent facilities, the best of any small city in Michigan.[12] Commodore Cornelius Vanderbilt had created a trunk line into Chicago by acquiring the Lake Shore and Michigan Southern in 1873 as the western extension of his New York Central.

The academic standards of Hillsdale College in the 1880s were outstanding. The faculty reported to the trustees in 1878 that "it is a gratifying indication to see the increased number who are turning their attention to the classical course." The total number of students in Professor J. H. Butler's Latin classes was 297! The Board of Visitors informed the Michigan Superintendent of Public Instruction in 1880–81 that "we have found the work of the institution of a very high order of excellence." The examiners claimed that one of the most noticeable things impressing any visitor was the excellent esprit de corps of the institution:

> One heart, one spirit animates all—president, faculty, and students. . . . One spirit pervades, a spirit of loyalty to and faith in the college, past, present, and future. Every one seems to feel he is a part, and expected to perform each duty so as to bring honor to the college. All are honest workers.

The Board of Visitors verified that Hillsdale had the only theological school in the state, with a faculty that contributed heavily to the Christian spirit pervading the campus.[13] The visitors reported that no Michigan college had so thorough a commercial and business department; also, they claimed that "no institution in the state, except the university, has better, if indeed so good, collections for instruction in natural history."[14]

Reports to the Michigan Superintendent of Public Instruction in 1880 revealed that Adrian College had 8 instructors and 169 students; Albion College, 9 instructors and 233 students; Kalamazoo

College, 7 instructors and 116 students; Olivet College, 12 instructors and 201 students; Michigan Agricultural College, 11 instructors and 232 students; and Hillsdale College, 15 instructors and 518 students. Hillsdale undergraduates in jest referred to Olivet as "a country school where Farmers' Alliances are wont to assemble" (i.e., a "cow college"); to Michigan Agricultural College as "somewhere near the University of Michigan"; to Kalamazoo as "a preparatory department"; and to their own institution as "the college which does more with the money at hand than any other school in the U.S."

The visitors' report in 1882 to the Michigan Superintendent of Public Instruction again complimented Hillsdale College highly. Board members considered the literary societies' outstanding work to be a marked feature of the institution, and they rated class instruction as "a high order of excellence." The examiners commented favorably on additions to the natural history collection and on the high standards of the commercial department.[15] In 1883 the evaluators reported that Hillsdale College was doing "work which ranks with any institution of its grade and facilities." As president of the Alumni Association, Joseph Mauck in 1887 asserted that none of the excellent institutions in the state, except the university, provided such varied instruction as Hillsdale. Mauck claimed that Hillsdale surpassed even the University of Michigan in music, art, theology, commerce, and telegraphy.[16]

After visiting Hillsdale College in 1882, the Committee of the Michigan Yearly Meeting of Freewill Baptists judged academic standards to be the highest in the history of the institution. The team credited professors with showing zeal for their students' advancement and praised faculty efforts "to display great truths in such a manner that they can be understood and retained." The students' excellent deportment was due partly to being treated as adults by the faculty, rather than with disdain. Hillsdale professors frequently took time to pursue advanced studies at schools such as Harvard and Union Theological Seminary. The college endowment had excellent security, and the committee concluded that "the funds are not ample—far from it—but what the college has at its disposal, you may rest assured is carefully guarded."[17]

A large percentage of students with advanced standing from other colleges or preparatory schools entered Hillsdale each year. Many new students in 1881, for example, had taken preparatory work at Oberlin. Requirements for admission to Harvard and Hillsdale in the 1870s and 1880s continued to be almost identical. For entrance to the classical collegiate course, Harvard required Caesar, Vergil, Latin prose, Roman history, Greek prose, Greek history, English composition, French or German, elementary physics, and geometry. Hillsdale's requirements were Caesar, Vergil, Cicero, Latin prose, Roman history, Greek prose, Greek history, geometry, English composition and rhetoric, French or German, elementary physics, and botany. A visitor to Hillsdale's Greek classes in 1884 judged the students to be well prepared. Observing Latin classes reading Juvenal and Caesar, the same scholar was convinced that "Hillsdale College affords instruction in Greek and Latin equal to that of any other college in the land."[18] As an advanced student in 1882, Lorenzo Dow taught a Latin class which he divided into two sections, because the enrollment reached 106. The Greek Library Association had about twenty-five members, who regularly ordered classical atlases, Greek histories, grammars, biographies of Greek authors, etc. A high percentage of Hillsdale students in the philosophical and scientific programs chose Greek as an elective.

Because enrollment increases were not accompanied by a larger faculty, professors frequently faced excessive class sizes. The department of mathematics with one professor (and a tutor teaching only two hours) had an enrollment of 300 students! Salaries at Hillsdale remained low. Ransom Dunn, acting president from 1884 to 1886, received $1200 annually; full professors' salaries in 1880 ranged from $600 to $1000. Will Carleton commented to President Dunn in 1885 that the Hillsdale professors' reward was satisfaction from assisting students rather than financial remuneration.[19] In the same era, Oberlin paid most professors $1400; Kalamazoo, $1200; Antioch, $1050; Amherst, $2500; Williams, $2000; Ohio Wesleyan, $2400; and Bowdoin, $1700. Lorenzo E. Dow, '85, received the same income from his first teaching position at Homer, Michigan, as senior Hillsdale professors.[20] Even more revealing was the fact that the average Hillsdale faculty salary remained basically unchanged from 1855 to 1900!

Low incomes, however, in no sense reflected inferior teaching. The faculty, dedicated to its students and to the college, voluntarily sacrificed the opportunity for material gain. Clarence Otis Williams, professor of Latin language and literature, exemplified Hillsdale faculty scholarship. An 1883 graduate of Brown University, he took postgraduate studies at the Theological School of Bates College before coming to Hillsdale in 1887. The young professor proved himself to be a superior teacher. He also gave to his fellow men "that greatest of all arguments for the Christian religion—the daily example of a life in harmony with its teachings." An excellent linguist, Williams had a thorough knowledge of Greek, Latin, and Hebrew, and in 1888 he began the study of Sanskrit. Tragically, the promising young scholar died on September 10, 1889, from malarial fever.[21]

Professor A. E. Haynes described his teaching methods in an article in the *Michigan School Moderator* (June 20, 1889). He questioned the effectiveness of one final examination per course and preferred to use daily recitations and periodic examinations. Haynes argued that his technique gave the students time to digest the subject matter. In geometry and calculus, he required each student to prepare a thesis in place of a final examination.

Speaking to alumni in 1885, Wallace Heckman observed that the greatest contribution by the Christian men and women who built Hillsdale College was character in education. He pointed out that the best security for the United States was men and women from schools like his alma mater, who lent dignity to common life. Hillsdale students attended daily services in the college chapel, decorated with the motto "We honor the men who wore the blue." Students regularly attended many churches; Hillsdale remained a Christian, nonsectarian institution. Trustee Ezra L. Koon in 1882 stated that Hillsdale, of all the colleges he knew, was least afflicted with vices such as drinking and smoking. He informed the student body that they would soon graduate "to drop down as stars in the dark spots of our country to light them up, to be good feeders of Hillsdale College, to know, as just now you do not know, what a place this college holds in the great Northwest. . . . I am yet to find one man who is sorry he came to Hillsdale."[22]

Lorenzo Dow in 1883 vividly described to his mother the moral impact of Hillsdale College:

> I remember that after trying to reason me out of my idea of coming West {from Maine], you at last said that perhaps it would be all for the best. . . . The influence here is of the best & has ever since I came led me to think of religious matters in a different light than ever before & last week I decided that the rest of my life shall with God's help be better than what I have lived. I have experienced no sudden change that led me to this step.[23]

College authorities sometimes called off afternoon classes to hold a half day of prayer. Evidence of moral leadership was active support for the Y.M.C.A. and the Y.W.C.A. in the late nineteenth century. Seventy-five students organized the local Y.M.C.A. in 1879, and the national organization soon reported that Hillsdale did "a larger and better work than any Christian college in the West."[24] At the time, 326 colleges had Y.M.C.A. chapters. Thirty Hillsdale College women formed their own organization separate from the men's in October 1883. The men and the women held joint and separate weekly meetings, conducted courses in Bible study, and had prayer meetings every Tuesday evening during the college year.[25] In 1885, the college sent twenty-one delegates to the state convention. Professor A. E. Haynes of Hillsdale was chosen chairman; and Miss Cassie Reamer, Lady Principal, was elected president of the state Y.W.C.A. In 1886, Professor Dunn's daughter Nettie became national secretary of the Y.W.C.A. Further proof of Hillsdale's moral posture was an occasional cancellation of classes for prohibition lectures. When a man got his throat cut in a Hillsdale barroom brawl, the college students immediately knew where to place the blame—on rum!

In 1886 George Frank Mosher, a native of Maine and resident of New Hampshire, became the first layman to serve as president of Hillsdale College. A volunteer nurse in field hospitals during the Civil War, Mosher was a Phi Beta Kappa and graduate of Bowdoin College in 1869. He served two terms in the New Hampshire legislature; and he was a United States consul in Europe, two years in France and two years in Germany.[26] At the age of forty-two, Mosher assumed the presidency of Hillsdale College. Admiring the character of the students and alumni of Hillsdale College, President Mosher stated:

> I was thrilled by her example of energy and vitality when she [Hillsdale College] arose twelve years ago from her very ashes. . . . I have also admired her faculty, men of devotion and self-sacrifice, who had consecrated themselves to their nobler work. . . . Relying upon the proved devotion of the faculty, which is always the heart of a college, and especially upon such blessing as God may bestow on our united and consecrated work, I have decided to accept the trust.[27]

Healthy enrollments are exemplified by contrasting the 75 freshmen entering the Hillsdale collegiate program in 1885 with the following institutions: Brown, 75; Union (at Schenectady, New York), 30; Amherst, 98, Rochester, 39; Trinity, 21; and the University of Pennsylvania, 100.[28] Hillsdale admitted men and women from thirty-seven states and territories in the 1880s. Most students, as previously, supported themselves by sawing wood, teaching, selling books, and doing farm work. G. B. Hopkins, '84, noticed that Hillsdale College students learned economy, good habits, and "push," and he argued that "the world needs educated men, trained in heart, as well as in intellect. Everywhere there are open fields for the enterprising, God-fearing, educated young man or young woman."[29]

Proud of their alma mater, most graduating classes contributed a memorial gift. The seniors of 1886 donated a magnificent bronze fountain, ten feet high. Decades later, a dynamite explosion unfortunately shattered the memorial at 12:30 a.m. on April 15, 1940. Wrappings of dynamite sticks were found, but no public announcement ever revealed who was guilty of the crime.[30] In addition to class gifts, seniors continued to improve commencement exercises. A special train from Lansing brought Governor Alger, the secretary of state, the state superintendent of public instruction, and various state senators and representatives to the ceremonies in June 1885. Governor

Alger told the crowd that "the history of Hillsdale College ranks among the foremost educational institutions." Former president Fairfield, who became the first chancellor of the University of Nebraska after leaving Hillsdale, also addressed the crowd: "An education that is not sanctified, that is not glorified with Christian principles, is not worth the getting. Were I to have life to live over again, I would never waste one year to build up a state university. We want consecrated learning."[31] We can assume that women at the ceremony reflected Victorian splendor, because merchants had run large advertisements on the front page of the local newspaper for graduation dresses made of black and colored silks and velvets.

The literary societies, meanwhile, continued their excellent work. In 1883 the State Board of Visitors observed that the societies were "a power for intellectual, moral, and social improvement." The organizations maintained a sense of public purpose, as when the Alphas celebrated the fiftieth anniversary of Michigan statehood. Society publications included *The Alpha Kappa Phi* (1858–62), *The Amateur* (1859–62), *The Souvenir* (1860–62), and three society histories in the late nineteenth century.

Although Delta Tau Delta formed their Kappa chapter at Hillsdale on October 19, 1867, it operated in secrecy in the woods north of town because of faculty disapproval; and no other men's fraternity was organized for nearly sixteen years. Hillsdale became known in the northern states as the nonfraternity college. In the 1870s, renewed faculty opposition caused Delta Tau Delta to suspend temporarily its active organization at Hillsdale.[32] By the 1880s, the professors began to relax their antifraternity policy, and four fraternities and two sororities functioned openly at Hillsdale during the decade. Phi Delta Theta was established in 1882 and Sigma Chi in 1883. Obtaining evidence of misbehavior by two Sigma Chis in rooms in the Flatiron Block downtown, Ransom Dunn deactivated the chapter in June 1886. Upset by their dismissal, the Sigma Chis decided to form an Alpha Tau Omega chapter. A southern fraternity hoping to reduce sectional bitterness, Alpha Tau Omega willingly accepted northern Hillsdale in 1888. Kappa Kappa Gamma was chartered on

June 9, 1881, following a planning session at Cold Spring Park. Pi Beta Phi was chartered on May 21, 1887.

High standards of student conduct notwithstanding, the *Detroit Evening News* reported in January 1883, a case of discipline under the headline "College Rumpus—Twenty Hillsdale Seniors Suspended for Sleighriding." Miss Shafer, a coed, had invited seniors to her father's farm five miles from campus for an oyster supper on Saturday evening. The faculty, not wishing to establish a precedent for late hours, refused to grant permission. Attempting to train character as well as the intellect, the professors found themselves supporting rules unacceptable to seniors. Without faculty permission, the students took their sleigh ride to the Shafer residence the next Wednesday evening! The issue became what the faculty would do with members of the graduating class. The professors finally voted to suspend the entire senior class, because the students intentionally had organized opposition against the college. The sleigh ride itself was relatively minor, but the faculty would not tolerate a direct challenge to their authority. Temporary suspension of the seniors nearly broke up the literary societies, who lost the upperclass officers' leadership.

In the same month as the sleigh ride incident, the faculty expelled Lyman Brewer of Hillsdale and Clara Frost of Jackson "for night-walking & sundry other offenses."[33] When Miss Frost's father arrived to take his daughter home on the 3 p.m. train, the faculty made an uncharacteristic decision to reinstate Clara. Two days later, however, the "rebellious" Miss Frost voluntarily withdrew from college after her involvement in the senior sleigh ride episode described above!

Another controversy, the "Little Door" dispute of the late 1870s and early 1880s, involved entrances to the Amphictyons' and the Alphas' new society rooms on the third floor of Knowlton Hall. The Amphictyon Society had obtained exclusive use of a landing at their hall entrance, which provided them two entry doors on the third floor of Knowlton Hall. The Alphas demanded easier access to their own society room, which had only one door on the third floor of Knowlton. Accordingly, the Alphas cut an extra door to their room through the landing wall. The college Prudential Committee ordered the Alpha Kappa Phi Society to close the illegal opening. When the Michigan legislature in 1880 passed an act providing for sufficient doors in public halls as a fire safety measure, the Alphas put pressure on the city authorities to recut a door through the wall. The Prudential Committee intervened, and several more times the door opening was replaced and then reconstructed. By December 22, 1883, college secretary-treasurer Charles B. Mills informed Alpha Kappa Phi of the Prudential Committee's decision that the societies "must make no opening in any walls of the College from their rooms and that whenever it shall become necessary to make such opening it will be done by the College Authorities."[34]

The student body enjoyed recreation, such as attending the county fair annually on a day when classes were dismissed. Pranks remained common, however. Students in 1884 carried the president's buggy to the top of the college tower. The next year, male students who hid classroom chairs were expelled. President Durgin complained openly when one of the tables in the dining hall became boisterous and noisy.

In May 1886, the local newspaper reported another episode: "Some of the bad, bad students got loose last week and gave vent to their pent up musical natures, by ridiculously serenading a new married couple." In the same month, a custodian was surprised to find a barbed wire fence dividing the sidewalk from Central Hall to College Street. On one side was printed in large letters LADIES AND MARRIED THEOLOGUES HERE, and on the other GENTS HERE. The obvious intent was to protest the strict policy against integration of the sexes in chapel lectures and literary society meetings. In November 1886, college men took the city hose cart, attached the hose to the campus hydrant, and directed water into a recitation room!

The sophomore class in 1882 pulled a prank on the seniors in retaliation for having being sold as slaves, with assigned labor. For several evenings, a magic lantern show (comparable to modern slides) had entertained the students at the college chapel. Sophomores meanwhile cleverly redesigned the seniors' photographs by placing their heads on comical bodies. On October 28, 1882, as a sophomore read a humorous poem about the senior class, the revised images were projected onto the chapel screen. One of the participants wrote, "The chapel was crowded with students, professors, & people from town, & they fairly went wild over the affair."[35]

College rules forbade the use of tobacco, but an anonymous student informed the Hillsdale faculty in 1886 that "Mr. James Davidson is in the habit of using tobacco at times, to an immoderate degree, and it is not infrequently that persons sitting near him in recitations are very much annoyed by the offensiveness of his breath and clothing."[36] Some future ministers raided melon patches and grape vineyards. More serious than such misconduct was the students' belief that Willis Moore had cribbed his literary society oration; integrity in the contests was equivalent to the strictest honor code.

The junior class in 1874 and 1875 published *The Crescent,* a periodical. This student publication marks the beginning of the oldest college newspaper in Michigan, although various changes in management and title followed. The publication lasted only a few years, but a proprietor/publisher proposed in 1878 to sponsor the *Hillsdale Herald,* a student newspaper advocating college interests. With the agreement that the faculty have general oversight of the copy, the first issue of the *Herald* was published on October 10, 1878. Cost of the four-page weekly newspaper was seventy-five cents a year. Because the publisher soon moved his operation to the center of the city, the college again lacked its own newspaper. The faculty consequently arranged to purchase the *Herald.* Under Michigan law, the Hillsdale College Publishing Association was organized on April 6, 1880, and any professor or administrator could purchase stock. The new college agency renewed publication of the *Herald* on April 8, 1880. Issued fifty-two weeks a year, the *Herald* almost immediately obtained the largest circulation of any college newspaper in the United States.[37] With over 1,200 subscriptions, the *Herald* exceeded the *Kansas University Courier,* which claimed earlier that its circulation of 900 was largest of 300 American college newspapers. The *Herald* also became the only American college sheet to be issued fifty-two weeks a year.[38]

An unfortunate controversy broke out in 1885 between the faculty and Professor A. C. Rideout, who held controlling stock in the newspaper. The administration had reason to believe that Rideout persistently misrepresented facts about the college. According to the *Cleveland Plain Dealer* of June 9, 1885, Rideout openly criticized the Prudential Committee for not obtaining fire escapes, as the Board of Trustees had requested. Rideout also revealed that Chauncey Cook, son of the late trustee and generous patron John P. Cook, had been denied a seat on the college board. The reason apparently was that John P. Cook before his death had revoked the part of his will containing a bequest to Hillsdale College. Rideout showed some prescience in this long-standing Cook controversy. William W. Cook, John's descendant who died in 1930, bequeathed fifteen million dollars to build the Law Quadrangle and Hutchins Hall at the University of Michigan![39] Rideout's conflicts with the college included more than the newspaper; for example, he accepted into his commercial department students who had been dismissed from the classical curriculum.

President James A. Garfield's death attracted national attention to Hillsdale College. S. D. Bates, college trustee, had inspired Garfield as a youth to begin his formal education at Geauga Academy in Ohio. When Garfield was making preparations for his journey to Washington and his inaugural address in 1881, he entertained Bates at his home in Mentor, Ohio.[40] Numerous Freewill Baptist teachers and religious leaders including Day, Marks, Mills, Dunn, Ball, Branch, and Fowler had served the Geauga Academy in Chester, Ohio, before its transfer to Hillsdale College. Because some of these Geauga instructors who moved to Hillsdale had taught Garfield, the memorial service at the college chapel following the president's assassination was particularly meaningful. Dr. George Ball, leader of the Freewill Baptists in the late nineteenth century, said in September 1881, that Hillsdale College rightfully claimed the slain president as a former student. The *Cleveland Leader* reported that the literary societies, faculty, and students at Hillsdale eagerly wanted to build Garfield Memorial Hall as a replacement for East Hall. The monument proposed by Dr. Ball to the memory of "our student, our friend, our statesman, our Christian brother, our President"[41] never was built, primarily because of the solid construction of East Hall. Also, many alumni opposed the demolition of East Hall, which was all that remained from the original building of 1853.

Hillsdale, making substantial progress in athletics for men and women in the 1880s, became the first college in the state, including the University of Michigan, to build a gymnasium. Women students persuaded the Prudential Committee in April 1884, to set up a gymnasium in a recitation room on the third floor of East Hall. Each professor voluntarily contributed to the project. Carpenters, masons, painters, and paperhangers prepared an excellent exercise room 38 by 14 feet, and by April 24 the "calisthenium" was ready for use. Indian clubs, wands, grace hoops, and a trapeze were the original equipment.[42] This was the earliest women's gymnasium in Michigan and one of the first in the West, and the ladies immediately organized the Calisthenic Association of East Hall.

After the success of the women's calisthenium, demands arose for a gymnasium building available to both sexes. F. B. Dickerson of Detroit in 1884 contributed $500 to start the project. Dickerson Gymnasium was built the next year at a cost of $2,254.50, plus $196.33 for equipment. The facility contained swings, rings, bars, ladders, chest weights, pounding bags, and boxing gloves. Resembling oversized bowling pins, Indian clubs were the rage in the late 1800s. They were named by British soldiers in India, who improved muscle tone by swinging the wooden clubs. The Dickerson Gymnasium, a pioneer for physical education in the United States, even had an indoor batting cage for baseball. The G. J. Kline Company of Hillsdale gave thirty-one yards of heavy duck fabric for a wrestling and boxing floor. Hearing of the completion of Dickerson Gymnasium, an Albion College student protested, "Don't see why we can't have one too."[43] Women and men participated in the facility at separate hours. The ladies' schedule was from 4 to 5 p.m., and a coed's gym suit cost three dollars. (One student later sold her suit for $3.75!)

The first Dickerson Gymnasium contest occurred on June 14, 1886, as the ladies engaged in freehand and dumbbell exercises. Gentlemen's contests included club swinging and performances on the horizontal and parallel bars and rings. The trustees recommended by

1886 that all students in the academic department be required to practice regularly under instructors approved by the faculty. The college employed student E. H. Barringer as director of the gymnasium and hired Miss Evelyn McDougal to instruct the young ladies in calisthenics.

Professor A. E. Haynes endorsed the beneficial effects of the Hillsdale gymnasium in a lecture to the thirty-ninth annual meeting of the Michigan State Teachers Association at Lansing on December 26, 1889. He argued that true education consisted of combining academic knowledge with useful and moral habits of body and soul. Haynes claimed that the gymnasium was necessary to ensure exercise, recreation, and self-reliance; and he dismissed the idea that the facility should be used primarily to train students for athletic contests. Hillsdale professors in 1890 agreed that all students should engage in physical exercise. Two years later, the faculty reported to the trustees that students who supported themselves by manual labor, who walked long distances to college, or who had recitations at the hours available for practice, could be excused from gym workouts.[44] Benefits from the new athletic activities at Hillsdale College included "the improved figure, the elastic step, the sparkling eye that only health can give."[45] A participant stated, "God has given us mind and muscle, and it is our duty to improve both."

Perhaps the students' physical conditioning was a factor in avoiding the diphtheria plague that threatened the community in 1886 and caused cancellation of many events: church services, literary society meetings, a Salvation Army procession, among them. Harmon R. Hyatt, a senior from Vermont, died from typhoid fever on October 11, 1888. The most prevalent illnesses during the 1880s in southern Michigan, including Hillsdale, were pneumonia, influenza, consumption, measles, typhoid fever, diphtheria, scarlet fever, diarrhea, bronchitis, rheumatism, neuralgia, whooping cough, dysentery, mumps, malaria, cholera, intermittent fevers, and croup.[46]

Hillsdale College played a central role in organizing the Michigan Intercollegiate Athletic Association. Delegates from Hillsdale, Michigan Agricultural College, Adrian, and Albion met in Jackson to establish a state intercollegiate baseball league on March 24, 1888.

The constitution specified: "No club can employ a player who is not a bona fide student or instructor in the college where the club is located. Nor can a club have more than one professional player on its list."[47] The new baseball conference soon expanded into the Michigan Intercollegiate Athletic Association, the oldest athletic conference west of the Appalachian Mountains. James Heckman of Hillsdale, who initially proposed the formation of the league, was considered to be the "father" of the M.I.A.A. E. H. Barringer of Hillsdale became the league's first president. A third Hillsdale sponsor was Professor Clark Herron, first league commissioner (judge advocate) from 1922 to 1931.[48]

Hillsdale athletes performed best in track and field events during the 1880s. Thirty-five Hillsdale men participated in the field day at Lansing in June 1887, and four of them won prizes: E. H. Barringer for heavyweight boxing, W. Moore for lightweight boxing, H. B. Woodward for swinging Indian clubs, and V. W. VanFleet for running (a gold medal).[49] Hillsdale College held its first field day on June 14, 1887. At the last minute, the faculties of Michigan Agricultural College and Albion College refused to let their students attend because of examinations, so events proceeded without them. With a shortage of contestants, ten local lads and ten college boys waged the tug of war. The student body shouted themselves hoarse, and local observers hissed and groaned during the townies' defeat.[50]

Hillsdale College athletes captured the first men's track championship at the M.I.A.A. field day at Lansing on May 31, 1888. They won the following events: 100-yard dash, 50-yard backward run, 220-yard dash, half-mile run, half-mile bicycle race, one-mile relay race, running high jump, Indian club swinging, parallel bar, and lightweight wrestling.[51] Hillsdale hosted the second annual M.I.A.A. field day in early June 1889, after the back campus had been graded for football and baseball the preceding fall. Almost 300 athletes from Olivet, Albion, and Michigan Agricultural College participated. Events included boxing, baseball, lawn tennis, jumping, running, tug of war, half-mile bicycle race, 880-yard dash, 50-yard backward dash, Indian club swinging, horizontal bar, parallel bars, wrestling, hundred-yard dash, baseball throw, three-legged race, 16-pound hammer throw, mile run, 17-pound shot put, standing broad jump, running broad jump, backward broad jump, standing hop, step, and jump, running high jump, high hand spring jump, 440-yard dash, pole vaulting, standing high kick, and high kick backward. John Collins of the Detroit Athletic Club was referee, and final scores were Hillsdale 41; M.A.C., 40; Albion, 21; and Olivet, 9.

"Their Early Aspirations Were Prophecies"[52]

The most important results of a college are seen in the records of its students. The first class to complete four years of collegiate study at Hillsdale graduated in 1860. The five men and eight women included two attorneys, a banker, an educator, and a telegraph operator. Best known of the class was Honorable J. T. Hoke, judge of the first judicial district of West Virginia. After obtaining his law degree from the University of Michigan, he opened a practice in Martinsburg, West Virginia. Hoke organized the first Union governments in Berkeley and Jefferson counties; before the end of the Civil War, he established the earliest Republican newspaper in that part of the state. As president pro tem of the West Virginia Senate, he led the state's ratification of the Fifteenth Amendment to the United States Constitution. Hoke also was delegate to three Republican national conventions.

Hillsdale graduates and former students built an impressive reputation in the late nineteenth century. The following selective list illustrates their achievements in politics, education, science, and other areas. Lieutenant Samuel A. Cherry, Hillsdale student before graduating from West Point in 1875, fought with the Fifth U.S. Cavalry against the Ute Indians. The *Chicago Sunday Times* reported that he commanded skirmishers in the engagement at Milk Creek in 1879: "He received the first of the attack and bore the brunt of the fierce onslaught for several hours. Cherry's conduct in that battle, and, indeed, in the whole of that campaign, was valiant to a striking degree." Lieutenant Cherry later was killed accidentally by a soldier attempting to murder another officer.

Henry S. Walworth, an early Hillsdale student, was agent for the Missouri, Kansas & Texas Railroad in 1860. He accompanied famous guests hunting with "Buffalo Bill" Cody and later returned home to help establish the Hillsdale Savings Bank. Bion J. Arnold, '84, known in his college days as "the little engine builder," was grandson of Jeremiah Arnold, one of the earliest pioneers in Hillsdale County. He became president of the American Institute of Electrical Engineers and designed two of the largest electrical engines in the West. Arnold used his patents to build power plants for the World's Fair and the Chicago Board of Trade. Civil engineer on the Chicago, St. Paul, & Kansas City R. R., Arnold also designed power plants for the North Shore and Suburban railroads in Chicago.

Lewis Emery, Jr., who entered Hillsdale College in 1856, went to Titusville following the discovery of oil in Pennsylvania. At age twenty-six he pioneered the production, refining, and marketing of oil, and he successfully resisted John D. Rockefeller's invitations to join Standard Oil for twenty-seven years. Ruined temporarily by the 1873 panic, Emery leased 14,000 acres of oil land, began boring, placed nearly 500 wells into operation, and built one of the largest refining plants in the world. President of the Octave Oil Company, he purchased and returned to production the property on which the original Drake oil well was located. The first millionaire from Hillsdale College, Emery rebuilt Knowlton Hall after it was gutted by fire in 1910. Interested in politics, he was elected to each house of the Pennsylvania legislature. His brother, David, served on the Hillsdale College Board of Trustees.

Other prosperous entrepreneurs were lumbermen Austin W. and William W. Mitchell, sons of Charles T. Mitchell. Attending Hillsdale College before developing timberlands in Michigan and Oregon, each brother became a millionaire. James L. Callard, a poor servant in the British army, came to the United States and graduated from Hillsdale with honors in 1880. Superintendent in the construction of numerous western railroads, in 1888 he became U.S. engineer on the great lock at Sault Sainte Marie, 800 feet long and 100 feet wide. D. M. Martin, '81, was engineer in charge of building some of the highest dams in the world.[53] Franklin Bailey, '73, gained national recognition for his astral lantern, an early planetarium that he perfected in 1881. The U.S. Naval Observatory endorsed Bailey's lantern as ingenious; and C. S. Lyman, professor of astronomy at Yale, claimed that the invention should find a place in every college. Arthur E. Haynes, Hillsdale alumnus and professor, was one of five Americans elected to membership in the London Mathematical Society. While a member of the Hillsdale faculty, Haynes was one of the few scientists to record accurately the transit of Venus on November 6, 1882.

The first Hillsdale graduate elected to Congress was Spencer O. Fisher from the neighboring town of Camden. Earning over a million dollars in lumbering and banking, he became mayor of Bay City and was elected to the House from the tenth district in 1884. Solomon R. Dresser from Litchfield also was elected to Congress; in addition, he invented various machines for the oil and gas industry. He and his brother Jasper had attended Hillsdale College on a $100 scholarship with perpetual tuition. Their father, an early supporter of Hillsdale College, contributed the scholarship during President Fairfield's personal visit to the family farm. John C. Patterson, '64, and A. R. Chapman, '67, were Michigan state senators. Charles E. Soule, '65, served as probate judge at Grand Haven, Michigan; and Moses A. Luce, '66, superior court judge and district judge at San Diego, California, played a major role in founding the city. S. G. Updyke, '69, and George Laybourne, '78, were leading members of the Dakota constitutional convention, and J. H. G. Weaver, '72, served as speaker pro tem in the California legislature.

Samuel Lappin, an early student at Michigan Central, became treasurer of the state of Kansas. M. H. Chamberlain was mayor of Detroit, beginning in 1885. Charles P. Lincoln, formerly consul for six years at Canton, China, became a prosperous lawyer in Washington, D.C., and argued cases before the United States Supreme Court. Hillsdale graduates taught at the state universities of Michigan, Illinois, Minnesota, Nebraska, and South Dakota, and others were professors at Harvard, Cornell, Oberlin, and Berea. The following were among the many who served as superintendent of schools: S. D. Crane, '74, in LaGrange County, Indiana; H. B. Larrabee, '75, in

Wayne County, Pennsylvania; John Wadhams in Cook County, Illinois; J. H. Felch in Portage County, Wisconsin; and Lewis W. Day for the Cleveland school system.[54]

Hillsdale College "exceeds all my expectations."[55]

During the 1880s, Hillsdale College had risen, phoenix-like, to new heights. The *Chicago Herald* reported that Hillsdale was second in standing to no denominational college in the United States.[56] Senior professors agreed that the college never had offered academic work of higher standing. The faculty continued to believe that Greek, Latin, and the modern languages were as practical as any study, and the science department made remarkable progress. The Harrington biological laboratory, first and largest in the state, contained seven rooms with excellent equipment such as dissecting tables and fourteen expensive microscopes. Mr. H. Harrington of Woodstock, Ontario, Canada, was the major benefactor. (A student, Lilian Kirkwood, complained in 1887 that she had to dissect a most horrible cat in physiology lab!)[57] What a contrast to the earliest years at Spring Arbor, when most of the scientific apparatus was handmade! The museum of natural science and the college library grew steadily, and the Dickerson Gymnasium was a successful pioneering project among western colleges. The commercial department had some of the finest equipment in the nation, and Professors A. C. Rideout and W. A. Drake advertised that "no other first-class school in the United States presents to the public a better course of study, or tuition, board, and other incidental expenses at rates so low." Many commercial graduates occupied responsible business positions, and the art and music departments also experienced steadily growing enrollments.

Hillsdale in the 1880s was virtually a free school; tuition became nominal with an increase in endowment each year. Students contributed at most a quarter of all institutional income. Colleges have personalities of their own, and Hillsdale took particular pride in strengthening the moral values of self-supporting Christian students. Ransom Dunn lectured in 1886 that "literature to be grand, to be interesting, must contain an underlying reference to God at heart. All the beauty of poetry depends upon it."[58] An alumnus proudly stated in 1885, "The high-souled men and women, who from schools like this, lend dignity to common life, are this land's best security."[59] Initiative always had motivated the college to put its convictions into practice. Perhaps Hillsdale's most distinctive feature was the drive to do what many colleges only theorized about; and the graduates—self-made men and women, shared the spirit of enterprise.

If Hillsdale College had a shortcoming by the end of the 1880s, it was its failure to publicize its unique record more widely. The ambitious college, less than half a century old, had demonstrated excellence in academic programs, moral leadership, and quality of the faculty, administration, and alumni. Many prominent guests who came to Hillsdale for the first time "look over our work, students, curriculum, chapel-faces, and breathe for a day the atmosphere of the college, and voluntarily say . . . in private conversation with an earnestness that carries small hint of adulation: 'Do you know I never dreamed there was *so much of a college here*. I had heard of Hillsdale often, but this exceeds all my expectations.'"[60] Intelligent, independent people repeatedly made such comments. An alumnus proudly called Hillsdale "a great American college," with graduates influencing the state and the nation. Modern educational concepts in the last decade of the century would present new challenges to the enterprising, traditional college.

Endnotes

1. *Hillsdale Standard,* September 4, 1883.

2. George N. Fuller, *Michigan: A Centennial History of the State and Its People* (Chicago, 1939), II, p. 445. The Old Northwest included Ohio, Michigan, Indiana, Illinois, Wisconsin, and part of Minnesota.

3. *Hillsdale Herald,* December 23, 1880.

4. The college held a memorial service in the chapel following Henry Waldron's death on September 13, 1880.

5. D. D. Ball, "Our Colleges," *Morning Star*, as reprinted in *College Herald*, November 17, 1887.

6. *Forty-Seventh Annual Report of the Superintendent of Public Instruction of the State of Michigan* (Lansing, 1886), p. 92.

7. Ransom Dunn, "Financial Values of Hillsdale College," *The Wolverine* (Cleveland, 1896), p. 29.

8. O. A. Janes left Hillsdale College to enlist in the Fourth Michigan Infantry, and he participated in most of the major eastern battles: the Wilderness, Spotsylvania, North Anna, Cold Harbor, etc. Losing his left arm at the siege of Petersburg, Janes returned to Hillsdale and graduated in 1868. Engaged in the practice of law in Hillsdale, Janes was elected to numerous public offices, headed the Grand Army of the Republic for Michigan, and served two decades as a trustee for Hillsdale College.

9. *Hillsdale Standard*, February 16, 1886.

10. *Chicago Herald*, 1891.

11. *Portrait and Biographical Album of Hillsdale County* (Chicago, 1888), p. 183.

12. Michigan County map by H. F. Walling (Detroit, 1874), original lithograph. AKG.

13. Unlike Hillsdale, many colleges began as theological schools and only later developed into four-year liberal arts institutions. My alma mater, Susquehanna University, for example, had its origin as the Missionary Institute in 1858. See *Addresses, Inaugurals and Charges, Delivered in Selin's Grove, Snyder Co., Pa., September 1st and November 24th, 1858, in Connection with Laying of the Corner Stone, and the Installation of the Professors of the Evang. Lutheran Missionary Institute* (Baltimore, 1859). AKG.

14. Report of the Board of Visitors to the Michigan Superintendent of Public Instruction on Hillsdale College, 1880–81, as published in *Hillsdale Herald*, December 7, 1882.

15. Report of the Board of Visitors to the Michigan Superintendent of Public Instruction on Hillsdale College for 1882, as published in *Hillsdale Standard*, September 27, 1883.

16. *Hillsdale Herald*, June 30, 1887.

17. Annual Report of the Committee of the Michigan Yearly Meeting on Hillsdale College, as published in *Hillsdale Herald*, September 14, 1882.

18. *Hillsdale Herald*, April 3, 1884.

19. Will Carleton to President Ransom Dunn, October 3, 1885. Ransom Dunn Collection, MHC.

20. *The Reunion*, May 20, 1885.

21. *Hillsdale Standard*, September 17, 1889.

22. Ibid., November 7, 1882.

23. Lorenzo Dow to Mrs. Wm. M. Dow, February 20, 1883. Dow Collection, loaned by Dr. Lilian Rick, professor emeritus of Spanish, Hillsdale College.

24. *Hillsdale Herald*, June 10, 1880.

25. *Students' Hand-Book, Compiled by the Y.M.C.A. and Y.W.C.A. of Hillsdale College* (Hillsdale, 1887), p. 4. Loaned by Dr. Lilian Rick.

26. *Educators of Michigan: A Choice Collection of Biographical Sketches and Portraits of the Teaching Profession* (Detroit, 1894), pp. 24–25. Three previous Hillsdale College presidents had fathers who fought in the War of 1812. George Mosher belonged to a new generation, and his grandfather had participated in the conflict.

27. Quoted in *Hillsdale Standard*, July 27, 1886.

28. *The Advance*, October 21, 1885.

29. *Morning Star*, August 27, 1885.

30. When I began teaching at Hillsdale College, some senior professors told me that they knew who was responsible for blowing up the memorial in 1940.

31. *The Reunion*, June 17, 1885.

32. *Fifth General Catalogue of the Delta Tau Delta Fraternity* (1884), p. 150.

33. Lorenzo Dow diary, entry for January 24, 1883. Dow Collection, loan from Dr. Lilian Rick.

34. Hillsdale College Secretary-Treasurer Charles B. Mills to Alpha Kappa Phi Society, December 22, 1883. Loan from Dr. Lilian Rick.

35. Lorenzo Dow to his sister, October 29, 1882. Dow Collection, loan from Dr. Lilian Rick.

36. "A Student of the Academic Department" to Hillsdale College faculty, May 23, 1886. Ransom Dunn Collection, MHC.

37. *Hillsdale Herald,* October 1, 1885.

38. *An Illustrated City Directory of Hillsdale, Michigan* (Hillsdale, 1894), p. 7.

39. Howard H. Peckham, *The Making of the University of Michigan, 1817–1967* (Ann Arbor, 1967), p. 174.

40. *Marion Independent,* as reprinted in *Hillsdale Herald,* March 3, 1881.

41. George H. Ball, "Garfield Hall," *Morning Star,* as reprinted in *Hillsdale Herald,* January 12, 1882.

42. *Hillsdale Herald,* April 24, 1884.

43. *Hillsdale Standard,* February 23, 1886. Both men and women used the Dickerson Gymnasium for much of its history. There is a common misconception that the facility was built for women only. The Dickerson Gymnasium was demolished in 1964 to provide space for the new Dow Leadership Development Center.

44. Minutes of June 6, 1892. Records of the Proceedings of the Board of Trustees of Hillsdale College from June 9, 1884, to August 20, 1901, with Proceedings of the Prudential Committee, June 18, 1884, to July 22, 1904. HCVPA.

45. *Hillsdale Herald,* March 24, 1887.

46. *Ninth Annual Report of the Secretary of the State Board of Health of the State of Michigan* (Lansing, 1882), pp. 262–63, 283. AKG.

47. *Hillsdale Herald,* March 22, 1888.

48. Thomas L. Renner, ed., *Celebrating a Century of the Student Athlete: The 100 Year History of the Michigan Intercollegiate Athletic Association* (MIAA, 1988), pp. 15–16; Thomas Oliver, ed., *MIAA Handbook* (Hillsdale, 1939),

p. 9; Todd E. Harburn and Gerald E. Harburn, *MIAA Football: The Illustrated Gridiron History of the Michigan Intercollegiate Athletic Association* (Chelsea, 1986), p. 1.

49. *Hillsdale Standard*, June 7, 1887.

50. Ibid., June 21, 1887.

51. Ibid., June 5, 1888.

52. This toast was made by W. W. Heckman, '74, at the 1890 banquet of the Hillsdale Alumni Association.

53. *Hillsdale Standard*, January 3, 1888.

54. Lewis W. Day left Hillsdale College to serve in the 101st Ohio Infantry until the close of the Civil War. He returned to Hillsdale to complete his degree and then established a record as an educator "which extended into every state in the Union." Superintendent of several Ohio school systems, he held important positions in national educational associations.

55. Quotation by Hillsdale College visitor in *Hillsdale Herald*, February 16, 1882.

56. *Chicago Herald*, April 7, 1891.

57. Lilian Kirkwood diary, entry for February 12, 1887. Loan from Dr. Lilian Rick.

58. Ransom Dunn, "Lectures in Theology," lecture notes taken in 1886 by Frank E. Kenyon, p. 1. HC.

59. Wallace Heckman, '74, as quoted in *Hillsdale Standard*, June 16, 1885.

60. Hillsdale College visitors' quotations in *Hillsdale Herald*, February 16, 1882.

NINE

Defense of Traditional Education

May earth be better and Heaven be richer because of the life and labor of Hillsdale College.
—Prayer enclosed in Hillsdale College cornerstones
1853 and 1874

Hillsdale was an attractive and thriving town in the 1890s. The railroad center had twenty-two passenger trains arriving and leaving daily. When the *New York World* conducted a poll at the end of the century to find the most desirable place of residence in Michigan, Hillsdale received the most votes. The *Chicago Herald* humorously described strong political sentiments by reporting in 1891 that Hillsdale was so solidly Republican that even a tornado of the previous fall had passed it by. In the late Victorian era, many families living in Italianate homes had live-in domestic help.[1] The pride of the community was the Freewill Baptist institution that was "second in standing to no denominational college in the country."[2] At a meeting between college personnel and members of the Presbyterian Church, Pastor Jacobs praised local interest in the college. Extending one arm toward college hill and the other toward town, he proclaimed, "What God hath joined together let not man put asunder."[3]

Hillsdale College was described widely as "the pioneer in the coeducational scheme." Irrespective of religious beliefs, the entire college community attended daily chapel services. The careful student's total cost (board, lodging, fees, and books) for a full year was about a hundred dollars, the lowest expense in the state.[4] The total number of professors increased to twenty-five, although some resigned to take positions at leading universities. William F. Tibbetts (Latin), L. A. Crandall (American history), Elias P. Lyon (physiology), and Clark Herron (mathematics) moved to the new University of Chicago, and Frank Smith (zoology) accepted professorships at Trinity College and at the University of Illinois. Hillsdale enrollment averaged 500 students annually during the last two decades of the nineteenth century. In contrast, Kalamazoo College in 1892 had a faculty of five professors and six instructors; an annual budget of less than $18,000; and an enrollment of 125 preparatory and 40 collegiate students.[5]

These and other descriptions of Hillsdale College at the opening of the decade seem almost idyllic. No wonder that a departing coed wistfully wrote in her diary, "I lay on the bed gazing out at the open window thinking that this might be the last Sunday I would ever spend in Hillsdale."[6] The campus of the hilltop college was acclaimed as the most beautiful in Michigan, and visitors could apply to a custodian for a tour escort. During the heyday of small rural colleges, Hillsdale's mission was to help students develop faith in God and respect for learning. Former secretary-treasurer Lorenzo P. Reynolds, who remained upset over his firing and published the vindictive *Story of Fifty Years*, made the only significant attack on the institution. For twenty years he even launched tirades against the venerable Ransom Dunn.[7]

By 1891, Michigan had 120 Freewill Baptist churches with a total membership of 5,233 to provide stronger financial support. The college endowment fund reached $216,763.63 in 1894. Hillsdale College held 281 mortgages on Michigan farm land, with an average interest rate of 7.26 percent. Refuting false charges of mismanagement of funds during the 1893 economic panic, the trustees' finance committee reported that the "percentage of loss will be found to be less than almost any other institution or business of the same character will show."[8]

As usual, the trustees exercised extreme prudence and excellent business judgment. Finances were tight during the 1893 panic, and by 1897 the income from endowments provided only $802.09 over costs! Nevertheless, some physical facilities were modernized. Water pipes from Baw Beese Lake to East Hall and the chemical laboratory had been laid by the fall of 1886. The committee on grounds and buildings in 1893 decided to place water closets in all campus buildings and to remove the outhouses. Electric lights were installed at each corner of the campus in December 1893, and steam heating replaced wood-burning stoves in Central Hall. Students who previously reported terribly cold weather at 25 degrees below zero undoubtedly appreciated the new comfort, although a central heating plant for the entire campus was not installed until 1910. (During the 1890s, there were some years when the students experienced snow and cold weather in late May.) The endowment reached $230,107.35 by 1896. Lawn mowers eliminated annual haymaking on the college green in 1898, the same year that the first concrete sidewalks were built on campus. The wooden fence, constructed on three sides of the college square in 1862 from 4" x 4" x 10' wooden rails and 8" x 8" x 7' oak posts, was removed in 1900 when grazing by livestock on campus was forbidden.

Academic standards of the college remained strong. Most significantly, Hillsdale by retaining traditional values was not susceptible to the new progressive "reforms" in education. The State Board of Visitors reported that Hillsdale biology students did more work in dissection than any other Michigan college except the medical schools. The Theological School perhaps had the highest standards of all the departments, many of which had gained outstanding reputations. In the entire history of the college, more graduates received the classical degree, or the Bachelor of Arts, than any other. The faculty reported to the trustees in 1892 that "while we feel the necessity of offering to our students as broad an elective course as any similar institution, we believe it to be good policy to adhere as closely as possible to such well-chosen classical and scientific studies as will give the broadest mental discipline. . . . "[9]

Hillsdale College chose to graduate broadly educated people, not specialists who were tradespeople within their own disciplines. Many alumni became physicians, lawyers, and engineers. The faculty believed strongly that such professionalization was premature, unless preceded by a liberal arts education. Although progressivism had begun to reduce the national emphasis upon traditional studies in favor of the utilitarian approach, Hillsdale resisted the trend. The 1897–98 catalogue, for example, emphasized courses in Greek, Latin, Hebrew, literature, history, political economy, logic, ethics, mathematics, chemistry, and biology.[10] A. W. Augir spoke at class day exercises on June 16, 1890, about the value of the classics. Opposing modern trends in education, he defended the liberal arts:

> Homer's *Iliad* is the model epic which Vergil copied and Dante and Milton imitated. Aeschylus and Sophocles made laws for the drama which neither Shakespeare nor Racine nor Schiller deemed best to alter.... Demosthenes is still the ideal towards whose power and beauty of expression every orator strives. Phidias is yet the greatest name in sculpture and architecture.... *Let our colleges and universities, then, beware of yielding too much to the present movement.... The great and increasing tendency toward specialization in every department of life renders some means of preventing intellectual narrowness indispensable.* [Emphasis mine.] The long and severe course of special training required as the first condition of success in any profession inevitably tends to narrow the mental vision and prevent a just estimate of kindred fields of activity. To check this tendency is the province of the thorough college course....

Hillsdale students maintained their outstanding oratorical reputations in the 1890s. The literary societies remained strong several decades into the twentieth century and weakened at Hillsdale the trend toward fraternities. Society members spoke on such topics as "The Study of History," "The Need of the Ideal," and "The Classics." The college Board of Trustees held annual meetings in Alpha Kappa Phi Hall, the society's old room in Knowlton Hall, as late as the 1940s.[11] Washington Gardner, a successful politician, claimed at the end of the century: "The Amphictyon Society gave me my first lesson in the knowledge and application of parliamentary law; in thinking and speaking on my feet; in discerning and measuring the capacities of men as revealed in the arena of debate."[12]

At the national oratorical contest on prohibition, Amos A. Ebersole of Hillsdale won first prize in New York City on June 29, 1894, by defeating students from schools including the University of Wisconsin and Brown University.[13] The State Oratorical League was organized at Hillsdale College in 1897. Two years later, Hillsdale won first honors at the state oratorical contest at Hope College, and the entire student body celebrated in front of Central Hall. Faculty and students declared that "Hillsdale's victory at Hope is worth fifty olive wreaths of the athletic field." At the same time, distinguished lecturers continued to visit the campus.

On June 20, 1895, the Alpha Kappa Phi Civil War Soldiers' Monument was dedicated. The project began when Judge Richmond W. Melendy, Civil War hero, died a pauper at the Eaton Rapids Sanitarium. Millionaires David and Lewis Emery promptly arranged to have their old college friend buried at Oak Grove Cemetery in Hillsdale. Just before Melendy's body was lowered into the grave, a crippled veteran stepped forward and asked to see the face of his beloved officer one more time. The request for a moving silent interview of the living and the dead was granted. The college flag draped the cupola of Central Hall.

Motivated by Melendy's plight, many alumni decided to memorialize all Alpha Kappa Phi veterans with a statue of a color-bearer holding in both hands the broken staff of "Old Glory." Lorado Taft, an eminent sculptor, had designed a statue of several Civil War soldiers for the University of Minnesota. Joe Cummins, chairman of the Hillsdale monument committee, arranged with Taft and the university to have the central figure, an unknown standard bearer, recast for Hillsdale College.[14] The best grade of granite was purchased from Barre, Vermont, and the American Bronze Co. of Chicago made the bronze castings. Johann Gelert, an outstanding Chicago sculptor, created the model for the bas relief of the "Surrender of Lee" at the base of the statue. The eight figures in the bas relief were generals Marshall, Rollins, Lee, Grant, Sheridan, Porter, Brown, and Grant's secretary. Professor Arthur Haynes, who had left Hillsdale to teach at the University of Minnesota, secured much of the $1,600 expense from 120 donors. Congressman A. J. Hopkins, Ransom Dunn, President G. F. Mosher, Mayor A. B. LaFleur, and Consul Charles P. Lincoln spoke at the dedication. Will Carleton composed "Bronze and Stone," with these closing lines, for the occasion:

> Stand, hero of our campus ground,
> And guard the classic-templed hill;
> While on the world still brighter glows
> This object lesson, sad but grand:
> That student boys the books can close,
> And die to save their native land.

Henry Magee, successful Chicago attorney who had served with his fellow students in the Michigan Fourth, expressed his hopes that the statue would "tell the simple, old, old lesson of truth and duty, again and always, to the endless line of boys and girls, the men and women, who shall tread this hill while Hillsdale College stands and make them all ever remember and rejoice that in the hour of their country's peril, Hillsdale College ... failed not to bring their share of noble sons to the sacrifice of human life on the altar of their country. And yet, we can build no monument for them, which shall be more enduring than the monument they built for themselves in our hearts, by their truth and self-sacrifice."[15]

U. S. Senator Albert J. Hopkins, Hillsdale alumnus, also spoke at the dedication of the Soldiers' Monument. He termed the years of sectional conflict one of the most important eras in the history of the college: "In the dark and stormy period of the Civil War it [Hillsdale College] was one of the first institutions in our country to patriotically respond to the call of the president. She gave to her country's service the very flower of her students. Those who returned ... have set apart this day to commemorate the memories of the ones whose bones lie bleaching upon southern soil."[16] At the same ceremony, Professor Arthur Haynes paid tribute to wartime sacrifices by the college and its young students:

> We here commemorate the same love of country, the same spirit of loyalty and heroism that characterized our forefathers on Lexington

Green, at Concord Bridge and on Bunker Hill, a spirit of which their descendants proved well worthy during the awful struggle from '61 to '65. Malvern Hill! Gettysburg! Chickamauga! Missionary Ridge! How these names thrill our souls! Men who left these college halls, and freely giving their all, dared to sleep the sleep of death to maintain the sacred principles represented by our glorious flag, and to preserve the integrity of our beloved country, and who thus advanced the holy cause of "the greatest of rights—an equality of rights."[17]

Hillsdale College in the 1890s expressed compassion toward the defeated Confederacy, as the new generation recognized bravery on both sides. Memorial services for veterans, North and South, were held annually in the college chapel, so crowded that spectators sat on the window sills. F. M. Webster at the literary societies' joint memorial service on May 30, 1893, acknowledged, "They who fought and died whether wearing the blue or the gray have earned a nobler fate than to become the stock in trade of partisan speeches. . . . Humanity will be no loser when the Christian heroism of such men as Stonewall Jackson is duly known. . . . " Congressman Washington Gardner, ex-Hillsdale student, expressed accord with the Confederacy in 1902 as he addressed a reunion of General Sherman's veterans. The *Daily Times* of Chattanooga, Tennessee, described the "absolute hush that pervaded as he paid a glowing tribute to General James Longstreet, the famous Confederate chieftain."[18] Congressman Gardner also introduced a bill in Congress to create a home for Confederate veterans, to be maintained by the national government. As a student at Hillsdale in the mid-1890s, southerner James E. Kirbye from Tennessee proudly defended his ancestry. After graduation, he lectured widely on Stonewall Jackson and became pastor of a Congregational church in Charleston, South Carolina.

M. H. Peters, Hillsdale student when the war began, became a Union major. His brother in the South enlisted under the Confederate flag, and both were wounded in combat. Major Peters composed "Brother and I" in 1894 to reveal compassion over the American conflict waged a generation earlier:

Both of us fought for what we thought was right,
        But of duty each took a different view;
Both of us entered the perilous fight
        And did our duty as patriots do—
        But he wore the gray and I wore the blue.

Let the awful past be buried from sight,
        As our comrades so noble, brave and true
Are buried on fields where they made the brave fight,
        Keeping their virtues alone in view—
        The chivalrous gray and generous blue.

In terms of physical expansion, the most significant progress by Hillsdale College in the 1890s was the acquisition of Griffin Hall from Professor Alexander Rideout. For years there had been trouble and litigation between the college and Rideout, editor of the *Hillsdale College Herald*. The *Reading Hustler* believed that the faculty established the *Hillsdale Collegian* because of bitterness toward Rideout. The first issue of the *Collegian* was distributed at chapel in December 1893, and Rideout was hanged in effigy from the college tower a month later. The faculty even arrested Rideout for attending chapel service, because they claimed that he was not a professor at the college, only at his own commercial school. A. C. Rideout replied on March 12, 1894, that the Michigan Supreme Court in the case of Hillsdale College vs. Rideout had recognized his ownership and right to use Griffin Hall on campus. [19]

By an agreement reached on May 25, 1896, Rideout's Hillsdale College Publishing Association and the *Hillsdale College Herald* were moved to the college, which came into full possession of Griffin Hall on June 30. The trustees then voted to transfer the building formerly occupied by Rideout's commercial classes to the Theological Department. Trustee Aaron Worthing, local manufacturer of fur coats, contributed $8,000; and Griffin Hall was renamed Worthing Divinity Hall in 1898.

Student behavior in the 1890s continued to reflect a strong work ethic and self-sufficiency. Both sexes commonly arose to study between 4:30 and 5:30 a.m. Coeds washed their clothes and hung them out to dry behind the East Wing. Poor conduct stood out as an exception to the Victorian norm, although Lady Principal Harriet Deering reminded male students of proper decorum when they called on young ladies, lest more restrictions be imposed. College authorities finally eliminated a formal list of twenty social regulations by 1890. Mixed couples now could eat at Smith's Hotel, play ball and croquet, use the toboggan slide, walk downtown, go boating on Baw Beese beyond the third lake, walk back to campus on the railroad tracks, share the parlor in East Wing during late evening hours, and so on.[20]

A group of college men, irritated by noise, dancing, and card-playing, invaded a party held by two boarding clubs at a home on Manning Street in April 1892. Their action upset college authorities, who claimed it was irresponsible for a disorderly mob to handle such violations. In the same month, the *Hillsdale Standard* revealed that "the usual spring revival of questions relating to college ethics is upon us. The Pres. and Lady Principal have both spoken to the students . . . and the opinion of the students seems to be that the restrictions laid down are a trifle harsh."[21]

Despite some flexibility, the professors continued to enforce discipline. The *Cincinnati Post* reported an unpopular ruling by the Hillsdale faculty effective January 10, 1894. Single students who entered college were not allowed to get married and remain in class. On the other hand, persons already married were admitted and permitted to stay. The student body protested that the ruling served no good purpose, because married men in the Theological Department consistently had demonstrated the highest scholarship.

Pranks were commonplace, as always. Upperclassmen seized the freshmen's new black caps and carefully placed them on a wire stretched across the chapel in May 1892. The student newspaper editor deplored this hazing as a relic of the dark ages and advocated police protection for freshmen. Students from two rooming houses in March of 1893 engaged in the "bloodiest snowball fight of the season."

One of the more outstanding pranks in Hillsdale history occurred in May 1893. A custodian spotted a skeleton with freshman cap and colors hanging from the peak of the Central Hall cupola. Two freshmen tried to rescue their "colleague," but they found the only entrance to the belfry, a trap door, nailed down from the top and secured by a piece of studding. The truth finally was revealed a year later. An anonymous upperclassman had taken a skeleton from the science laboratory on the upper level of East Hall. Using a ladder, he inched across the precarious gap between East Hall and Central Hall. After securing the skeleton on the top of the tower, the daring student nailed down the trap door and descended the outside of the dome and walls of Central Hall. Ingeniously using the ladder to cross numerous chasms, he reached the roof of East Hall and descended the outside walls.[22] The prankster's climbing and crawling all had taken place *outside* the high tower!

A major departure in college social policy permitted the Alpha Tau Omega fraternity in September 1892, to rent a private residence for a chapter house.[23] Fraternities gradually gained at least a formal acceptance from the faculty, unlike earlier years when Delta Tau Delta gave fictitious mailing addresses when attending fraternity conventions. Fraternities by the 1890s invited professors to their activities, and the college in turn allowed the brothers to host coeds at social events. Phi Delta Theta, for example, entertained female students with a sleigh ride in January 1896.

Athletics became an important student activity for the first time in the 1890s, and a committee of students and faculty selected ultramarine as the college color in November 1893. Duncan M. Martin, professor of mathematics, used statistics to indicate that 75 percent of those who participated in Hillsdale sports were superior students; he denied that athletics and scholarship were incompatible.[24] The *Collegian* reported in 1894 that Hillsdale policy had always been "not to encourage athletics at the expense of scholarship, and it is now true that the leaders in athletics are among the best students in the college."[25] Interclass football games, often impromptu, gained popularity as a leading men's sport. The juniors and seniors (including two professionals) probably waged the first interclass contest in November 1890. The literary societies and the men's fraternities also played amateur football with high emotion. The local newspaper observed in 1891. "Football is the leading pastime among the boys in this fine weather. No bones have as yet been broken, but the dry goods have suffered some."[26]

Early Hillsdale intercollegiate football teams were organized, managed, and coached entirely by students. The student-athletes formed their college athletic association (the Athletic Club) and elected officers to a board of control. In 1898 the board voted to award an "H" letter only to men who played regularly: "This will mark very clearly the distinction between the real athlete—the man who is willing to get out and work —and the one who does little but talk."[27] Responsibility for football gradually shifted toward the faculty and a part-time coach. The men trained themselves in 1893 but secured a coach from Cornell for one week. J. L. D. Morrison, who had played football at the University of Michigan and coached the Notre Dame team, arrived in Hillsdale in late October 1894 to coach for several weeks. The next step would be a department of athletics with a full-time coach, Henry C. McRae, in 1904.[28] The college proudly declared in 1919 that its coach had "Y.M.C.A. ideals."[29]

Olivet and Albion played an exhibition "football match" at the second annual M.I.A.A. Field Day in 1889. The first official intercollegiate football contest in the league, however, was Hillsdale College's home loss by 36–4 to Albion in 1891. This game began the oldest rivalry in the conference until Hillsdale withdraw from the league in 1960.[30]

Although Notre Dame was already a football power, Hillsdale enjoyed playing them three years in a row, once to a 0–0 tie. The Irish gave the Hillsdale players fine accommodations, a big dinner, and cigars to smoke on the train ride home![31] Other major teams that played Hillsdale included Purdue, the University of Michigan, and Michigan Agricultural College (now Michigan State University).

Another Hillsdale victory over a well-known power came in the twentieth century, when Coach Dwight Harwood's squad traveled to Stagg Field at the University of Chicago on September 26, 1931. The Maroons were led by the legendary Amos Alonzo Stagg, rated first among all college football coaches (followed by Fielding Yost, Knute

Rockne, and Fritz Crisler) in a poll of sportswriters in 1990. The squad of twenty-two men defeated Chicago by 7 to 0, as Hillsdale gained fourteen first downs to Chicago's two.[32] Hillsdale College received Stagg's assistance frequently in the early twentieth century. When the need to hire a new football coach arose in 1908, Hillsdale authorities asked Stagg at Chicago for his recommendation. Coach Stagg also interpreted a questionable ruling by a referee in Hillsdale's favor.

On Thanksgiving, 1892, Hillsdale achieved a lop-sided victory by defeating Adrian in an away game, 56 to 0. On October 16, 1893, Hillsdale overcame Albion by 18 to 0 with an effective play called the "turtle creep," in which the runner and offensive line together formed a slowly moving but unstoppable mass. Students greeted the Hillsdale athletes returning to campus with a fireworks display. The team was carried by wagon up Howell Street, where the sheriff and his deputy temporarily tried to stop the festivities and jailed one student. Prominent citizens cleared up the problem, and the students proceeded up College Hill where hundreds attended a bonfire in front of the fountain. The college paper reported that "even one of the faculty was mounted upon a box and praised the boys for their victory."[33] Hillsdale won a second game from Albion by the identical score of 18–0 and claimed the 1893 M.I.A.A. championship. The decisive victory was Hillsdale's third shutout of the season. The players on the 1893 championship team, whose average weight was 171 pounds, deliberately let their hair grow long to provide extra protection![34]

The sports editor of the *Marion Star* in 1950 interviewed Jesse P. Robinson, '96, a member of the 1893 team. Robinson claimed that Hillsdale football in the 1890s was less complicated but much rougher than now. Slugging on the line and piling on a player who was down were routine. For headgear, the players wore heavy leather helmets and rubber nose guards. Forward passing was prohibited, and most of Hillsdale's plays were end sweeps or plunges through guard and tackle. The Hillsdale team perfected the "flying wedge," with which the men lined up in an upside down V and hit the opposing line at full speed.

President Mosher attended a college conference at Jackson,

Michigan, on March 16, 1894, which adopted a resolution urging the avoidance of unnecessary brutality in sports. By fall of 1894, the faculty was willing to buy uniforms for the first team but not for the substitutes. Part-time coach J. L. D. Morrison, ex-player for the University of Michigan, led Hillsdale to a 34–6 victory over Olivet in October. Perhaps because of the president's earlier warning, Hillsdale's 28 to 4 victory over Adrian in November was "devoid of all slugging and unnecessary roughness." Halfback Rapp, however, left the game with stomach trouble caused by boarding at the Fat Men's Club![35] When Hillsdale defeated Kalamazoo on November 24, 1894, with twelve touchdowns and ten goals, the referee called the game twelve minutes early to allow the victors to catch their train home. The final varsity contest of the successful 1894 season was on Thanksgiving, when Hillsdale defeated Adrian 28 to 4, although their opponents used many players from Ann Arbor and other schools. The Adrian coach, an ex-University of Michigan player, played fullback and called the plays. The college boys (the "holy terrors") and the townies later held a club game on December 27.

A segment of the college community continued to oppose violence in athletics, and they staged the "funeral of Mr. H. C. Football" in November 1897. The glee club sang "There'll be no football in the old town tonight," but most Hillsdale citizens dismissed the affair as a college prank. The local newspaper reported earlier that "football and other athletics are popular at Hillsdale College with the students and faculty and are not likely to be suppressed. There is, too, another point which each college may consider: a first class team is a fine advertisement, and the liberalizing and reciprocal advantage of visits to other colleges is not to be overlooked."[36]

Annual track and field days of the Michigan Intercollegiate Athletic Association retained their popularity in the 1890s, and Hillsdale won its first championship in 1891. The University of Michigan, incidentally, did not hold an intercollegiate track meet until 1893.[37] College students graded the one-fifth mile track, almost completed by September 1893. The faculty reported to the trustees that "during the year considerable work has been done by the students making the race track, which shows that they can handle the shovel and hoe, as well as the dumb bells and Indian clubs." In May 1894, B. F. Green of Hillsdale ran the 100-yard dash in 10 seconds flat.[38] Cinder was placed over the original dirt track in 1895; inside the oval was the football field, flooded in the winter for a skating rink. Mathematics professor Duncan Martin gave much of his time, labor, and money for the fine athletic facility. The improved athletic grounds on the back campus, named Martin Field, commonly were described as the best in Michigan and had capacity for 2,500 fans.[39]

Baseball remained a major sport at Hillsdale in the 1890s. An unusual feature of the new baseball diamond at Martin Field was an extremely steep bank in deep right field next to the gymnasium.[40] The earliest outstanding pitcher was Eddie Storms; in 1896, the "farmers" of Michigan Agricultural College couldn't touch him in a 4 to 1 Hillsdale victory. Third baseman Frank Wells, hit in pre-game practice, played the entire game with a broken right thumb. Men's wrestling became a popular sport, Charles Macomber won the M.I.A.A. men's tennis singles title for Hillsdale in 1891, and a college cycling club was organized in 1894.

Hillsdale students began playing basketball in October 1895, less than four years after James Naismith invented the game at Springfield, Massachusetts. Hillsdale played intercollegiate basketball as early as 1898, a year after Yale and the University of Pennsylvania held the first contest.[41] The University of Michigan, meanwhile, did not start an intercollegiate basketball program until 1917.

"The Alumnus at Large"[42]

According to a University of Wisconsin survey, Hillsdale was one of seven western universities and colleges having the largest percentage of graduates from the late nineteenth century listed in *Who's Who in America*. The other six institutions were Oberlin and the universities of Michigan, Wisconsin, Indiana, Illinois, and California. By 1900, Hillsdale had graduated more than one hundred clergymen. An additional three hundred students became ministers without completion of their theological degrees. Sixty-four missionaries worked in locations including Jamaica, India, China, and Africa.

Education was another major profession for Hillsdale alumni. Seven graduates became college presidents. John R. H. Latchaw, '81, served presidencies at Findlay College and Defiance College. Fifty alumni in the latter half of the century held professorships at leading colleges and universities, and Hillsdale graduates in the 1890s served on the faculties of Harvard, Cornell, Michigan, Minnesota, and Nebraska. John F. Downey, who fought under Sherman in the Atlanta campaign and paid his college costs by teaching, harvesting, painting, and doing masonry work, became a highly respected professor of mathematics and astronomy at the University of Minnesota. Arthur E. Haynes, who helped to construct Central Hall by carrying eighty-pound hods of brick to the top floor, joined Downey in the mathematics department of the University of Minnesota. Dr. James N. Martin, '80, served with distinction on the medical faculty of the University of Michigan for many years.

Harry C. King, Hillsdale student in the 1870s, began teaching at Oberlin College in 1898 and held the chair in religion first occupied by Charles G. Finney, prominent revivalist of the Second Great Awakening. N. J. Corey, '76, was organist at Harvard College. Aaron A. Myers, Hillsdale student in the 1860s, became a Congregationalist minister and opened the Harrow School near the Cumberland Gap in 1890. His purpose was to educate youth in the rural mountains. General O. O. Howard, formerly head of the Freedmen's Bureau, joined Myers in expanding the Harrow School into Lincoln Memorial University, chartered by Tennessee as a liberal arts institution in 1897. The temperance views of George W. Lawrence, Hillsdale, '80, caused a drunk to shoot him. Recovering his health, Lawrence became mathematics instructor at Lincoln Memorial University in 1897.

Leroy Waterman, '98, taught Hebrew at Hillsdale from 1902 to 1910 and became a renowned Biblical scholar and translator of the Old Testament. Head of the department of Semitic languages and literature at the University of Michigan for thirty years, he directed an expedition to Mesopotamia that uncovered the old wall of Nebuchadnezzar. He headed archaeological excavations in Tel Umar, Iraq, from 1927 to 1931.[43] Duren James H. Ward, '84, received an M.A. from Harvard University and a Ph.D. from the University of Leipzig. In the late 1880s he became superintendent of the Workingman's School of New York City, an excellent academy with 15 teachers and 350 pupils. Author of thirty-six books and pamphlets, Dr. Ward later taught philosophy at the University of Colorado. Jason E. Hammond and Theodore Nelson each served as Superintendent of Public Instruction in Michigan.

County school superintendents included Alfred Bayless, '70, at Sterling, Illinois, and O. J. Steward at Delevan, Minnesota. Charles H. Gurney, '73, superintendent of public schools at Marengo, Iowa, wrote *Opening Exercises for Schools*. O. S. Dolby, '86, who was superintendent of schools at Lake Charles, Louisiana, developed a large irrigation system for flooding thousands of acres of rice in bayou country.[44] James W. Simmons, superintendent of schools in Owosso, wrote a popular textbook entitled *Qualitative Chemical Analysis*.[45] Other educators did home mission work, frequently as teachers among blacks in the South or with Indians in the West. Dr. F. P. Woodbury became secretary of the American Missionary Association, a leading philanthropic organization to assist blacks.

More than twenty former Hillsdale students became journalists by 1890. William F. Kelley, reporter for the *Nebraska State Journal*, was one of three newspaper correspondents at the battle of Wounded Knee. When attacked by an Indian, Kelley grabbed a Winchester from a fallen soldier and killed three braves. Kelly later earned his law degree and served as consul in Rome. Hillsdale journalist Charlie Root wrote for the *Nebraska State Journal*, Maurice Perkins was editor of the *Indianapolis Sun*, Luther M. Hall was a publisher in San Diego, California, Oscar Rakestraw was editor-publisher of the *Steuben Republican*, and Arthur Randall published the *Tekonsha News*.

One hundred and two attorneys graduated from Hillsdale College, and many of them joined other alumni in providing public leadership during the 1890s. General Marvin E. Hall was elected national commander-in-chief of the Sons of Veterans in August

1892.[46] O. A. Janes, chairman of the Republican state convention at Detroit on May 7, 1896, informed his audience: "The difference between the Republican and Democratic administrations of governmental affairs is that under a Republican administration the receipts of the government exceeded the expenses, and the public debt was diminished. Under the Democratic administration the expenses exceed the receipts, and the public debt is increased."[47] Washington Gardner informed Hillsdale County Republicans on September 1, 1898, that he felt at home because of having attended the college after the Civil War: "I came here a young boy, having laid aside my knapsack and my musket and haversack and canteen; the battles were over, the victories were won. . . . I came over to Michigan to school, and I have never had any occasion to regret it. It was here in this city that I drank in the lessons of Republicanism as a young boy, before I had reached my majority. . . . Over in front of yonder courthouse, many years ago, I heard that stalwart Republican, then Senator, Zachariah Chandler; right down here below the flatiron [Flatiron Building] I heard that honored son of Ohio, Benjamin Wade."[48] Gardner became Michigan Secretary of State and was elected six times to the United States Congress as a Republican.

Albert J. Hopkins, '70, served in Congress for nearly eighteen years, almost became speaker of the House of Representatives, and was U.S. Senator from Illinois. General Jasper Packard, distinguished Civil War officer, was Congressman for six years as successor to Schuyler Colfax. John R. Foster, '65, served in the Kansas state legislature; Frank P. Wiley, '73, in the Missouri legislature; and George Laybourn in the Minnesota legislature. David Allen, student in 1857, was a member of the Dakota territorial legislature; and Joseph Arnold, another of the earliest Hillsdale students, attended the Nebraska territorial legislature in 1865–66. J. S. Drake and J. M. Dresser both were elected to the Indiana Senate. Henry V. Perrin, '60, helped to organize the Jackson County Bank in 1872 and later served in the Michigan legislature.[49] J. B. Moore, Eugene H. Belden, G. W. Thompson, and A. W. Westgate also were chosen to the Michigan legislature; and H. L. Wood, '69, was a member of the Michigan Senate. Many Hillsdale College attorneys moved to the West. Charles

Witherel practiced law in Carson City, Nevada; John M. Rice, in Los Angeles; John M. Melendy, in Eureka, California; Orman J. Bates, in Trinidad, Colorado; and S. H. Hullinger in Denver. Spencer G. Millard, '78, became Lieutenant-Governor of California. J. E. Reynolds traveled south to practice law in Acadia, Louisiana.

Thirty Hillsdale alumni were judges by 1900. J. T. Hoke served on the Virginia Supreme Court, and M. B. Koon on the Minnesota Supreme Court. W. H. Sherman, '61, was circuit judge at St. Louis, Missouri; Charles S. Bently, '70, circuit judge in Ohio; and R. W. Melendy, '70, circuit judge in Michigan. Joseph B. Moore and C. D. Long became members of the Michigan Supreme Court in the 1890s. In the early twentieth century, Walter French, '96, became Chief Justice of the Supreme Court of the state of Washington; and Walter H. North, '96, joined the Michigan Supreme Court.

During the Indian Wars on the Great Plains, Frank D. Baldwin courageously claimed that the United States Army shared the blame for the Wounded Knee tragedy of December 29, 1890. In later fighting against the Moros in the Philippines, President Theodore Roosevelt complimented General Baldwin "for the splendid courage and fidelity which have again carried our flag to victory." Major General Baldwin was one of six Hillsdale students to attain the rank of general in the nineteenth century. Former Hillsdale students who served in Roosevelt's Rough Riders included Major Charles M. Brodie, Captain Buckie O'Neill, and Lieutenant Duncan M. Martin.

The most renowned naval hero from Hillsdale College was Charles V. Gridley, who left the Hill early in the Civil War to attend the U.S. Naval Academy. Graduating as an ensign on October 1, 1863, he served in the West Gulf Squadron from 1863 to 1865. Official naval records reported that Gridley's conduct aboard the U. S. steam sloop-of-war *Oneida* at Mobile Bay on August 5, 1864, was "beyond all praise."[51] He also participated in operations that captured Forts Powell, Gaines, and Morgan. After the war he served on the steam sloop *U.S.S. Kearsage,* which earlier had sunk the Confederate raider *Alabama.* At the 1903 celebration in Hillsdale marking half a century since the college had relocated from Spring Arbor, Gridley's flag from the *Kearsage* adorned the speaker's stand. Promoted to lieutenant commander in 1868, Gridley taught seamanship, naval tactics, and naval construction at the U.S. Naval Academy from 1875 to 1879.[52]

In the Spanish-American War, Gridley became famous as commanding officer of Admiral George Dewey's flagship *U.S.S. Olympia* during the battle of Manila Bay in 1898. Five thousand yards from the Spanish fleet at 5:40 a.m. on May 1, 1898, Dewey gave his order, "You may fire when you are ready, Gridley." The eight-inch gun on the forward turret of the *Olympia* signaled the other ships to join the action, and Dewey's command became a famous war slogan. Captain Gridley personally conducted the gunfire from his conning tower throughout the battle, ending with the complete destruction of the Spanish Philippine fleet. Already ill from an incurable liver disease, Gridley collapsed when the fighting ended and murmured, "The battle of Manila has killed me." Removed to Hong Kong, he died at Kobe, Japan, on June 5. His body was cremated and the ashes taken home by steamer.[53] Admiral Ramsey described Gridley as "one of the brainiest and pluckiest officers in the naval service." Hillsdale held memorial services on July 31, 1898, at St. Peter's Episcopal church, which was filled to capacity.[54] A bronze plaque in the Naval Academy's Hall of Fame at Annapolis commemorates Captain Gridley. President Joseph Mauck had good reason to remind a Hillsdale audience in 1903 that "this college, the child of the church militant, is a college militant, throbbing with patriotism when the oppressor comes and man is wronged."[55]

Science was another significant profession of Hillsdale alumni. Some of the earliest Michigan Central College students, including Dr. Orrin Fowle, became physicians. Fowle graduated from Western Homeopathic College in Cleveland in 1859. The Amphictyon Literary Society alone had 28 physicians among its members by 1890. S. E. Root, M.D., studied medicine at Harvard and became professor of anatomy and physiology at the Medical College of Maine. Henri Ambler, '64, was professor of dental surgery in Cleveland. Leaving Hillsdale College in 1859, Dr. Albert Hartsuff served in the Army Medical Corps in the Civil War, Indian wars, and Spanish-American War. He won a series of promotions from lieutenant to brigadier general. Dr. Frank B. Smith, '85, did graduate work at Johns

Hopkins and Harvard and taught for many years at the University of Illinois. The first scientist to make a systematic study of the classification of earthworms, Dr. Smith was an internationally recognized zoologist. Continuing his research in Hillsdale after retirement, Smith contributed some land for the college arboretum.

Elias Potter Lyon, '92, served as biologist on Dr. Frederick A. Cook's Arctic expedition of 1894, which set sail from New York on the iron steamship *Miranda*. Off the coast of Labrador, the vessel collided with a huge iceberg but finally reached Greenland. Cook led the scientists to within 800 miles of the north pole. Damaged again by hitting a large rock on the return voyage, the *Miranda* sank in the open sea, and the crew took refuge on a small schooner. Lyon saved some photographs by carrying them in his pockets.[56] After the Arctic expedition, Lyon earned his Ph.D. from the University of Chicago in 1897 and served as dean of the St. Louis University Medical School from 1907 to 1913.[57] A. W. Dorr, '96, joined the biology staff of the University of Michigan and did research at Woods Hole, Massachusetts. W. W. Payne, '63, professor at Carleton College and an eminent astronomer, was partially responsible for the system of standard time in the United States.

Many Hillsdale alumni traveled to the frontier. A. J. Wilber, for example, obtained his M.D. and then practiced medicine in Greeley, Colorado. Silas S. Sears, '80, sought adventure and gold in the Klondike; H. C. Abbott turned to ranching in New Mexico; James E. Davidson operated a steamboat; and E. R. Blackmar became a mining engineer in Leadville, Colorado.

Hillsdale College: The "West Point of Our Civil Life."[58]

Writing to alumni attending the 1890 reunion, former President Fairfield claimed that the Emersonian combination of "plain living and high thinking" had characterized the early days of the college at Spring Arbor and Hillsdale.[59] Dr. L. A. Crandall told the same reunion that "the only test of the tree is its fruit, and of a college the results . . . . Strong, self-reliant, earnest, truly cultivated manhood and womanhood, the warp and woof of civilization, this has been and is the product of the small college. . . . An observant foreigner has said of Americans that they are apt to mistake bigness for greatness. A college may be small and yet great; great and yet small. Out of the 345 colleges in this country bigness can be attributed to only eight or ten; but greatness rightfully belongs to many more. . . . Their students receive an education not to be bought with money, an education of the *will*." Crandall concluded by affirming that only a small college like Hillsdale could teach self-reliance, vigor, persistence, and other qualities needed to give character to our national life.

Will Carleton informed the class of 1892 that a large enrollment does not constitute a great college: "If greatness means mere largeness in a physical sense, then John L. Sullivan is a greater man than Dr. Holmes and Ralph Waldo Emerson put together." He argued that "poverty is considered here as merely a temporary inconvenience, and not an implied reproach—much less a disgrace."[60] The college in 1896 advertised itself as "a school that places an education in the reach of every young man and woman of ordinary ability, who has energy, industry and economy. A school for the poor and a school for the rich." Hillsdale remained a national leader in providing young people the opportunity to gain an education at lost cost. The *Free Baptist* of Minneapolis in 1896 claimed that there was no one so poor but that he could find a welcome home at Hillsdale, "where the only aristocracy known is that of scholarly attainment. . . . It is this stern, self-reliant spirit, born of self-denial and persevering effort, that has made Hillsdale's sons and daughters so marvelously successful." John Collier explained to the Alumni Association in 1895 that the college mission had been "to lend a helping hand to many a young man and young woman whose hands were well nigh empty, but whose soul was athirst for knowledge. . . . So many first-class young people found their way to Hillsdale College."[61] By the 1890s Hillsdale had attracted students from thirty-seven states and territories. Also, international students attended from Prussia, Bulgaria, India, Japan, Canada, Cuba, England, Germany, Ireland, and other countries.

Odelia Blinn, M.D., who studied at Hillsdale in the early 1860s, wrote from Chicago in 1896 that Hillsdale College had "brought forth greater mental and moral worth and vigor than three-fourths of the literary institutions of our country. It has worthy representatives in every state and in every honorable avocation in life. . . . Estimates can be placed upon buildings, but never on mental and moral values of colleges and universities."[62] The *Chicago Times Herald* in 1895 described Hillsdale College as "one of those educational institutions that are the glory of the Northwest, where pupil and teacher are brought in close personal contact with each other, where the intellect is not only developed and trained, but where character is formed and strengthened." Attorney Wallace Heckman of Chicago in 1899 claimed that Hillsdale College "helped me to look out on creation from a higher window and to enjoy it more largely."[63]

Retaining traditional values, Hillsdale was not susceptible to progressivism in education. The college in 1856 had placed the motto "Virtus Tentamine Gaudet" ("virtue rejoices in the challenge") on the original circular seal. A new trefoiled design replaced the former pattern in 1898, but the motto remained permanent. Unlike most American colleges, Hillsdale retained Greek or Latin as a requirement for the bachelor of arts degree throughout the 1890s. Washington Gardner, former Hillsdale student and Michigan Secretary of State, warned the student body of the threat to education presented by new technical and professional schools. He argued that *"young people who take these short cuts to learning are likely to find themselves at a serious disadvantage in all those relations where variety and fullness of knowledge are required in preference to the technicalities of a narrower curriculum."*[64] [Emphasis mine.]

While institutions such as the University of Michigan, Brown, Union, Oberlin, and Antioch adopted the elective system, pragmatism, and other progressive ideas, Hillsdale maintained its classical curriculum. James Garfield, who received his first formal education at Geauga from future Hillsdale professors and trustee Dr. George H. Ball, commented, "Given a log with Mark Hopkins at one end and a boy at the other, and you have a college." George Roche, today's president of Hillsdale College, has reaffirmed the founders' goals by emphasizing individuality and by defining education as "nothing if not the teaching of one person at a time."[65] President Roche teaches the political economy seminar for graduating seniors, as did his predecessor George F. Mosher in the 1890s.

A student editor in 1896 boasted that his college had only begun to make history and would be several hundred years in completing it. The Committee on Education of the State Association in 1898 unanimously applauded "the moral and spiritual advantages of Hillsdale College over all institutions under state control." The committee's report also cited financial advantages: "The colleges are furnishing, free of cost to the state, full collegiate courses of study, while the people are taxed for practically the same work in state schools."[66] The Michigan Superintendent of Public Instruction reported in 1895 that "no educator in Michigan is doing better work for the cause than is President Mosher," and the Hillsdale city directory of 1901 expressed pride that the local college occupied "a position second to none in the land, for thoroughness of training and moral influence."[67] Forged from adversity, Hillsdale continued in the 1890s to rank high as a leader of higher education in the West. Despite the disappearance of the frontier, Hillsdale retained enterprise and traditional values.[68]

Extensive undergraduate competition offered by tax-supported institutions in the 1890s adversely affected many small colleges, as eight leading state universities in the West increased their attendance over 200 percent from 1886 to 1896. Joseph W. Mauck, soon to become president of Hillsdale College, wrote in 1894 that "to conduct one of those colleges [like Hillsdale] successfully in these days of great state appropriations and enormous personal donations is a good deal like making bricks without straw."[69] Hillsdale could have resolved the challenge of bigness by accepting an offer to affiliate with the University of Chicago and its faculty of 170 in 1895.[70] Hillsdale would have sent examinations to the university for grading, and its students would have received their degrees from Chicago. Cherishing independence, the Hillsdale trustees rejected the attractive offer, although there had been only slight increases in faculty salaries for over thirty years.

Hillsdale enthusiastically maintained its moral and religious convictions. According to Joseph Mauck, the nonsectarian college appealed widely not only to Baptists but to Congregationalists, Episcopalians, Catholics, Presbyterians, Unitarians, Methodists, the Church of God, and many others. National membership in the Freewill Baptist church peaked at 90,000 by the end of the nineteenth century, and in 1911 the Freewill Baptists merged formally with the American Baptist Convention.[71] Will Carleton's "College and Nation," written for the fiftieth anniversary of the 1853 ground-breaking, ended with these significant lines:

> So shall we work for high Heaven and further
>   our Maker's intention;
> For though man must run the machinery,
>   the college is God's own invention.

To improve financial strength, the college appointed S. E. Kelley, '94, as field agent in 1897. He traveled as far as Minnesota, North Dakota, Nebraska, and Kansas. The trustees, according to a principle first proposed by Professor Dunn in the 1850s, refused to spend endowment money for current expenses. Total receipts from all tuition and matriculation fees in the three years after 1893 averaged only $3,196.83 annually. Complete charges for men in the 1890s never were more than $6.50 per term; costs for women, $4.25. Ever since 1844, tuition had been practically free. Hillsdale proudly claimed that no other college in the country offered such superior facilities for a liberal education at so low an expense. Book costs almost equaled college fees. One student's books in a single term cost $1.35 for geometry, $2 for philology, $1 for moral philosophy, $.90 for Horace, and $.75 for Greek prose.[72]

Largest college in the state for almost half a century, Hillsdale by 1894 had more students than ever before in its history.[73] Some reduction in enrollment resulted from eliminating the commercial program, which had attracted annually about a 150 students for a short course. Another factor was the rapid expansion of public high schools, which reduced the preparatory program. In effect, the traditional pre-collegiate program now operated as a private Christian academy. The direction of college policy therefore was toward higher quality at the expense of quantity. The classical course remained the academic anchor, and the largest numbers of classical graduates to that time appeared in the classes of 1892, 1896, and 1897. Half a dozen students discovered that Greek was not impossibly difficult and switched from the philosophical to the classical course in 1893. Because of high enrollment, the beginning Latin class in 1899 was divided into two sections. Committed to a strong liberal arts program, the Hillsdale trustees refused to adopt a curriculum with vocational emphasis. The four standard degrees remained the Bachelor of Arts, the Bachelor of Philosophy, the Bachelor of Letters, and the Bachelor of Pedagogy. Two decades into the twentieth century, the twelve majors at Hillsdale College included classical languages, modern languages, English, history, mathematics, social sciences, religion, chemistry, biology, business administration, and music.[74]

Few founding fathers remained, but their spirit of enterprise permanently shaped the independent college. Succeeding generations in the twentieth century owed a debt that never could be repaid. Frederick M. Fowler, for example, had moved by oxen team through unbroken wilderness to Michigan territory with his parents in 1834. The Fowlers sacrificed to build the first log schoolhouse in Adams Township on their farm the following year. (Over half of American children attended one-room schools as late as 1913. The accomplishments of the nineteenth century underscore the effectiveness of teaching the 3 R's and moral standards.) Young Frederick, riding horseback over an Indian trail, regularly accompanied the female teacher to work.[75] As a lad of eighteen years, Fowler helped to cut the road from Jonesville to Hudson, and he worked to clear off and grade the Michigan Southern Railroad east of Hillsdale. Fowler later served in both houses of the Michigan legislature. A successful businessman, he was a major figure in obtaining Central Michigan College for Hillsdale. Fowler served almost half a century as a Hillsdale College trustee from the first election on March 22, 1855, until his death on November 17, 1902.[76] The college trustees' testimonial expressed appreciation for Fowler's "wise counsels, his fidelity to all interests of the college, his generous benefactions to the institution, and his uniform courtesies to his associates on this board." Founders like Fowler were self-made men who willingly demonstrated public spirit and sacrifice.

Professor Charles H. Churchill, another founding father, was educated at Dartmouth and Oberlin. He had supported the removal of Michigan Central College to Hillsdale in 1853. Churchill made his final public remarks about Hillsdale College in July 1903:

> Hillsdale is a glorious institution. It has proceeded on a sound basis. It has been fortunate in having good teachers. It has been fortunate in its management in every respect. *For basic instruction as a typical small college it cannot be surpassed. Hillsdale can do that just as well as any other institution in the world, I fully believe.*[77] [Emphasis mine.]

Many founders and early supporters of the college were buried in Oak Grove Cemetery, established north of campus by four Hillsdale professors. Henry Waldron, college trustee and generous donor, had the only private vault. Long-time trustee Colonel Frederick M. Holloway was born in Bristol, New York, and came to Michigan in 1833. County register of deeds, postmaster, and mayor of Hillsdale, he served as college trustee from 1853 until his death and burial at Oak Grove in 1891.[78] Ezra L. Koon, born in 1832 in Tyrone, New York, also is buried at Oak Grove. Arriving in Hillsdale County in 1844, he was admitted to the bar in 1858 and served as prosecuting attorney, state senator, and mayor of Hillsdale. Koon belonged to the Prudential Committee of the college's Board of Trustees from 1875 until his death on February 9, 1892.[79]

Chauncey Reynolds, who died on May 22, 1890, had moved to Michigan from Genessee County, New York, in 1828. Recognizing the necessity for better education on the frontier, he supported Michigan Central College. Henry J. King, first secretary-treasurer of Hillsdale College, died on November 12, 1890. Educated at Oberlin College, he served Hillsdale as general manager and supervisor of the construction of the first college buildings. Franklin P. Augir, born in Herkimer County, New York, was educated at Hillsdale College from 1855 to 1860. Augir served churches in states from Michigan west to the Rocky Mountains. A college trustee for many years, he returned to Hillsdale for his children to receive an education from 1869 to 1875. F. P. Augir died in early July 1893.[80]

The greatest loss at the turn of the century was the death of Professor Ransom Dunn, who resigned because of declining health on June 13, 1898, at the age of eighty. Dunn had been a dynamic leader from the beginnings at Spring Arbor. The trustees unanimously recognized that "to his energy and enthusiasm in its early days are due its [the college's] origin and growth more than to any other man."[81] At the close of commencement exercises, every eye was moistened by tributes to Professor Dunn, whose life reflected a quotation from Longfellow: "I shall pass through this world but once; any good thing, therefore, that I can do or any kindness that I can show, let me do it now. Let me not defer it nor neglect it, for I shall not pass this way again." Dunn's last public appearance in Hillsdale was at the 1900 commencement, when the large crowd instinctively rose, stood silently, and then gave a last rousing cheer for the "Grand Old Man" of Hillsdale College. Eighty-two years of age, Dunn remained alert to the end. Death came in early November at his family's home in Scranton, Pennsylvania. On November 11, the faculty and students formed a procession to Dunn's home in Hillsdale, where his body lay in state. The students served as honor guard, and a hearse carried the body to the College Church and then to Oak Grove Cemetery. The memorial speeches emphasized Dunn's faith in Hillsdale College and its students.

A licensed minister at the age of sixteen, the "boy preacher" Dunn had left his New England home two years later for the frontier.[82] With eight borrowed dollars, the young evangelist told a friend, "I give my life to the West." Well acquainted with leading personalities such as John Greenleaf Whittier, Charles Sumner, William Lloyd Garrison, Henry Ward Beecher, Edward Everett, Joshua R. Giddings, John P. Hale, and Benjamin Wade, Dunn permanently accepted the challenges of the Michigan frontier. He agreed with Thoreau's statement, "Eastward I go only by force; but westward I go free." The fearless professor, more than anyone, was responsible for building and managing the small, enterprising college at

Hillsdale. President Joseph W. Mauck later wrote that faculty like Dunn were greatly underpaid at best and showed a devotion unknown in the twentieth century.[83] A student described the professor leading a prayer meeting in 1883 as "very earnest and enthusiastic and well-attended."[84] When theological students were forced to miss lectures because of pastoral responsibilities, Dunn willingly took time to repeat the material in individual conferences.[85] Now the senior professor's chair on the Hillsdale College platform was draped in black.[86] President George F. Mosher's resignation came the following year.

Throughout the nineteenth century, the essential purpose of Hillsdale College had been to produce Christian men and women. The hilltop institution that had been forged from adversity emphasized morality, honor, independence, and devotion in an environment of rising modern skepticism. An alumnus described Hillsdale as the "West Point of our civil life," because graduates with their education of the *will* faced life's duties with self-reliance, vigor, and persistence. Resisting the pressures of progressivism, pragmatism, and materialism toward the end of the century, the college retained the high standards of a classical education. An alumnus proudly claimed in 1890 that Hillsdale would go on forever, because it had "within itself the condition of its own immortality.... The college still entertains a broad and comprehensive view of its future." With traditional values and the new presidency of Joseph W. Mauck in 1902, Hillsdale College faced the twentieth century.

Endnotes

1. Willfred O. Mauck, "Dear Hearts and Gentle People" (n.p., n.d.), III, p. 2. Manuscript loaned by Mrs. Charles Buchanan.

2. *Chicago Herald,* April 7, 1891.

3. *Collegian-Herald,* February 10, 1898.

4. Even with low boarding fees, Sunday dinners featured turkey, gravy, oyster dressing, sweet potatoes, pie, cake, and fruit!

5. Arnold Mulder, *The Kalamazoo College Story* (Kalamazoo, 1958), p. 15.

6. Lilian Kirkwood diary, entry for June 5, 1887. Loan from Dr. Lilian Rick.

7. Lorenzo P. Reynolds became secretary and treasurer of Hillsdale on August 18, 1862. The trustees, by a narrow vote, released Reynolds from his position in 1877. In 1874, he had successfully championed the plan to rebuild the college with a group of structures. Implications about possible dishonesty probably were responsible for his dismissal. *Portrait and Biographical Album of Hillsdale County, Mich.* (Chicago, 1888), pp. 323–24.

8. *Hillsdale Standard,* June 19, 1894.

9. Minutes of June 8, 1892. Records of the Proceedings of the Board of Trustees of Hillsdale College from June 9, 1884, to August 20, 1901, with Proceedings of the Prudential Committee, June 18, 1884, to July 22, 1904. HCVPA.

10. An unsuccessful innovation in the curriculum was the Department of Military Science and Tactics. The 115 students who enrolled were "Hillsdale College Cadets," for whom the United States government provided two 3-inch field pieces and 115 rifles. Lieutenant Eli A. Helmick, an 1888 West Point graduate, became professor of military science and tactics at Hillsdale in January 1894; but the college dropped the program in 1897 due to lack of student interest. In 1921, incidentally, Helmick was promoted to major general. A near tragedy occurred on November 21, 1895, when a fire was discovered among boxes stored in the basement of Central Hall. The students soon extinguished the fire, only to find that the Military Department had stored over a hundred pounds of gunpowder in the adjacent room!

11. Hillsdale College commencement program, June 6–9, 1941. Gift from Mrs. Marie E. Davis, North Adams, Michigan. AKG.

12. *History of the Amphictyon Society of Hillsdale College*(Hillsdale, 1890), p. 72.

13. *Chicago Herald,* as quoted in *Hillsdale Herald,* July 5, 1894.

14. *The Hillsdale Alumnus* (May 1935), p. 60. Lorado Taft's sculpture on West Michigan Avenue in Jackson, Michigan, is judged to be one of the

finest Civil War monuments in the United States. The sculpture, made in 1904, portrays three soldiers in a lifelike position. George S. May, "Michigan Civil War Monuments" (Lansing, 1965), pp. 36–37.

15. *Hillsdale Collegian,* October 11, 1895.

16. Ibid., p. 244.

17. Ibid., p. 246.

18. Quoted in the *Hillsdale Leader,* September 26, 1902.

19. *Hillsdale Herald,* March 15, 1894.

20. Lilian Kirkwood diary, entry for June 3, 1887. Loan from Dr. Lilian Rick.

21. *Hillsdale Standard,* April 19, 1892.

22. *Hillsdale Herald,* March 1, 1894. With approval from the college authorities, Dean of Students Kevin Andrews and I recently climbed the tower by the interior route. Crawling up a series of steps and ladders, we finally passed through the trap door nailed down by the anonymous students almost a hundred years ago. Emerging at the top of the cupola, we viewed the countryside far beyond Jonesville. The audacity and physical strength to scale the *outside* of the tower seem unbelievable.

23. *Hillsdale Standard,* September 13, 1892.

24. Ibid., January 9, 1894.

25. *Hillsdale Collegian,* June 8, 1894.

26. *Hillsdale Standard,* October 6, 1891.

27. *Hillsdale Herald,* January 20, 1898.

28. One of the earliest fulltime coaches at Hillsdale in the twentieth century was W. J. Boone. After playing football at Hillsdale College, he transferred in 1905 to the University of Chicago and became star halfback for Coach Amos Alonzo Stagg. Unfortunately, Boone was declared ineligible on November 11, on the basis of having played his four allotted years of college football at Hillsdale. Coach Stagg replied, "Chicago's chances against Michigan look dark with Boone out of it." The details of Boone's ineligibility are unknown. A lifelong leader for honesty in athletics, Stagg always went by the rules, disliked professionalism in sports, and opposed smoking.

29. *Directory of Hillsdale County, Michigan* (Philadelphia, 1919), p. 252.

30. Thomas Oliver, ed., *M.I.A.A. Handbook* (Hillsdale, 1939), p. 9.

31. *Hillsdale Alumnus* (May 1950), p. 40.

32. *Hillsdale Daily News,* September 28, 1931. Having coached at the University of Chicago for 40 years, Amos Alonzo Stagg left in 1932 because of mandatory retirement at age 70. Serving as head coach at the College of the Pacific from 1933 to 1946, he was name N.C.A.A. Coach of the Year in 1943. I was privileged to become personally acquainted with Stagg when he assisted his son Alonzo at Susquehanna University from 1946 to 1951. Knute Rockne once said, "All football comes from Stagg." The legendary coach spanned the Civil War (born in 1862) to the atomic age (died in 1965), served as head coach for more than 57 years, and won 314 games. Most importantly, he endorsed the highest moral standards for amateur athletics.

33. *Hillsdale Herald,* October 19, 1893.

34. *Hillsdale Standard,* November 21, 1893. For an excellent description of early collegiate football rules and formations, see Fielding H. Yost, *Football for Player and Spectator* (Ann Arbor, 1905).

35. *Hillsdale Standard,* December 4, 1894. Many Hillsdale College men in the 1890s ate at boarding clubs located off campus.

36. Ibid., January 9, 1894.

37. Howard H. Peckham, *The Making of the University of Michigan, 1817–1967* (Ann Arbor, 1967), p. 90.

38. *Hillsdale Standard,* May 29, 1894.

39. The area behind Central Hall was called the back campus until after World War I, and the scenic area south of the circle drive to Knowlton, Worthing, Central, East, and Fine Arts Halls was referred to as the front campus.

40. Hillsdale College played baseball at Martin Field until after World War II. Mr. Harold Stock, All-M.I.A.A. quarterback in 1908 and Hillsdale College benefactor, donated funds to construct bleachers and dugouts in 1939. The famous hill in right field was levelled a few years later. I have interviewed college baseball players from the 1930s who claim that the deep

right field bank along Dickerson Gymnasium presented a more difficult challenge than the famous left field wall in Fenway Park, Boston.

41. Gorton Carruth and Eugene Ehrlich, *Facts & Dates of American Sports from Colonial Days to the Present* (New York, 1988), p. 59.

42. Toast given by Mrs. Lottie Bailey Ewing, '92, at the Hillsdale College Alumni Association banquet on June 20, 1900.

43. Dr. John Meigham, another outstanding scholar in Semitics, taught at Hillsdale College in the early twentieth century. Dr. Meigham previously taught Hebrew and Greek at the University of Chicago and was scholar in Semitics at the University of Pennsylvania. With his thesis "Hebrew and Aramaic Words Recovered from the Cuneiform Records," he was the first person other than a Hebrew to receive a Ph.D. degree from Dropsie College. By finding Hebrew words in cuneiform records, Meigham disproved the claims by Bible critics that the history of the Jewish people in the Book of Genesis was the invention of a later age. He concluded that cuneiform records from the fifth century B.C. to the twenty-eighth century B.C. supported the information in the Old Testament concerning the migrations of the Hebrew people. While teaching at Hillsdale College, Dr. Meigham got into a public dispute with Luther Burbank, who declared that the doctrine of immortality was impossible. *Philadelphia Ledger*, March 1, 1918. (Information provided by Mrs. Winnie Young, Hillsdale.)

44. *Jennings* (Louisiana) *Times*, as quoted in *Hillsdale Herald*, September 19, 1895.

45. Clarence M. Burton et al., *Educators of Michigan: A Choice Collection of Biographical Sketches* (Detroit, 1894), p. 77.

46. *Hillsdale Standard*, August 28, 1892.

47. Ibid., May 19, 1896.

48. Ibid., September 6, 1898.

49. *History of Jackson County, Michigan* (Chicago, 1881), pp. 690–91.

50. Robert H. Steinbach, *A Long March: The Lives of Frank and Alice Baldwin* (University of Texas Press, 1989), pp. 9, 96, 163, 182.

51. *Official Records of the Union and Confederate Navies in the War of the Rebellion* (Washington, 1892–1922), series I, XXI, p. 480. Master mate Julius L.

Williams from Hillsdale College also served in the U.S. Navy during the Civil War.

52. John Robertson, *Michigan in the War* (Lansing, 1880), p. 249.

53. "History of Ships Named Gridley" (Navy Department, Office of the Chief of Naval Operations, Division of Naval History, Ships' Histories Section), pp. 1–2. Another ex-Hillsdale student who fought in the Spanish-American War was W. E. Nason.

54. *Hillsdale Standard*, August 1, 1898.

55. President Joseph Mauck, address of July 4, 1903, published in *The Collegian*, September 30, 1903.

56. *Hillsdale Democrat*, July 1894.

57. President William G. Spencer to Dr. Frank Padelford, April 21, 1924. ABAC.

58. A Hillsdale College alumnus quoted in *Hillsdale Herald,* July 3, 1890.

59. *Hillsdale Herald,* July 24, 1890.

60. Ibid., September 29, 1892.

61. Ibid., July 11, 1895.

62. Ibid., June 17, 1896.

63. *Collegian-Herald,* February 2, 1899.

64. Ibid., October 27, 1898.

65. George Roche, *One by One; Preserving Values and Freedom in Heartland America* (Hillsdale, 1990), pp. 20–21.

66. *Collegian-Herald,* November 3, 1898.

67. *Hillsdale City Directory* (Chicago, 1901), p. 23.

68. The population of Michigan had increased more than 600 percent between 1850 and 1900.

69. *Hillsdale Collegian,* March 9, 1894.

70. Ibid., April 12, 1895.

71. Joseph W. Mauck made the following observation about the Baptist

merger of 1911: "I still maintain that, among the many good and great things that the Free [Will] Baptists did, the greatest was the gallant and devoted spirit in which they recognized the truth that . . . there was no longer a defensible ground of continuous separate existence." Mauck to Judge Lindley Webb, October 14, 1931. Joseph W. Mauck, papers, ABHS. President Mauck considered his leadership in joining the Freewill Baptists with the Northern Baptist Convention to be one of his greatest contributions. Earlier in the twentieth century, he had conferred with the Bishop of Michigan about the possibility of making Hillsdale an Episcopalian institution.

72. Memorandum, Lorenzo Dow 1883 diary. Dow Collection, loan from Dr. Lilian Rick.

73. Clarence M. Burton, *Educators of Michigan*, p. 25.

74. Hillsdale College publicity brochure, 1918. Donated by Martha Leonard. HC.

75. William Kirby, "Pioneer Life in Hillsdale County," *The Sauk Trail Historian* (January 1991), p. 10.

76. Gary and Sue Fowler, eds., *Oh Sir'll Be Home: Civil War Correspondence and History of a Union Soldier* (n.p., 1892), pp. 52–53. Typed manuscript. MPL.

77. *The Collegian*, February 10, 1904.

78. *Hillsdale Standard*, September 15, 1891.

79. Ibid., February 16, 1892.

80. Ibid., July 11, 1893.

81. *Collegian-Herald*, June 23, 1898.

82. *Hillsdale Leader*, November 16, 1900. Unfortunately, ex-President Edmund B. Fairfield of Mansfield, Ohio, was too feeble to attend the funeral. Of the college leaders, he had given Dunn the strongest assistance during the early years of the frontier institution.

83. Joseph W. Mauck to William Slayton, June 16, 1924. HC.

84. Lorenzo Dow diary, entry for January 9, 1883. Dow Collection, loan from Dr. Lilian Rick.

85. Lura A. Mains, *Mizpah: Autobiographical Sketches* (Grand Rapids, 1892), p. 30.

86. Helen Dunn Gates, *A Sketch of the Life and Labors of Rev. Ransom Dunn, D.D.* (Boston, 1901), pp. 281–319.

Sesquicentennial Epilogue

> Education is precisely the preservation, refinement and transmission of values from one generation to the next. Its tools include reason, tradition, moral concern and introspection. . . . Education seeks meaning in human life, justice in human affairs, dignity in human aspirations. . . .[1]
>
> —President George Roche

Two decades ago, George Roche brought to the presidency of Hillsdale College an unyielding conviction that ideas have consequences.[2] He knew that a strong college could be built upon traditional values and principles. During his presidency, Hillsdale College has emerged as a leader in American higher education, and the institution consistently has been ranked high on the lists of the most outstanding liberal arts colleges in the United States.[3]

Much of the recent progress reflects principles basic to Hillsdale College during the nineteenth century. On the eve of the 1994 sesquicentennial, an analogy between past and present values of pioneering Hillsdale College is significant. Addressing national audiences about the necessity of returning to traditional moral, political and economic principles, President Roche frequently endorses convictions that guided the college founders. The foundations of Hillsdale College today—the work ethic, traditional moral values, individual freedom and responsibility, and emphasis upon the classical curriculum—were defended vigorously by earlier college leaders such as Ransom Dunn and Edmund Fairfield.

Independence characterized the ministers and small Freewill Baptist congregations who established Michigan Central College at Spring Arbor. Small churches, such as Cook's Prairie Freewill Baptist, founded the institution in 1844 and showed distrust for hierarchy. Only several years later did the annual state denominational meeting endorse the Spring Arbor institution. An autonomous Board of Trustees, created on March 19, 1845, exercised independent authority over the college. By breaking the monopoly of the University of Michigan over higher education, the founders in 1850 again practiced self-sufficiency. The Freewill Baptist endeavor at Spring Arbor was the first successful private college in Michigan. Facing adversities such as physical relocation to Hillsdale in 1853, enormous sacrifices in the Civil War, the great fire of 1874, and near-foreclosure of mortgages from the 1930s to the 1950s, the college remained self-reliant. During the Great Depression, an independent, self-appointed committee selected Hillsdale as one of three small American colleges that most successfully developed citizenship. (The other two were Swarthmore and Carleton.) Strength in adversity had become commonplace, and the college rejected public revenue as a solution to its needs.

The most striking feature of early Hillsdale College was leadership in opening higher education to blacks, women and members of all religions. The antebellum college also was a leading force for abolitionism in the American West, and there is no doubt about the historical dedication of Hillsdale to individual freedom and dignity. President Edmund Fairfield in his July 4 oration at Hillsdale in 1853 insisted that *"national greatness is but the aggregate of individual greatness."* [Emphasis mine.] He continued: "Not all men have equal tact, equal talents, or must necessarily have equal wealth; but all men should have equal rights and an equal chance. . . . Give man his freedom to think, to do and to acquire, and you have made him a man. . . . The highest national prosperity, whether in the acquisition of wealth or the spread of general intelligence, is inseparably connected with the fullest enjoyment of personal liberty."

It was at best ironic, and perhaps tragic, that the Department of Health, Education and Welfare in 1975 ignored Hillsdale's contributions as one of the earliest colleges providing equal admission for blacks and women. To accept race and gender as proper criteria in admitting students and hiring faculty was unacceptable and inappropriate for the enterprising college that had pioneered integration and equality of opportunity. Had not Hillsdale been the first college in the nation to insist that its charter include nondiscrimination on grounds of race, sex and religion? What purpose could Title IX of the Education Act Amendments of 1972 hold for the proud institution that voluntarily had had banned discrimination for more than a century?

In a firm decision consistent with Hillsdale tradition, President Roche refused to sign the compliance form and rejected affirmative action, artificial quotas, and, by implication, federal control. The small heartland college's struggle, including action in the highest court in the land, against federal funding and control remains a matter of principle. Believing that traditional freedom cannot coexist with federal funding and bureaucratic guidelines, small Hillsdale College refuses to compromise its independence. The stakes today are much higher than during the nineteenth century, but the enthusiasm with which the college defends its self-reliance is part of a proud tradition. Friends across the nation join Hillsdale in sharing Daniel Webster's sentiment as he defended the private charter of Dartmouth College before the U. S. Supreme Court in 1818: "It is, sir, as I have said, a small college, and yet there are those who love it."[4]

The founders of the nineteenth-century college had strong religious faith, and their primary goal was to provide nonsectarian Christian education. They believed with Daniel Webster that "the greatest thought of my life is that of my individual responsibility to God." The Christian Studies program today is consistent with the early values of the institution. Moral responsibility motivated a majority of the 13,000 students who attended Hillsdale College before 1900 to exercise leadership in fields of public service. As judges, college presidents, professors, teachers, school superintendents, businessmen, physicians, attorneys and military officers, Hillsdale graduates established goals that superseded material and personal success.[5] The alumni today have strong precedents for assuming leadership positions and for providing public service. Another continuing principle of

Hillsdale College—patriotism—was exemplified by a superlative Civil War record. President Fairfield stated in 1853 that "the college is the friend of the republic, and the republic should be the friend of the college."

During the Civil War era, Hillsdale College became a leading forum in the West for nationally prominent orators, politicians and statesmen. In recent decades the Center for Constructive Alternatives and the Ludwig von Mises lecture series have brought hundreds of outstanding leaders to the campus on an even more impressive scale. In American higher education, Hillsdale College has developed unique speakers' programs. Through the Shavano Institute for National Leadership and college publications, such as *Imprimis*, the college successfully has advocated traditional ideals to a growing audience across the country. *Imprimis* circulation is expected to reach half a million by 1994–95.

Hillsdale College traditionally has maintained excellence in athletics, and the outstanding recent record includes a national small college football championship, dozens of All-Americans and Academic All-Americans, and numerous national champions in track and cross-country.[6] The student-athletes have a high graduation rate, and teams earn some of the highest academic averages on campus. Competitive and successful, the college athletic program retains a wholesome amateur quality reminiscent of early teams in the 1890s. Another Hillsdale tradition, the Board of Women Commissioners, has played a major role by providing substantial support for the institution every year since 1893.

Exercising sound financial management, college authorities throughout the nineteenth century realized maximum benefits from their assets and accounted for every dollar raised. The Board of Trustees continues to endorse thrift, excellent management of resources, and construction of new facilities only when supported by available capital. Physical improvements, recently or soon to be constructed, include the sports complex, new dormitories, a fine arts center and additions to the science building and the library.

The rise of Hillsdale College to the status of one of the nation's most respected liberal arts colleges is evidence of President Roche's leadership. The important ingredients of the small heartland college are traditional principles and values. As George Gilder observed, George Roche at Hillsdale has waged a "courageous and visionary battle . . . to preserve the values of a true American education against educational and legal bureaucracies run amok."[7] Robert Penn Warren once observed that our ancestors, before the rise of modern skepticism, materialism and a hundred other "isms," were "more real" in their consciousness and in the very constitution of their being. They understood permanent ideals and moral values that have been abandoned or overlooked in an age of modernity. A century and a half ago, Hillsdale began establishing an historical identity with distinctive traditions. In an age of affluence and moral relativism, small but independent Hillsdale College proudly accepts the challenge of continuing to make a difference in American higher education.

Endnotes

1. George Roche, *A World Without Heroes: The Modern Tragedy* (Hillsdale, 1987), p. 213.

2. In this analogy between the old and the new, it is appropriate to mention that George Roche, in office since 1971, soon will surpass the longest presidency in Hillsdale College history. Edmund B. Fairfield, one of the founding fathers, served from 1848 to 1869.

3. In March 1991, Hillsdale College was named first among eighty-seven colleges and universities by the John Templeton Foundation Honor Roll for Free Enterprise Teaching. Selected by college presidents and academic deans, the awards are given to schools with an "institutional commitment to traditional Western political and economic philosophies." *U.S. News and World Report*, the *New York Times*, *Barron's*, and *National Review* have in recent years consistently named Hillsdale among the top schools in the nation.

4. The Hillsdale College student body of the nineteenth century greatly admired Daniel Webster because of his brilliant defense of nationalism in the 1830s. Of all public figures, he was most highly esteemed. With Calhoun and Clay, Webster comprised the great triumvirate in the Senate,

and conservatives in New England referred to him as "the godlike Daniel." Hillsdale literary societies publicly honored Webster long after his death in 1852.

5. The excellent literary societies of Hillsdale College encouraged members to develop oratorical skills as preparation for careers in law, education, business, etc. Today the debating and forensics teams and the Tower Players maintain interest in public speaking, debating, drama, original and impromptu oratory, and reading of prose and poetry. Hillsdale students have won numerous oratorical prizes; and the Hillsdale Invitational Debate Tournament, with attorneys as judges, is held annually at the county courthouse.

6. The athletic program at Hillsdale College follow the high moral standards set almost a hundred years ago by Amos Alonzo Stagg. I have photographed our All-American athletes, and the murals line one of the hallways of the new Health Education and Sports Complex. Hillsdale College student-athletics have won 145 All-American and 80 Academic All-American awards. In indoor and outdoor track and field competition, 14 Hillsdale male athletes have won individual national small college championships since 1978. Three Hillsdale female athletes captured individual national titles in outdoor track, and one woman won a national championship in cross-country. Most recently, Hillsdale College athletes claimed national small college championships in the men's indoor 600-yard dash, the women's indoor two-mile relay, and the women's indoor distance medley in March 1991.

7. George Roche, *A Reason for Living* (Washington, DC, 1989), p. ix.

Bibliography

Primary Sources: Archival

Ames, Emily. Letter to Sophia Randolph, n.d. Donated by Mrs. Marie E. Davis, North Adams, Michigan. AKG.

Bailey, Franklin H. Diaries and papers, 1862, 1866, 1870, 1871, 1874, 1875. Franklin H. Bailey Collection. MHC.

Bissell, Francis M. Civil War pension papers. NA.

Blair, Austin. Governor's appointment of Professor Ransom Dunn as Michigan military agent for the U. S. Sanitary Commission, July 7, 1864. Ransom Dunn Collection. MHC.

Blair, Austin. Autobiographical notes, n.d., typescript. Austin Blair Collection. MHC.

Bowen, Jerome. Military service record. NA.

Buck, Andrew N. Correspondence, 1862–63. Andrew Newton Buck Collection. MHC.

Churchill, Charles H. Correspondence, 1854. Ransom Dunn Collection. MHC.

Cochran, Varnum, Michigan Superintendent of Public Instruction. Appointment certificate for state examiners to Hillsdale College, November 22, 1882. RHC.

Dow, Lorenzo. 1883 diary. Dow Collection. Loan from Dr. Lilian Rick.

Dow, Lorenzo. Letter to sister, October 29, 1882. Dow Collection. Loan from Dr. Lilian Rick.

Dow, Lorenzo. Letter to Mrs. Wm. M. Dow, Feb. 20, 1883. Dow Collection. Loan from Dr. Lilian Rick.

Dunn, Francis Wayland. Correspondence, 1857–64. Francis Wayland Dunn Collection. MHC.

Dunn, Francis Wayland. Diaries, 1860, 1861, 1862, 1863, 1864, 1866, 1867, 1869, 1871, 1872, 1874. Francis Wayland Dunn Collection. MHC.

Dunn, Ransom. "Lectures in Theology," 1886. Lecture notes taken by Frank E. Kenyon. HC.

Dunn, Ransom. Papers, 1853–1900. Ransom Dunn Collection. MHC.

Dunn, Ransom. Subscription list for construction of Hillsdale College, 1853–55. Ransom Dunn Collection. MHC.

Dunn, Ransom, Jr. Correspondence, 1861–62. Newell Ransom Dunn Collection. MHC.

Dunn, Ransom, Jr. Journal, 1860. Newell Ransom Dunn Collection. MHC.

Fairfield, Edmund B. Correspondence, 1852–61. Ransom Dunn Collection. MHC.

Fairfield, Edmund B. "The Essentials of a College." Speech delivered at Oberlin College in 1887. NL.

Ford, Henry M. "Alumni History of Hillsdale College," 1910. Ransom Dunn Collection. MHC.

Ford, Henry M. "Some Reminiscences of the College Church and Its Pastors," June 10, 1934. HC.

Fourth Annual Concert of the Beethoven Society, Hillsdale College. Program, June 14, 1865. AKG.

Freewill Baptist Home Mission Society, 1840s and 1850s. Annual reports. ABHS.

Freewill Baptist Ministry in the West, 1854. Minutes. Free Will Baptists, Michigan Association Collection. MHC.

Hadley, Cornelius. Abstract of military service record. SAM.

Hawley, James. Correspondence, 1862. Ransom Dunn Collection. MHC.

Hillsdale College. Records of the Proceedings of the Board of Trustees from July 18, 1855, to September 20, 1869, with Proceedings of the Prudential Committee, September 29, 1855, to June 10, 1870. HCVPA.

Hillsdale College. Records of the Proceedings of the Board of Trustees from June 13, 1870, to September 18, 1883, with Proceedings of the Prudential Committee, June 20, 1870, to June 3, 1884. HCVPA.

Hillsdale College. Records of the Proceedings of the Board of Trustees from June 9, 1884, to August 20, 1901, with Proceedings of the Prudential Committee, June 18, 1884, to July 22, 1904. HCVPA.

Hillsdale College catalogues. 1855–1900. HC.

Hillsdale College circular. September 1, 1856. MHC.

Hillsdale County map, 1857. Cartographers: S. Geil and S. L. Jones. Daniel Kellogg: Philadelphia. SAM.

Hillsdale County map, 1874, original lithograph. Cartographer: H. F. Walling. Tackabury: Detroit. AKG.

Hillsdale village map, ca. 1845. Cartographer: Joel McCollum. MHC.

Hillsdale village and College Hill, 1866. Sketch by unknown artist. Property of Robert Keefer, Hillsdale.

Hubbell, Don A. Correspondence, 1862–63. RHC.

Humphrey, Gen. William. Abstract of military service record. SAM.

King, Henry J. Correspondence, 1856–61. Ransom Dunn Collection. MHC.

Kirkwood, Lilian. Diary, August 12, 1885-December 31, 1886. Loan from Dr. Lilian Rick.

Kirkwood, Lilian. 1887 diary. Loan from Dr. Lilian Rick.

Luce, Moses A. Correspondence, 1861. Ransom Dunn Collection. MHC.

McKnight, Joseph. Correspondence, 1863. Ransom Dunn Collection. MHC.

March, Edwin J. Correspondence, 1864–65. Edwin J. March Collection. MHC.

Mauck, Joseph W. Letter to Sophia Randolph, December 9, 1871. Donated by Mrs. Marie E. Davis, North Adams. AKG.

Mauck, Joseph W. Letter to William Slayton, June 16, 1924. HC.

Mauck, Joseph W. Paper on Michigan Central College, November 7, 1916. Free Will Baptists, Michigan Association Collection. MHC.

Mauck, Joseph W. Mauck papers. ABHS.

Mauck, Willfred O. "Dear Hearts and Gentle People," n.d., 3 parts. Manuscript loaned by Mrs. Charles Buchanan.

Mauck, Willfred O. Memoirs entitled "Hometown," n.d. HC.

Merritt, E. V. Correspondence, 1855. Ransom Dunn Collection. MHC.

Michigan, 1844 map, original lithograph. Cartographers: Sidney Morse and Samuel Breese. AKG.

Michigan and Wisconsin, 1853 map, original lithograph. Cartographer: Roswell Smith. Daniel Burgess and Co., New York. AKG.

Michigan Central College at Spring Arbor. Records of the Proceedings of the Board of Trustees from the year 1853 to July 9, 1855. HCVPA.

Michigan Southern and Northern Indiana Railroad Companies, 1849. Directors' report soliciting a quarter of a million dollars to extend the railroad west from Hillsdale. CHS.

Michigan Southern and Northern Indiana Railroad Companies, 1853. Directors' report. CHS.

Michigan Yearly Meeting of Freewill Baptists at Franklin Center. Record book, June 7, 1844. Free Will Baptists, Michigan Association Collection. MHC.

Michigan Yearly Conference of Freewill Baptists at Commerce, June 11, 1847. Constitution and Records. Free Will Baptists, Michigan Association Collection. MHC.

Mills, Charles B. Letter from Hillsdale College Secretary-Treasurer to Alpha Kappa Phi Society, December 22, 1883. Loan from Dr. Lilian Rick.

North Reading Baptist Church. Notes from the clerk's record book. Copy donated by Kevin Andrews, Hillsdale College Dean of Men.

Patterson, John C. "History of the Freewill Baptist Church of Cook's Prairie," n.d. John C. Patterson Collection. MHC.

Patterson, John C. Speech to Alpha Kappa Phi, May 4, 1863. John C. Patterson Collection. MHC.

Patterson, John C. Speech to Alpha Kappa Phi, January 29, 1864. John C. Patterson Collection. MHC.

Patterson, John C. Speech to Hillsdale College Alumni Association, 1880. John C. Patterson Collection. MHC.

Perrine, Livonia Benedict. List of graduates from Michigan Central College, n.d. Michigan Central College Collection. MHC.

Railroad Map of Ohio, Indiana, & Michigan with Steamboat Landings, ca. 1860. Cartographer: G. Woolworth Colton. SAM.

Reynolds, William H. Diaries, 1857–61. William H. Reynolds Collection. MHC.

Rhines, Levant C. Abstract of military service record. SAM.

Slayton, George A. Autobiography, n.d. Slayton Family Collection. MHC.

Slayton, George A. Correspondence, 1868–71. HC.

Spencer, William Gear. Correspondence, 1924–28. ABAC.

Stark, Jacob H. Correspondence, 1861–65. Ransom Dunn Collection. MHC.

Steward, Lillian. Letter to friend, October 1, 1871. Donated by Mrs. Marie E. Davis, North Adams, Michigan. AKG.

Tottis, James W., Department of American Art, The Detroit Institute of Arts. Letter to author, March 9, 1989.

Tuttle, William. Correspondence, 1861. RHC.

Wellington, Horace. Letter to friends at Lynn, Massachusetts April 19, 1847. Michigan Central College Collection. MHC.

Western Ministerial Conventions. Records, n.d. Western Ministerial Collection. MHC.

Whipple, Henry E. Correspondence, 1854–77. Ransom Dunn Collection. MHC.

Whitney, Orville. Letter to family, April 15, 1873. Loaned to author by Margo Shidaker, Sarasota, Florida.

Primary Sources: Printed

Acts of the Legislature of the State of Michigan, Passed at the Annual Session of 1845. Detroit, 1845.

Acts of the Legislature of the State of Michigan, Passed at the Annual Session of 1850. Detroit, 1850.

Acts of the Legislature of the State of Michigan, Passed at the Annual Session of 1855. Detroit, 1855.

Addresses, Inaugurals and Charges, Delivered in Selin's Grove, Snyder Co., Pa., September 1st, and November 24th, 1858, in Connection with Laying of the Corner Stone, and the Installation of the Professors of the Evang. Lutheran Missionary Institute. Baltimore, 1859. AKG.

Atlas of Hillsdale County Michigan. Cartographer: D. J. Lake. Philadelphia, 1872. AKG.

Bailey's Astral Lantern. Description of F. H. Bailey's early planetarium. Boston, n.d. Franklin H. Bailey Collection. MHC.

Baldwin, Alice B. *Memoirs of the Late Frank D. Baldwin, Major General, U.S.A.* Los Angeles, 1929.

Berlin, Ira, ed. *The Black Military Experience (Freedom: A Documentary History of Emancipation, 1861–1867, Series II)*. Cambridge, 1982.

Blake, Sophia Jex. *A Visit to Some American Schools and Colleges.* London, 1867.

Bouton, William. "The Study of Language." *The Amateur* (June 1861).

Bovee, E. W. "Chronicles of a Pioneer Family." *The Sauk Trail Historian* (January 1991): 5–9.

Brown, Harry and Frederick Williams, ed. *The Diary of James A. Garfield.* 2 volumes. East Lansing, 1967.

Carleton, Will M. *Poems.* Chicago, 1871. AKG.

A Catalogue of the Officers and Students of Brown University, 1854–55. Providence, 1854. AKG.

Catalogue of the Officers and Students of Michigan Central College, at Spring Arbor, 1845–6. Jackson, 1846. Michigan Central College Collection. MHC.

Catalogue of the Officers and Students of the Michigan Central College, at Spring Arbor, for the Year Ending July, 1850. Jackson, 1850. Michigan Central College C ollection. MHC.

Catalogue of the Officers & Students of the Michigan Central College, at Spring Arbor, for the Year Ending January, 1852. Detroit, 1852. Michigan Central College Collection. MHC.

Directory of Hillsdale County, Michigan. Philadelphia, 1919. AKG.

Dunn, Ransom. *A Discourse on the Freedom of the Will.* Dover, NH, 1850. HC.

Dunn, Ransom. "Financial Values of Hillsdale College." *Wolverine* (1897 yearbook). AKG.

Exercises of the First Annual Commencement of Hillsdale College. Hillsdale, June 18, 1856. HC.

Fairfield, Edmund B. Address at college chapel, May 19, 1904. *The Collegian* (May 25, 1905).

Fifth General Catalogue of the Delta Tau Delta Fraternity. 1884.

First Quinquennial Record of the Alumni Association of Hillsdale College. Hillsdale, 1876.

Forty-Seventh Annual Report of the Superintendent of Public Instruction of the State of Michigan. Lansing, 1886. AKG.

Fourteenth Annual Report of the Freewill Baptist Home Mission Society. Dover, NH, 1848. ABAC.

Fowler, Gary and Sue, ed. "Oh Sir'll Be Home: Civil War Correspondence and History of a Union Soldier." N.p., 1982. Typed manuscript, MPL.

Freewill Baptist Connection. Minutes of the Twenty-Second General Conference. Dover, NH, 1874.

Fuller, Harvey A. *Where Dark Shadows Play.* Milwaukee, 1890. AKG.

Gazetteer of the St. Joseph Valley, Michigan and Indiana. Chicago, 1867.

General Catalogue of Bates College. 1931.

Goodell, William. *Slavery and Anti-Slavery.* New York, 1852. AKG.

Graves, Alvah. *The Voice, in Conversation, Speech, and Song.* Lansing, 1882. Loaned by Dr. Lilian Rick.

Hawley, James. "Sumner and Sumter." *The Amateur* (June 1860).

Heckman, Wallace. "Character in Education." *The Reunion* (June 17, 1885).

Hillsdale City Directory. Chicago, 1901. AKG.

Hillsdale College catalogues. 1855–1900. HC.

Hillsdale College circular. September 1, 1856. HC.

Hillsdale College brochure. Hillsdale, ca. 1900. Loaned by Dr. Lilian Rick.

Hillsdale College publicity brochure. Hillsdale, 1918. Donated by Martha Leonard. HC.

Hillsdale College, 1897–8. Hon. George F. Mosher, LL.D., President. Hillsdale, 1897. Loaned by Dr. Lilian Rick.

History of the Alpha Kappa Phi Society of Hillsdale College. Hillsdale, 1890. AKG.

History of the Alpha Kappa Phi Society of Hillsdale College. Hillsdale, 1915.

History of the Amphictyon Society of Hillsdale College. Hillsdale, 1890. AKG.

Kidd, J. H. *Personal Recollections of a Cavalryman with Custer's Cavalry Brigade in the Civil War.* Ionia, Michigan, 1908. 1983 reprint by Time-Life Books Inc.

Kirby, William. "Pioneer Life in Hillsdale County." *The Sauk Trail Historian* (January 1991): 10–12.

Lawrence, William R., ed. *Extracts from the Diary and Correspondence of the Late Amos Lawrence.* Boston, 1855. AKG.

Mains, Lura A. *Mizpah: Autobiographical Sketches.* Grand Rapids, 1892. AKG.

Manual of the Theadelphic Literary Society of Hillsdale College. Hillsdale, 1900. AKG.

The Michigan Almanac, 1871. Detroit, 1871. AKG.

Ninth Annual Report of the Secretary of the State Board of Health of the State of Michigan. Lansing, 1882. AKG.

Official Records of the Union and Confederate Navies in the War of the Rebellion. 30 volumes. Washington, 1892–1922.

"Our Great Loss." *The Crescent* (April 1874).

Perry, Arthur L. *Elements of Political Economy.* New York, 1871. AKG.

Plat Book of Hillsdale County. Chicago, 1894. SLM.

Portrait and Biographical Album of Hillsdale County, Mich. Chicago, 1888. AKG.

Randolph, Matilda Blackman. *Plantation Pictures: Colored Views.* Grand Rapids, 1890.

Randolph, P. P. "Life in Michigan Twenty Years Ago." *The Amateur* (June 1862).

Report of the Boards of Directors of the Michigan Southern and Northern Railroad Companies. New York, July 30, 1853. CHS.

Report of the Superintendent of Public Instruction of the State of Michigan for the Year 1863. Lansing, 1863. AKG.

Robertson, John, compiler. *Michigan in the War.* Lansing, 1880. AKG.

Smith, Adelaide W. *Reminiscences of an Army Nurse during the Civil War.* New York, 1911. AKG.

Smith, Edward P. *Incidents of Shot and Shell.* New York, 1868. AKG.

Solid Shot: The Facts and the Arguments on the Liquor Traffic. Springfield, OH, 1889. AKG.

Songs of the Amphictyon and Union Societies of Hillsdale College. Hillsdale, 1887. AKG.

Students' Hand-Book, Compiled by the Y.M.C.A. and Y.W.C.A. of Hillsdale College. Hillsdale, 1887. Loaned by Dr. Lilian Rick.

System of Public Instruction and Primary School Law of Michigan. Lansing, 1852. AKG.

Tenth Annual Report Relating to the Registry and Return of Births, Marriages, and Deaths, in Michigan for the Year 1876. Lansing, 1881. AKG.

Third Record of the Alumni Association of Hillsdale College. Hillsdale, 1908.

Thirty-Fifth Annual Report of the Superintendent of Public Instruction of the State of Michigan. Lansing, 1871.

Thirty-Sixth Annual Report of the Superintendent of Public Instruction of the State of Michigan. Lansing, 1872. AKG.

Transactions of the Forty-First Annual Meeting of the Alumnae Association of the Woman's Medical College of Pennsylvania. Philadelphia, 1916.

Twelfth Annual Report of the Freewill Baptist Home Mission Society. Dover, NH, 1846. ABAC.

Twenty-Second Annual Report of the Freewill Baptist Home Mission Society. Dover, NH, 1856.

Twenty-Seventh Annual Report of the Superintendent of Public Instruction of the State of Michigan. Lansing, 1863. AKG.

Twenty-Eighth Annual Report of the Superintendent of Public Instruction of the State of Michigan. Lansing, 1864. AKG.

Walker, Amasa. *The Science of Wealth: A Manual of Political Economy.* 7th edition. Philadelphia, 1872.

"War." *The Souvenir* (June 1861).

War of the Rebellion: A Compilation of the Official Records of the Union and Confederate Armies. 128 volumes and index. Washington, 1880–1901.

Whaley, Alvin M. "An Ancient of Days." *The Advance* (December 2, 1885).

Wheelock, Julia S. *The Boys in White: The Experience of a Hospital Agent in and around Washington.* New York, 1870. AKG. '

The Wolverine, volume 1. Hillsdale College class of 1897 yearbook. Cleveland, 1896. AKG.

Woman's Medical College of Pennsylvania. Annual announcement for the session of 1867–68. Philadelphia, 1867. AWM.

Yost, Fielding H. *Football for Player and Spectator.* Ann Arbor, 1905. AKG.

Newspapers and Periodicals

The Advance (Hillsdale College), 1885–86. HC.

The Alpha Kappa Phi, 1861–62. HC.

The Amateur (Amphictyon Society), 1859–62. HC.

The American Citizen (Jackson), 1849–1853. JPL.

Chicago Herald, 1891. CHS.

The Collegian (Hillsdale College), 1903–06. HC.

Collegian-Herald (Hillsdale College), 1896–99. HC.

The Crescent (Hillsdale College), 1874–78. HC.

Detroit Advertiser and Tribune, 1864. BHC.

Freewill Baptist Quarterly. Volumes 1–15 (1853–67). HC.

Hillsdale College Herald, 1878–96. HC.

The Hillsdale Collegian, 1893–96. HC.

Hillsdale Democrat, 1894. MPL.

Hillsdale Leader, 1900. MPL.

Hillsdale Standard, 1855–1900. MPL.

Inter-Ocean (Chicago), 1872–75. CHS.

Jackson Patriot, 1848–49. JPL.

Michigan Baptist, 1923. ABHS.
Morning Star (Freewill Baptist periodical), 1885. ABAC.
The New Collegian (Hillsdale College), 1899–1902. HC.
The Reunion (Hillsdale College), 1885. HC.
The Souvenir (Ladies' Literary Union), 1860–62. HC.

Secondary Sources: Books

Abram, Ruth J., ed. *Send Us a Lady Physician: Women Doctors in America,*
   1835–1920. New York, 1985.
Adams, George W. *Doctors in Blue: The Medical History of the Union Army in*
   the Civil War. Dayton, Ohio, 1985.
Addenda to Memorabilia of the Class of 1887. Number Five. Hillsdale, 1944.
Addenda to Memorabilia of the Class of 1887. Number Eight. Hillsdale, 1947.
Anderson, James D. *The Education of Blacks in the South, 1860–1935.* Chapel
   Hill, 1988.
Anderson, William M. *They Died to Make Men Free: A History of the 19th*
   Michigan Infantry in the Civil War. Berrien Springs, MI, 1980.
Bald, F. Clever. *Michigan in Four Centuries.* New York, 1954.
Bartlett, Richard A. *The New Country: A Social History of the American Fron-*
   tier, 1776–1890. Oxford, 1974.
Belknap, Charles E. *History of the Michigan Organizations at Chickamauga,*
   Chattanooga, and Missionary Ridge. Lansing, 1899.
Beyer, Walter and Oscar Keydel. *Deeds of Valor: How America's Heroes Won*
   the Medal of Honor. 2 volumes. Detroit, 1901–2.
Blockson, Charles L. *The Underground Railroad.* New York, 1989.
Booraem, Hendrik. V. *The Road to Respectability: James A. Garfield and His*
   World, 1844–1852. Lewisburg, PA; 1988.
Brown, Alan, John Houdek, and John Yzenbaard, ed. *Michigan Perspectives.*
   Dubuque, IA, 1974.
Burton, Clarence M. et al. *Educators of Michigan: A Choice Collection of Bio-*
   graphical Sketches and Portraits of the Teaching Profession. Detroit, 1894.
   AKG.
Carruth, Gorton and Eugene Ehrlich. *Facts & Dates of American Sports from*
   Colonial Days to the Present. New York, 1988.
Centennial Book Committee, chairman Eugene Fry. *Hillsdale Area Centen-*
   nial. Hillsdale, 1969.

Chamberlain, John. *Freedom and Independence: The Hillsdale Story.* Hillsdale, 1979.

Conwell, Russell. *The Life, Speeches, and Public Services of James A. Garfield.* Portland, ME, 1881. AKG.

Cornish, Dudley Taylor. *The Sable Arm: Black Troops in the Union Army, 1861–1865.* Lawrence, KS, 1987.

Cremin, Lawrence A. *American Education: The National Experience, 1783–1876.* New York, 1988.

Current, Richard Nelson. *Those Terrible Carpetbaggers.* New York, 1988.

Davis, William C. *Battle at Bull Run.* New York, 1977.

Dorfman, Joseph. *The Economic Mind in American Civilization, 1606–1865.* 2 volumes. New York, 1946.

Dunbar, Willis, ed. *Michigan Institutions of Higher Education in the Civil War.* Lansing, 1964.

Dunbar, Willis F. *The Michigan Record in Higher Education.* Detroit, 1963.

Early Michigan Paintings: Kresge Art Center, Michigan State University, East Lansing. Michigan State University, 1976.

Feeman, Harlan et al. *The Story of a Noble Devotion.* Adrian College, 1945.

Fish, Carl Russell. *The Rise of the Common Man.* New York, 1927.

Fletcher, Robert. *A History of Oberlin College.* 2 volumes. Oberlin, 1943.

Foner, Eric. *Free Soil, Free Labor, Free Men: The Ideology of the Republican Party before the Civil War.* New York, 1971.

Foner, Eric. *Reconstruction: America's Unfinished Revolution.* New York, 1988.

Franklin, John Hope and Alfred A. Moss, Jr. *From Slavery to Freedom: A History of Negro Americans.* New York, 1988, sixth edition.

Friedman, Lawrence J. *Gregarious Saints: Self and Community in American Abolitionism, 1830–1870.* Cambridge, 1982.

Frothingham, Paul R. *Edward Everett: Orator and Statesman.* Boston, 1925.

Fuller, George N. *Michigan: A Centennial History of the State and Its People.* 5 volumes. Chicago, 1939.

Gates, Helen Dunn. *A Consecrated Life: A Sketch of the Life and Labors of Rev. Ransom Dunn, D.D.* Boston, 1901. AKG.

Gaustad, Edwin. *Historical Atlas of Religion in America.* New York, 1976.

Gienapp, William E. *The Origins of the Republican Party, 1852–1856.* New York, 1987.

Gildart, Robert. *Albion College, 1835–1960.* Albion, 1961.

Gillard, Kathleen. *Our Michigan Heritage.* New York, 1955.

Harburn, Todd E. and Gerald E. Harburn. *MIAA Football: The Illustrated*

Gridiron History of the Michigan Intercollegiate Athletic Association. Chelsea, 1986.

Harris, Wilmer C. *Public Life of Zachariah Chandler, 1851-1875.* Lansing, 1917. AKG.

Hathaway, Richard J., ed. *Michigan: Visions of Our Past.* East Lansing, 1989.

Hayne, Coe. *Baptist Trail-Makers of Michigan.* Philadelphia, 1936.

Hemans, Lawton T. *History of Michigan.* Lansing, 1906.

Hillsdale Area Centennial, 1869–1969. Hillsdale, 1969.

Hillsdale County Historical Society and Hillsdale County Bicentennial Commission. *150 years in the Hills and Dales.* 2 volumes. Hillsdale, 1976 and 1978.

History of Hillsdale County. Philadelphia, 1879. AKG.

History of Jackson County, Michigan. Chicago, 1881. AKG.

Hopkins, Alphonso A. *The Life of Clinton Bowen Fisk.* New York, 1969 reprint of 1888 edition.

Horowitz, Helen. *Campus Life: Undergraduate Cultures from the End of the Eighteenth Century to the Present.* Chicago, 1987.

Hosford, Frances J. *Father Shipherd's Magna Charta: A Century of Coeducation in Oberlin College.* Boston, 1937.

Illustrated City Directory of Hillsdale, Michigan. Hillsdale, 1894.

Jonesville: Sesquicentennial Historical Record. Jonesville, MI, 1978.

Kigar, Donald F. et al. *Small Arms Used by Michigan Troops in the Civil War.* Lansing, 1966.

Lake Shore & Michigan Southern Railway System and Representative Employees. Buffalo, 1900.

Lanman, Charles. *The Red Book of Michigan.* Detroit, 1871.

Levin, Beatrice S. *Women and Medicine.* Metuchen, NJ, 1980.

McKivigan, John R. *The War against Proslavery Religion: Abolitionism and the Northern Churches, 1830–1865.* Ithaca, NY, 1984.

McLaughlin, Andrew C. *History of Higher Education in Michigan.* Washington, 1891.

McPherson, James M. *Battle Cry of Freedom: The Civil War Era.* New York, 1988.

Madison, James H., ed. *Heartland.* Bloomington, 1988.

Mason, Philip and Paul Pentecost. *From Bull Run to Appomattox: Michigan's Role in the Civil War.* Detroit, 1961.

May, George S. *Michigan: An Illustrated History of the Great Lakes State.* Northridge, CA, 1987.

Millbrook, Minnie Dubbs. *Michigan Medal of Honor Winners in the Civil War*. Lansing, 1966.

Mitchell, Reid. *Civil War Soldiers*. New York, 1988.

Moberg, David. *The Great Reversal: Evangelism and Social Concern*. Philadelphia, 1977.

Moore, Vivian Lyon. *The First Hundred Years of Hillsdale College*. Ann Arbor, 1943. AKG.

Mulder, Arnold. *The Kalamazoo College Story*. Kalamazoo, 1958.

National Geographic Society. *Historical Atlas of the United States*. Washington, 1988.

Oliver, Thomas, ed. *MIAA Handbook*. Hillsdale, 1939. AKG.

Parks, Robert J. *Democracy's Railroads: Public Enterprise in Jacksonian Michigan*. Port Washington, 1972.

Peckham, Howard H. *The Making of the University of Michigan, 1817–1967*. Ann Arbor, 1967.

Peddycord, Will F. *History of the Seventy-Fourth Regiment, Indiana Volunteer Infantry*. Warsaw, Indiana, 1913. IHS.

Reading Centennial, 1873–1973. Coldwater, 1973.

Renner, Thomas L., ed. *Celebrating a Century of the Student Athlete: The 100 Year History of the Michigan Intercollegiate Athletic Association*. MIAA, 1988.

Reynolds, Elon G., ed. *Compendium of History and Biography of Hillsdale County, Michigan*. Chicago, 1903. AKG.

Roberts, Windsor H. *A History of the College Baptist Church, 1855–1955*. N.p., n.d. Donated by Dr. Charles Johnson, pastor of College Baptist Church. AKG.

Roche, George. *Going Home*. Ottawa, IL, 1986.

Roche, George. *One by One: Preserving Values and Freedom in Heartland America*. Hillsdale, 1990.

Roche, George. *A Reason for Living*. Washington, DC, 1989.

Roche, George. *A World Without Heroes: The Modern Tragedy*. Hillsdale, 1987.

Roland, Charles P. *An American Iliad: the Story of the Civil War*. New York, 1991.

Smith, Donald L. *The Twenty-Fourth Michigan of the Iron Brigade*. Harrisburg, 1962.

Smith, Page. *Trial by Fire*. Volume 5 of *A People's History of the Civil War and Reconstruction*. New York, 1990.

Smith, Timothy L. *Revivalism and Social Reform: American Protestantism on the Eve of the Civil War*. Gloucester, MA 1976.

Starr, Stephen Z. *The Union Cavalry in the Civil War*. 3 volumes. Baton Rouge, 1979, 1981, 1985.

Steinbach, Robert H. *A Long March: The Lives of Frank and Alice Baldwin*. University of Texas Press, 1989.

Streeter, Floyd. *Political Parties in Michigan, 1837–1860*. Lansing, 1918. AKG.

Taylor, George Rogers. *The Transportation Revolution*. New York, 1951.

Terman, William J., ed. *Spring Arbor Township, 1830–1980*. Spring Arbor, 1980.

Tewksbury, Donald. *The Founding of American Colleges and Universities before the Civil War*. New York, 1932. Reprint edition by Arno Press, Inc., 1969.

Tuttle, Charles R. *General History of the State of Michigan*. Detroit, 1873. AKG.

Tyler, Alice Felt. *Freedom's Ferment*. New York, 1962.

Ward, John T., ed. *Free Baptist Cyclopaedia*. Boston, 1886.

Weber, Thomas. *The Northern Railroads in the Civil War, 1861–1865*. Westport, CT, 1970.

Williams, Frederick D. *Michigan Soldiers in the Civil War*. Lansing, 1988.

Woodford, Frank. *Lewis Cass*. Rutgers, 1950.

Secondary Sources: Articles and Pamphlets

Bigelow, Martha M. "Michigan: Pioneer in Education." Michigan Historical Collections Bulletin No. 7, June, 1955. AKG.

Butchart, Ronald E. "Recruits to the 'Army of Civilization': Gender, Race, Class, and the Freedmen's Teachers, 1861–1875." Paper delivered at the 1990 annual meeting of the Organization of American Historians.

Davidson, James F. "Michigan and the Defense of Knoxville, Tennessee, 1863." East Tennessee Publications No. 35, 1963.

Day, Judson LeRoy, Jr. "The Baptists of Michigan and the Civil War." Lansing, 1965.

Fallon, Jerome A. "The Will Carleton Poorhouse." Hillsdale, 1989.

Fisk, D. M. "The Story of the Planting," I, II, III, IV, V, VI. *The Reunion* (May 6, 13, 20, 27, June 3, 10, 1885).

"The Hillsdale Crew." *Harper's Weekly* (June 10, 1882).

"History of Ships Named Gridley." Navy Department, Office of the Chief of Naval Operations, Division of Naval History, Ships' Histories Section.

Hopkins, John. "A Full and Reliable History of the Alumni and Alumnae of Our Alma Mater." *First Quinquennial Record of the Alumni Association of Hillsdale College*. Hillsdale, 1876.

Janes, O. A. "The Chickamauga and Chattanooga National Military Park." *The Hillsdale Collegian*, November 22, 1895.

"Lives of the Founders and Builders of Hillsdale College." *The Advance* (June 23, 1886).

May, George S. "Michigan Civil War Monuments." Lansing, 1965.

Michigan and Wisconsin territories, 1836 map. Cartographer: John Farmer. Copy, AKG.

Norton, S. W. "Hillsdale College, Hillsdale, Michigan," in *Michigan Pioneer and Historical Society Historical Collections*, XXXII (1903).

Patterson, John C. "History of the Freewill Baptist Church of Cook's Prairie," in *Michigan Pioneer and Historical Society Historical Collections*, X (1888): 33–51.

Patterson, John C. "History of Hillsdale College," reprint of 1883 article in *Collections of the Pioneer Society of the State of Michigan*, VI (1907): 137–65. AKG.

Potter, Laurens Baldwin. "Lives of the Founders and Builders of Hillsdale College." *The Advance* (April 28, 1886).

Ringenberg, William C. "The Vocations of the Alumni of the Early Michigan Denominational Colleges." *Michigan History* (September-October 1980): 12–16.

Walker, Francis A. "The Hon. Amasa Walker, LL.D." *The Historical and Genealogical Register* (April 1888): 133–41.

Dissertations

Killion, Mead W. "A History of Spring Arbor Seminary and Junior College." University of Michigan M.A. thesis, 1941. JPL.

Potts, David B. "Baptist Colleges in the Development of American Society,

1812–1861." Harvard University Ph.D. dissertation, 1967. Published: New York, 1988.

Ringenberg, William C. "The Protestant College on the Michigan Frontier." Michigan State University Ph.D. dissertation, 1970.

Index

ARLAN GILBERT was a member of the History
Department at Hillsdale for thirty-eight years. He
served a decade as department chairman, and the
seniors elected him Professor of the Year in 1984.
He served seven years as senior faculty member
at Hillsdale, and his awards include the Alumni
Association's honorary alumnus in 1992 and the
annual Charger Award for his contributions to
athletics. During the College's sesquicentennial,
he was presented with an honorary doctor of philosophy degree. He is also a member of Hillsdale's
President's Club, which recognizes outstanding
supporters of the College. Dr. Gilbert has written three books on the history of Hillsdale College. Soon after retiring from teaching, he assumed
the position of Hillsdale College Historian.